PRAISE FOI

M000189745

"Travis Bookout has given us an insightful series of lessons in *King of Glory* which are designed for reflection and for deepening our trust in Jesus Christ. He is a deep thinker, and a great Bible student. In his book, he leads readers to see the many-sided glory of Jesus!"

— **Dan R. Owen**, Minister Broadway Church of Christ, Paducah, Kentucky and author of *That You May Believe: Lessons that Challenge Us To Personal Discipleship From The Gospel of John*

"John's Gospel was written by the disciple who had a particularly close, loving relationship with Jesus. Travis Bookout's *King of Glory* explores this amazing record of the life of Christ. I have great respect and appreciation for Travis and am confident his study will bless your life."

— **Chuck Monan**, Minister Pinnacle Church of Christ, Little Rock, Arkansas

"In his concluding remarks, the 'beloved disciple' told us that the book of John was written 'so that you may believe that Jesus is the Christ, the Son of God; and that by believing you may have life in His name.' Reading these 'reflections' by my friend has not only strengthened my faith, it has helped me to fall in love with Jesus even more. Travis Bookout is a young preacher who has wisdom that is far advanced for his age. I can't wait to read this book again and more fully drink from the insights contained in it. *King of Glory* will cause every reader to praise God for the precious gift of His Son and to rejoice because we have life in His name!"

— **Jeff Jenkins**, Minister Lewisville Church of Christ, Lewisville, Texas

"*King of Glory* is the product of a year-long quest to reflect on the Gospel of John. Readers should not rush through the pages like a novel. Instead, it is wise to read while reflecting on our relationship with the Lord. Stop and consider the questions at the end of each section. Whether you read this book privately or as part of a group project, it will impact your life if you let it. Thanks to Travis Bookout for producing a masterpiece for both seasoned believers and new Christians."

— **Ted Burleson**, Associate Professor of Bible, Amridge University, Montgomery, Alabama and Preacher, Hamilton Church of Christ, Hamilton, Alabama

"*King of Glory* is ideal for personal study, use in Bible class, as well as in small groups. It is also an effective tool for evangelistic outreach. It is written in a compelling style that not only highlights the unique structure of John's Gospel but also emphasizes some of the fourth Gospel's most important themes. Travis Bookout exposes readers to fresh new insights while providing practical applications for everyday life. The discussion questions at the end of each chapter encourage personal reflection and aid in group discussion. Much like the author, King of glory glorifies the King!"

— **Tim Lewis**, Preaching Minister North MacArthur Church of Christ, Oklahoma City, Oklahoma

KING OF GLORY

52 REFLECTIONS ON THE GOSPEL OF JOHN

TRAVIS J. BOOKOUT

CYPRESS
PUBLICATIONS

Copyright © 2021

Manufactured in the United States

Cataloging-in-Publication Data

Bookout, Travis J.

King of glory: reflections on the gospel of John / by Travis J. Bookout

p. cm.

Includes Scripture index.

ISBN 978-1-7347665-5-4 (pbk,); 978-1-7347665-6-1 (ebook)

I. Bible. John—Criticism, interpretation, etc. I. Author. III. Title.

226.506—dc20 Library of Congress Control Number: 2020920806

For information:
Cypress Publications
3625 Helton Drive
PO Box HCU Florence, AL 35630
www.hcu.edu

For Lauren, my witty, beautiful, and amazing wife.
You are my strength and helper, a constant encouragement,
travel buddy, dearest friend, and true love.

ACKNOWLEDGMENTS

The writing of this book could not have been completed without the assistance and encouragement of many along the way. To start, I want to thank my wife, Lauren Bookout, and dear friend Jeff Jenkins, along with the readers of my blog, who all encouraged me to continue, expand, and rework this study into book form. I am indebted to Lauren for her patience during the many hours I spent in my office studying and writing.

I am appreciative of Dr. Denny Petrillo and Dr. Dan Owen whose classes on John enriched my soul and opened my eyes to the wonders and mystery of this magnificent Gospel. I must also express gratitude to the Jackson Street Church of Christ for the many classes and sermons they sat through related to topics covered in this book.

I appreciate all who read this book, or sections of it, and offered helpful and constructive criticism. A special thanks to Chase Turner, Garrett Bookout, Kyle Savage, Jeff Jenkins, Dr. Dan Owen, Dr. Ted Burleson, Tim Lewis, Chuck Monan, and Dr. Ed Gallagher, each of whom are teachers, ministers, and/or professors I hold in high esteem, who took the time to read through the manuscript and share their thoughts with me.

I am grateful to Anna James Zeigler and Katie Allen for their time and proofreading skills. I'm sure my first drafts were no picnic to sludge through. Finally, I want to express my gratitude to Jamie Cox, Autumn Richardson, Brad McKinnon, Brittany Vander Maas, and the entire team at Cypress Publications, whose dedication and efforts made the hope of this book a reality.

LIST OF ABBREVIATIONS

Old Testament

Gen	Genesis
Exod	Exodus
Lev	Leviticus
Num	Numbers
Deut	Deuteronomy
Josh	Joshua
Judg	Judges
Ruth	Ruth
1–2 Sam	1–2 Samuel
1–2 Kgs	1–2 Kings
1–2 Chr	1–2 Chronicles
Ezra	Ezra
Neh	Nehemiah
Esth	Esther
Job	Job
Ps	Psalms
Prov	Proverbs
Ecc	Ecclesiastes

Song	Song of Solomon
Isa	Isaiah
Jer	Jeremiah
Lam	Lamentations
Ezek	Ezekiel
Dan	Daniel
Hos	Hosea
Joel	Joel
Amos	Amos
Obad	Obadiah
Jonah	Jonah
Mic	Micah
Nah	Nahum
Hab	Habakkuk
Zeph	Zephaniah
Hag	Haggai
Zech	Zechariah
Mal	Malachi

New Testament

Matt	Matthew
Mark	Mark
Luke	Luke
John	John
Acts	Acts
Rom	Romans
1–2 Cor	1–2 Corinthians
Gal	Galatians
Eph	Ephesians
Phil	Philippians
Col	Colossians
1–2 Thess	1–2 Thessalonains
1–2 Tim	1–2 Timothy
Titus	Titus
Phlm	Philemon
Heb	Hebrews

Jas	James
1–2 Pet	1–2 Peter
1–2–3 John	1–2–3 John
Jude	Jude
Rev	Revelation

FOREWORD

The Gospel of John is a strange book, and it introduces us to a rather strange Jesus. I recognize that "strange" is in the eye of the beholder, but for someone accustomed to the Synoptic Gospels of Matthew, Mark, and Luke, the Fourth Gospel is, at least, different. Jesus' interactions with people are sometimes mystifying—to me, anyway. Why, upon meeting Nathanael for the first time, does he describe him as an "Israelite in whom there is no guile" (1:47)? What does that have to do with anything? Or, a few verses later, what does he mean that Nathanael "will see heaven opened and the angels of God ascending and descending upon the Son of Man" (1:51)? His first miracle is turning water into wine at a wedding feast (2:1–11). Seems odd—a bit ... non-Jesusy. One of the religious leaders, Nicodemus, apparently wants to engage him in genuine conversation (3:1–2), but Jesus abruptly tells him, seemingly out of the blue, "verily, verily, I say unto you, except a person be born from above, he cannot see the kingdom of God" (3:3). When Nicodemus expresses bafflement, Jesus offers an explanation that only deepens Nicedemus' bewilderment (3:4–10). Later, when some people complain that Jesus is ignoring the Sabbath command, Jesus replies, "My Father is still working, and I also am working" (5:16–17). What kind of answer is that? The fact that you're working is the whole problem. Like Nicodemus, I find the Jesus of the Gospel of John confusing. I confess that the Fourth Gospel has long been my least favorite book of the New Testament.

I have no doubt all of this is by design. The somewhat more earthbound (mundane?) Synoptic Gospels resonate deeply with me, while the heavenly and mystical qualities of John's Gospel, which I find so confounding, challenge me to raise my spiritual perceptions. I recognize that the way to gain an appreciation for something is (usually) to study it. Readers left in the dark by this Gospel of Light need to spend more time with it. Had the servants brought Jesus' newly-made wine to me rather than to the chief steward in Cana (2:8–10), I would have had no idea whether it was good wine or bad wine or mediocre wine: I have not spent enough time with wine to be able to tell the difference. I'm not telling you to go to wine-tastings, I'm telling you to go to John-tastings. If you want the Fourth Gospel to be meaningful to you, the only way to get there is to spend time in John.

That's why you've picked up this book, which offers a year's worth of John-tastings. Our guide is Travis Bookout, an experienced Christian minister with graduate training in biblical interpretation. Travis was my student several years ago at Heritage Christian University, which makes me especially proud and gratified to be writing this Foreword to his wonderful book on John. I love Travis' approach to Scripture, his openness to think creatively, his respect for tradition and his determination to press beyond traditional understandings when something more seems to be happening in the biblical text, and his realization that there's always something more happening in the biblical text. Travis gives us bite-size tastes of John's Gospel for every week of the year.

Here's what each tasting is like: each chapter is a little over a thousand words (2–3 pages), and all those thousand words are aiming to help you become more familiar with the language and themes of John's Gospel, or, rather they are aiming to connect you to the eternal Word revealed in John's Gospel. Each tasting ends with a couple discussion questions. The chapters use Greek when appropriate and are conversant with scholarly literature but are written for regular people who want to grow in their appreciation of Scripture. And, yes, these chapters are helpful. There are three chapters on Nicodemus, the first of which retells his conversation with Jesus as a first attempt to demystify the encounter. The subsequent discussion over the next couple chapters highlights several aspects of the story: the phrase "born again," the further appearances of Nicodemus in the Gospel, the significance of the timing of the visit at night, Jesus' words to Nicodemus about the Spirit, the allusion to the brazen serpent from Numbers 21, and more.

How should you use this book? If I were you, I would first use it for personal devotion. Read the relevant passage from John's Gospel, and then read the discussion here. You should also consider teaching the material here in a church Bible class or discussing it in a small group.

Similar to many parts of the Bible, so also with John's Gospel we can study this profound account of our Lord all our lives and still fail to plumb its depths. But I bet Travis will help you along the way. As Jesus says early in this Gospel, "Come and see" (1:39).

Ed Gallagher
Florence, Alabama
November 2020

CONTENTS

Prologue   1

Reflection 1   5
The Logos and the Son

Reflection 2   11
Signs, Belief, and Eternal Life

Reflection 3   16
His Testimony Is True

Reflection 4   20
The Beloved Disciple

Reflection 5   26
Come and See

Reflection 6   30
You Follow Me

Reflection 7   35
Feast Days

Reflection 8   40
Misunderstanding Jesus (Part 1)

Reflection 9   45
Misunderstanding Jesus (Part 2)

Reflection 10   50
Reading the Signs

Reflection 11   54
Water into Wine

Reflection 12   59
Cleansing the Temple

Reflection 13   63
Jesus as the Temple

Reflection 14   67
Healing the Royal Official's Son

Reflection 15   72
Healing at Bethesda

Reflection 16   77
Bread from Heaven (Part 1)

Reflection 17   82
Bread from Heaven (Part 2)

Reflection 18   87
Walking on Water

Reflection 19   92
Healing the Blind Man (Part 1)

Reflection 20   97
Healing the Blind Man (Part 2)

Reflection 21   101
Healing the Blind Man (Part 3)

Reflection 22   105
Healing the Blind Man (Part 4)

Reflection 23   110
Raising Lazarus (Part 1)

Reflection 24   115
Raising Lazarus (Part 2)

Reflection 25   120
Meeting Nicodemus

Reflection 26   124
Nicodemus at Night

Reflection 27   128
Nicodemus and Snakes

Reflection 28   132
The Samaritan Woman at the Well

Reflection 29   138
Meeting God at the Well

Reflection 30   143
Equality with God

Reflection 31   148
Before Abraham Was, I Am

Reflection 32   153
Finally, A Good Shepherd

Reflection 33   158
I and the Father Are One

Reflection 34   163
Passover

Reflection 35   168
Washing Feet—The Incarnation

Reflection 36   172
Washing Feet—Let Go and Let God

Reflection 37   176
Washing Judas's Feet

Reflection 38   180
More than Clean Feet

Reflection 39   184
In My Father's House

Reflection 40   189
The Way, the Truth, and the Life

Reflection 41   193
I Am the True Vine

Reflection 42   198
You Are My Friends

Reflection 43   203
Persecution and Religious Violence

Reflection 44   208
The Holy Spirit and the World

Reflection 45   213
Grief Will Be Turned Into Joy

Reflection 46   217
Farewell Prayer

Reflection 47   222
Betrayed, Arrested, and Denied

Reflection 48   227
The King and His Kingdom

Reflection 49   232
Crucified

Reflection 50   237
The First Day of the Week

Reflection 51   242
Doubts and Fears

Reflection 52   247
Fishing with Jesus

Appendix 1   252
The Woman in Adultery

Appendix 2   257
Decide

Bibliography   261

Scripture Index   263

PROLOGUE

Origin and Goal

This book began as a blog series with a simple goal—once a week for one year I wanted to post something related to the Gospel of John. It may have been one of the major themes throughout the Gospel or just a thought on one particular character, story, or verse. My hope was at the end of the year, these fifty-two reflections would have aided my walk with God and served as a helpful introduction to some of the major ideas presented by John. It was primarily for me as I read, reflected, and wrote on the Gospel of John. I wanted to grow. I wanted to challenge myself. I wanted to spend a year focused on Jesus.

As a teacher, I thought it'd be useful to be able to go back and remember this dive into the fourth Gospel; I want you to as well. While working through this study of John's Gospel, and posting occasional blogs, I was encouraged to put them together into a collection for publication. Thus, this book was born and my journey can now become your journey. Whether you are reading straight through, taking a year for a slower meditative journey, or using it to teach a Bible class or small group study, I hope this causes everyone to appreciate, understand, and embody the call of John's Gospel. I hope you experience the same growth I have.

Well, life got real, and it took longer than a year to finish. Having two children, taking on a teaching job along with my ministry responsibilities, and entering into another graduate degree program all had a way of slowing down the project. However, those experiences also gave me fresh insights and ideas while reflecting and writing. I began the book with no children and finished it with a three and a two-year-old. As you'll see, they pop up from time to time.

Why Study John?

The Gospel of John has been profound in my life, ministry, and understanding of Jesus. It is my favorite evangelism tract ever produced. It is one of my favorite books in the Bible to read, study, teach, preach, and now write about. I want this book to put Jesus front and center in everything. This is not just a commentary on the Gospel of John. It's not just for you to learn more linguistics, history, or dispassionate theology. This is about Jesus. I want to glorify Jesus in all that is written. When this book is read, studied, and taught I want Jesus to be honored and worshiped. I want His brilliance, wisdom, and divinity to drip from every page. I pray everything written is pleasing to Him.

I also pray everything written respects the intentions of the original author. Again, this is not simply a commentary. It is not merely exegesis (the critical examination and interpretation of a text to draw out the author's original intention). This includes personal reflections on the Gospel of John. These are the thoughts and meditations which arouse my mind when I read about the Logos of God. I want them to be contextual, exegetically sound, and theologically true. I want them to honor the meaning of the original Greek, historical context, and authorial intent. Yet for me, this book is more personal than that. I hope it is for you also.

Disclaimer

There are things I ponder within this book that I cannot prove John specifically had in mind. There are ideas I present that may reflect my heart more than strict, rigorous exegesis. I admit that. I try to present none of those reflections dogmatically. I try to know when I have left exegesis and venture into speculation. I use the word "perhaps" over 60 times in this book. That is on purpose. I do not believe, however, any of these reflections would be offensive or unwelcomed by John. I pray each of them honors this Gospel and honors Jesus above all. Imagination is a gift from God, and I have done my best to portray a scripturally shaped and theologically sound imagination. You may not agree with everything written herein and that's okay. If your reflections lead you in another direction, I pray it is one that honors God and produces fruit for the kingdom. I'm truly thrilled if this book causes you to stop, read, think, meditate, and reflect on Jesus.

Admitting that, it's still not meant to be entirely subjective. I hope you actually learn the Gospel of John. I hope you walk away knowing the major themes presented. I hope you develop a greater understanding of the context, flow, and intentions of the author. I hope you learn more about Jesus. Many Scriptures have been cited and expounded upon. Without faithful interpretation of Scripture, the inspired transformative message loses its effect. Most Scripture citations come from the NASB, ESV, NRSV, or my own translation.

There is some Greek discussed in this book. You do not have to know Greek to follow the arguments and presentations in this book, but I do think it can help you to see some of the Greek words and texts for yourself. I will leave most of them in Greek script with my translation right beside it, but some words I transliterate into English so anyone can read it.

Organization and Structure

This book is arranged thematically rather than in the order John presents the information. It follows a loose structure similar to John's, but it jumps around thematically. The first 10 reflections introduce you to ideas and themes presented throughout the entire Gospel. They focus just as much on the end of the Gospel as the beginning. So, when you get to the conclusion of the Gospel of John, you'll see themes emerging you've already been introduced to and have hopefully been searching for. You'll see passages cited you've already studied. I think that can be beneficial.

Because it is not a verse by verse commentary, not every verse is discussed. I tried to make sure major stories, conversations, and major themes receive attention. Almost every paragraph is addressed either directly or is referenced as it relates to one of those major stories, conversations, or themes.

At the end of each reflection are two sets of questions. I challenge you to answer them for yourself or discuss them as a small group. These questions are to cause you to reflect on how the story of Jesus can transform you. Please do not skip this part. Some of the questions you may breeze right through. Some of them may require more time and thought. Take that time and give it that thought. That's where growth really occurs. I can personally attest to the fact that I have grown while considering these things. My prayer is you will also.

The Gospel of John is a testimony about Jesus written that you may believe. The signs call us to deeper understanding and recognition of who Jesus is and what He is doing in the world. This book serves the same purpose. Whether you are already a believer or not, I hope this book will challenge you to believe and take seriously the call of Jesus, following Him wherever He leads. Following Him where you don't want to go. Following Him to the cross. It is there you will find eternal life.

REFLECTION 1
THE LOGOS AND THE SON

John 1:1–18

The Logos of God

The Gospel begins with a shocking declaration: "In the beginning was the Word, and the Word was with God, and the Word was God" (John 1:1). The "Word" (Logos) existed before the world, existed with God, and existed as God. Throughout John, there is mass confusion about where Jesus came from (John 3:13, 31; 6:32–40, 51; 7:41–42, 52; 16:27–29, etc.). The reader knows from the beginning, He came from being with God. Yet to say someone was "with God" is quite different than saying someone "was God." How is it possible to be the person you are with? If someone is with you, they cannot be you. It is understandable that this difficult and frustrating concept will forever remain a source of conflict and tension when it comes to Jesus.

Interestingly, Jesus does nothing to ease the tension. He constantly speaks of God as His Father but then says things that only God can say (John 8:58). He speaks as though the Father is distinct from Him, but then says, "I and the Father are one" (John 10:30). Most characters reject these statements as blasphemy (John 8:59; 10:31), but some, though the journey is long and arduous, begin to see in Jesus something truly divine. Some will look upon Him and say "My Lord and My God" (John 20:28).

Seriously, that's almost an impossible thing to believe. I cannot imagine what it must have been like. I've been shaped by 2000 years of Christian tradition. It doesn't shock me like it should. Imagine you've never heard of Jesus. You've never heard of the incarnation. You've never heard of Christianity. What would it take to convince you some kid who grew up down the street from you, you knew his parents, you saw every awkward stage of his life, was "in the beginning with God and was God?" Could you ever believe He literally came down out of heaven? It's certainly understandable the crowds say, "Is this not Jesus, the son of Joseph, whose father and mother we know? How does He now say, 'I have come down out of heaven?'" (John 6:42). That is why it is so imperative to pay close attention to His signs (Reflection #2 and #10). They reveal the impossible. They show you what you'd otherwise never believe.

This prologue frames the Gospel of John and reframes everything we thought we knew about the world and God. God exists and He also speaks. His "Word" is what He speaks. His "Word" is how He created the world. His "Word" perfectly reflects His mind. His being. His "Word" is Him. The two are linked together as One in fascinating ways. This idea is not completely unique to the Gospel of John. The supremacy of the Word, the Logos, has deep roots both in Jewish wisdom tradition and Greco-Roman philosophy, particularly Stoicism, which saw logos as the rational force animating the whole cosmos.

Wisdom and New Creation

For John's readers, the Jewish Bible will prove a more reliable backdrop to the prologue.[1] The Old Testament equates God's

Wisdom with God Himself and His creative nature. Wisdom is personified in Proverbs as having been with God from creation:

> I, wisdom dwell with prudence ...When He established the heavens, I was there, When He inscribed a circle on the face of the deep, When He made firm the skies above, When the springs of the deep became fixed, When He set forth the sea its boundary So that the water would not transgress His command, When He marked out the foundations of the earth; Then I was beside Him, as a master workman; And I was daily His delight, Rejoicing always before Him, Rejoicing in the world, His earth, And having my delight in the sons of men (Prov 8:12, 23–31).

If you were asked, "Who was with God when He created the world? Who was the 'master workman' with God in creation? Who was 'His delight' before He created the world?" how would you answer? If you say, "Jesus" I think that's probably a good answer (though not exactly what Proverbs has in mind). In fact, the early church always read Proverbs 8 to be about Jesus and it was quite the controversial passage. Most of the early church read the Old Testament in Greek although it was originally written in Hebrew. This means they were reading a translation, just like we do. And anytime you read a translation there are difficulties that arise.

The Greek Old Testament, called the Septuagint (LXX), says God "created" wisdom in Proverbs 8:22. The Hebrew Old Testament says God "possessed" wisdom in that passage. The LXX translators translated the Hebrew word for "possessed" (קָנָנִי) with the Greek word for "created" (ἔκτισέν). If you assume Proverbs 8 is about Jesus, and you're reading the LXX, you have a homerun argument that Jesus is a created being, which was a crucial argument for Arianism, an early church controversy saying Jesus is not co-eternal with God, but was created by God. If it's about Jesus, and you're reading the Hebrew Bible, you simply have Jesus coexisting with God at the beginning. Early Christians argued about the best way to interpret this passage, but interestingly, no one ever really argued Proverbs 8 wasn't about Jesus.

Proverbs 8 in its original context, however, isn't so much talking about Jesus, but wisdom personified. God's wisdom has always been with Him. It is part of Him. Wisdom was active when God created. The same is true for His Word: "By the word of the Lord the heavens were made" (Ps 33:6). In fact, in Jewish writings, the word and wisdom of God are often linked together, especially in creation! The Wisdom of Solomon, a beautiful collection of Jewish poetry, begins a special prayer for wisdom with these words: "God of our ancestors, Lord of mercy, who by your word have made all things, and in your wisdom you have formed man to rule the creatures that have come from you, to govern the world in holiness and justice, and in honesty of soul to wield authority ..." (Wisdom 9:1–2). God created the world and formed man by His logos and sophia, His word and wisdom. There are many ways one can describe the divinity of Jesus, but I think John has picked up on this idea and is bringing them together in his introduction to Jesus.

The word and wisdom of God are eternal and coexistent with God. There was never a time God was without His wisdom or His word (Or Spirit for that matter). They are inexorably linked to each other because God's word without exception contains His wisdom. God has no words without wisdom. Together, God and His wisdom and His word created the world. In joining all of these together in the person of Jesus, John begins to retell the creation story of Genesis 1.

"In the beginning" is not some accidental, throwaway phrase. It is meant to call you back to creation itself. John reads and retells Genesis 1 with the word of God personified: "All things came into being through Him, and apart from Him nothing came into being that has come into being" (John 1:3). If you open your Bible to Genesis 1, you'll see the phrases "And God said..." or "God called..." repeated over and over again (Gen 1:3, 5, 6, 8, 9, 11, 14, 20, 22, 24, 26, 28, 29). Just think about how much God speaks in Genesis 1. There are so many words and each one is dripping with wisdom. By taking God's creative word and wisdom and joining them in Christ, John is beginning His gospel with a call to radically rethink everything you thought you knew about the cosmos and everything God created. Jesus' fingerprint is everywhere.

The Word has become a character in John's creation story. God's Word exists with and as the Creator, from whom also comes the light which shines in the darkness. When all was darkness upon the face of the deep primordial waters of earth, God said, "Let there be light" (Gen 1:2–3). In John's retelling of the creation story, Jesus is the Light of the World (John 9:5) which shines in the darkness (John 1:5; Gen 1:2–5). God's wisdom and word, in Jesus, illuminate the world through new creation. In John 1:1–5, God's new creative work to transform the world through Jesus is being introduced.

God in the Flesh

The most shocking part of this text, which separates it from Genesis, Jewish wisdom tradition, and Greek philosophy, is when "the Word became flesh, and dwelt among us, and we saw His glory" (John 1:14). The Logos which produces new creation became part of old creation. God became flesh. The word "dwelt" (ἐσκήνωσεν) in verse 14 literally means "He tabernacled" among us (see Rev 21:3). The Word became the new tabernacle on earth, which housed the glory of God. Remember the Exodus story? Moses prays, "I pray you, show me Your glory!" (Exod 33:18). The glory of the Lord passed by Moses briefly in the cleft of the rock (Exod 33:22). The glory of God was seen in the tabernacle, a cloud by day and fire by night (Exod 13:21; 40:35). The glory of God is now seen in His new tabernacle. As John continues, we will see Jesus is not only the life-giving force of new creation, He is the new tabernacle, temple, and presence of God on earth. The glory of God is seen in Him, "full of grace and truth."

If you want to see God, look to Jesus. If you want to see God's grace, truth, and glory, look to Jesus. "No one has ever seen God; the only God, the One who is in the bosom of the Father, He has made Him known" (John 1:18). Jesus "has made Him known" or literally exegeted (ἐξηγήσατο) God. He has embodied God and shown Him to the world; who He is, what He says, and how He lives. Jesus, the Logos of God, is everything we need to know about God. He has come. He is transforming the world. Come and see how.

Reflection Questions

1. In what ways has God remade the world through Jesus? How is the life of Jesus like the beginning of Genesis? How many connections can you make between the coming of Adam into the world and the coming of Jesus into the world?

2. What has the life of Jesus revealed to you about God? In what ways do you think about God differently because of Jesus?

---

1. For a good discussion on Jesus as the Word and Wisdom of God, see Richard B. Hays, *Echoes of Scripture in the Gospels* (Waco: Baylor University Press, 2017), 308–10.

REFLECTION 2

SIGNS, BELIEF, AND ETERNAL LIFE

∽

That You May Believe

Let's begin at the end and work our way from there, shall we? "Therefore, many other signs Jesus also performed in the presence of the disciples, which are not written in this book; but these have been written so that you may believe that Jesus is the Christ, the Son of God; and that believing you may have life in His name" (John 20:30–31). Don't you just love it when you're reading the Bible and searching for the occasion or purpose of a book and you come across a verse like this? It does all your thinking for you. He doesn't leave it ambiguous. John just comes right out and tells you why he wrote this book, why he included the signs he did, and what his goal is for the reader. John was written with an agenda; he lays his biases and motivations right out on the table.

Modern histories are written with the goal of objectivity. They attempt to avoid agendas and slants and just give facts and history. They want to hide their bias, though they always fail. Everything ever written has bias. John wants you to know his. He wants you to pick up this book, read it through, and at the end become a follower of Jesus. He wants you to believe. He wants you to find eternal life. To achieve this, he records a series of signs performed by Jesus. We'll talk a lot more about these signs throughout this book, but always remember John's signs have a purpose. They are to bring about belief.

After miraculously turning water into wine, John records, "This beginning of His signs Jesus did in Cana of Galilee, and manifested His glory, and His disciples believed in Him" (John 2:11). The first sign recorded produced belief. A little later Jesus says, "Unless you people see signs and wonders, you simply will not believe" (John 4:48). Then, He heals a Nobleman's son, "and he himself believed and his whole household. This is again the second sign that Jesus performed when He had come out of Judea into Galilee" (John 4:53–54). John counts the first two and invites you to count the rest. He also notes when each of these signs is honestly observed they each result in belief.

From Signs to Belief to Life

There is a constant connection between the signs of Jesus and belief in His name. In fact, if you search for the word "signs" in the Gospel of John, there is a pretty good chance you'll find the word "belief" close in the context. Nicodemus learns Jesus came from God as a teacher because "no one can do the signs that You do unless God is with him" (John 3:2). Jesus convinced the crowds that He "is truly the Prophet who is to come into the world" because "the people saw the signs which He had performed (John 6:14). "Many of the crowd believed in Him; and they were saying, 'When the Christ comes, He will not perform more signs than those which this man has, will He?" (John 7:31).

Sadly, however, not everyone is convinced: "Though He had performed so many signs before them, yet they were not believing in Him" (John 12:37). This could be a good summary statement of the first half of the Gospel of John. He did so many signs, from turning water into wine to raising Lazarus, but many just could not believe. John informs us this lack of belief actually fulfills Scripture (John

12:38–41). To those with eyes to see, to those who are not blind, to those in light rather than darkness, the signs are visible and amazing. They produce belief. To those who love darkness and are blind, they are blind to the signs. They care more about whether the sign was performed on Sabbath than if Jesus actually did it. The connection between signs and belief continues throughout the entire Gospel (John 6:30; 11:45–48; 20:20–29).

This connection makes a lot of sense. It's not an easy thing those who meet Jesus are asked to believe. It's not an easy thing John's readers are asked to believe. It's hard. And dangerous. It's actually a terrifying thing to believe. What would it take for you to call a man "God"? You know what happens if you're wrong, right? That's blasphemy. That's idolatry. That's an insult to your Creator and puts your life in jeopardy. That's what the pagans do! That's what the kings of Rome and other ruthless, godless pagan nations do. They elevate men to the status of gods. A man made of mere flesh and blood. A man who bleeds when you cut him. Any faithful Jew would immediately reject this idea. If king David claimed to be a god, as powerful as he was, he should be rejected as king and punished for his blasphemies. Abraham, Moses, David, Xerxes, Augustus, Nero, Domitian, it doesn't matter, none of them should ever claim to be equal to God.

But what about that one guy from insignificant little Nazareth? A king? No, I think he was a small-time carpenter. He wasn't wealthy. Not noticeably handsome. Looked human in every way. Never held a political office or any powerful position in society. He was actually a criminal. He was arrested and tried and crucified. He cried. He bled. He died. Do you think He is God?

What could possibly convince someone of that? Thank God for signs. They are necessary. What if He claimed to be God and then backed it up by doing things only God can do? What if He could turn water into wine and heal the sick by merely speaking a word (John 2, 4)? What if He miraculously multiplied bread to feed thousands and so controlled nature as to walk on water (John 6)? What if He gave life and light to the world through raising the dead and giving sight to the blind (John 9 and 11)? If nothing else, that certainly makes Him worth listening to. What if, after they crucified Him, He victoriously raised from the dead, vindicated His radical claims, and offered that same eternal life to all who would put their trust in Him? Would you listen? Could you believe? Signs make belief possible. They put the reality of belief right in front of you. They challenge you to believe the impossible.

The goal of the signs is to produce this frightening, dangerous, impossible belief. And the goal of this belief is to produce life. "For God so loved the world that He gave His only begotten Son, that whoever believes in Him shall not perish, but have eternal life" (John 3:16). That sounds a lot like John's stated purpose: "That believing, you may have life in His name" (John 20:30–31). The God who gives life is offering it through His Son and proving it through His signs. Will you believe it?

Evangelizing with John

All of this (signs, belief, life, etc.) will be discussed in much more detail in the ensuing Reflections. For now, I want to close with this thought: If John's goal was to write a book that would cause people to have faith in Jesus and eternal life, do you think he reached it? Do you think this book can produce belief? Can it produce eternal life? This question shifted the way I do personal evangelism.

I trust John is both a competent writer and inspired by God. If he thinks this book can bring someone to eternal life, then I bet he's right. If John were the only book in the Bible, we might know a lot less, but we should still be able to have eternal life through Jesus. So, one of the ways I like to study with people and evangelize is simply to go through the Gospel of John. You don't have to flip to 400 verses throughout different books of the Bible. You don't even need to leave this one gospel. Just read through it and study it together. Discuss it together. By doing this, people can see everything in context and appreciate how seriously you take the words of Scripture.

John is structured in such a way that all the information you need about Jesus to receive eternal life is there. If interpreted properly, this book leaves nothing out that is essential to life. Rather than me coming up with my own way of telling the story of Jesus, I let the inspired writer do it. I follow his lead. And at the end of the book I can be confident there has been enough taught "that you may believe."

Reflection Questions

1. Do you believe Jesus is the Christ, the Son of God? If so, list your reasons why. If not, list your reasons why.

2. What benefits do you see in evangelizing by studying through John? Do you think this is a helpful way to introduce people to Christianity? What are the pros and cons of this method?

REFLECTION 3

HIS TESTIMONY IS TRUE

~

His Testimony is True

As you read John, it becomes apparent that recording signs was not John's only method in producing belief. Consider this statement John makes about witnessing the crucifixion: "And he who has seen has testified, and his testimony is true; and he knows that he is telling the truth, so that you also may believe" (John 19:35).

The purpose of this testimony is "so that you also may believe" (John 19:35), which is the same stated purpose as the signs: "that you may believe" (John 20:30). In addition to signs, a second strategy John employs to produce faith in the reader is testimony. He records a series of testimonies about Jesus and as an eyewitness claims "his testimony is true" (John 19:35; 21:24).

John the Baptist

One way John reveals Jesus' identity is by telling stories where the characters offer profound testimony about Jesus. It starts all the way back with John the Baptist, introduced as "a man sent from God, whose name was John. He came as a witness, to testify about the Light, so that all might believe through him" (John 1:6–7). The first human character in the gospel is a "witness" who "testifies." The word "witness" could be translated "testifier," and the word "testify" could be translated "bear witness." Whenever you see the words "testify" or "bear witness," those are the same Greek word (μαρτυρέω). It's pronounced martureo, and it's used repeatedly. Notice also, he came to testify "so that all might believe" (John 1:7). Just like the signs, testimony is intended to produce belief and belief is intended to produce life.

But what did John testify about Jesus? Just reading through the first Reflection, you find several things John the Baptist testified about Jesus (John 1:15, 19, 32, 34). John testified that Jesus ranks higher than him, because of His preexistence (John 1:15, 30). He testified that he is unworthy to even untie the thong on Jesus' sandal (John 1:27). He testified that Jesus is the Lamb of God who takes away the sin of the world (John 1:29, 36). He testified that the Spirit descended upon Jesus at His baptism (John 1:32). He testified that Jesus is the Son of God (John 1:35). Not only that, but when his own disciples heard his testimony, they left him to become followers of Jesus (John 1:37). That is his goal. Don't follow John, follow Jesus.

The List of Witnesses

John the Baptist is an excellent witness about Jesus. His testimony led to followers, but he was not the only one to do this. Andrew testifies to Peter, "We have found the Messiah" (John 1:41). Philip testifies to Nathanael, "We have found Him of whom Moses in the Law and also the Prophets wrote—Jesus of Nazareth, the Son of Joseph" (John 1:45). Nathanael then testifies saying, "Rabbi, you are the Son of God; You are the king of Israel" (John 1:49). Each of these testimonies produces more followers!

Adding up all the things you learned about Jesus in these testimonies: He was preexistent, He is greater than John the Baptist,

He is the Lamb of God who takes away the sin of the world, the Holy Spirit came upon Him, He is the Son of God, He is the Messiah, the Law and Prophets write of Him, He is the King of Israel! When John compiles these testimonies he gives you a great look into the identity of Jesus. And that's only John 1!

As the Gospel continues, more characters meet Jesus and testify great things about Him!

Nicodemus says, "Rabbi, we know that you have come from God as a teacher..." (John 3:2). The woman at the well says to her fellow Samaritans, "Come, see a man who told me all the things that I have done; this is not the Christ, is it?" (John 4:29). Then we find out "many of the Samaritans believed in Him because of the word of the woman who testified, 'He told me all the things I have ever done'" (John 4:39). Her testimony produced belief! In fact, once the Samaritans meet Jesus, they all testify, "we have heard for ourselves and know that this One is indeed the Savior of the world." (John 4:42).

It is intentional the way John structures his Gospel. It's a major theme that cuts through the whole story, and it's teaching us about Jesus. In John 5, during a discussion about His relationship with the Father, Jesus clearly and dangerously articulates His equality with God (John 5:18-30). Then He supports His claim with His own list of witnesses: John the Baptist testified about Him, His works testify about Him, the Father testifies about Him, Scripture testifies about Him (John 5:31–47; cf. John 8:12–19).

After feeding the 5,000 the crowds testify: "This is truly the prophet who is to come into the world" (John 6:14). Peter proclaims, "We have believed and have come to know that You are the Holy One of God" (John 6:68). During disputes, some would say, "'This certainly is the Prophet.' Others were saying, 'This is the Christ'" (John 7:40–41). Even Jesus testifies about Himself (John 8:18) in His famous "I Am" statements.

I Am the bread of life (John 6:35, 48)
I Am the light of the world (John 8:12; 9:5)
I Am the door (John 10:7, 9)

I Am the good shepherd (John 10:11, 14)
I Am the resurrection and the life (John 11:25)
I Am the way, the truth, and the life (John 14:6)
I Am the true vine (John 15:1–11)

The list of testimonies is extensive and grows and culminates in the post-resurrection testimony of Thomas: "My Lord and my God!" (John 20:28).

So, who is Jesus? If you look at the testimonies from all the eyewitnesses, you get to see Jesus in all His glory. I wish I could have been there myself. I wish I could have seen the signs and heard the testimonies, but I'm 2000 years removed from the incarnation. That's why I love the Gospel of John. These testimonies are written down for me. And you. And anyone who picks up the Gospel of John. And they are intended to produce faith in all of us who couldn't see it for ourselves. That's why we need the testimonies. That's why they are recorded. That's also why Jesus tells Thomas, "Blessed are they who did not see, and yet believed" (John 20:29).

That's us. That's a call to us. How can we believe without seeing?

Trust the testimonies and follow the signs. Those who do are blessed. Those who do inherit eternal life.

Reflection Questions

1. What do you find to be a profound testimony about Jesus? Why? Who do you know who needs to hear that testimony? Are you willing to share it with them?

2. Why do signs and testimonies work so well together in bringing about belief? What do you think of John's apologetic method? Is it still convincing in our modern world?

REFLECTION 4
THE BELOVED DISCIPLE

~

The Unnamed Disciple

In John 13:23 we are introduced to a disciple who becomes a major figure in the second half of the Gospel of John. In fact, the anonymous Gospel of John concludes by saying this unnamed disciple is the one who "is testifying to these things and wrote these things" (John 21:24). I've been calling him "John" so far in this book, but the Gospel notably referred to him by the descriptions "the beloved disciple" or "the disciple whom Jesus loved" or even just "the other disciple" (John 13:23; 18:15–16; 20:2–4). There seems to be a particularly special relationship between him and Jesus. He is held up as the prime example of discipleship and what it means to be a follower. Perhaps it is a display of his humility that he leaves his name unmentioned.

To me it's always a little funny when a biblical author intentionally leaves something ambiguously unresolved, but scholars come along years later refusing to accept the ambiguity. If we were supposed to know who this "beloved disciple" was, we would know. He could easily tell us but apparently, doesn't want to. Not only do so many discussions of his identity ignore authorial intent (the author didn't intend to say his name), but they have also had the tendency to turn contentious: "You must say it's John or you're a liberal!" "Only a fundamentalist could claim this was actually written by the disciple John!" The truth is, we are not certain who the beloved disciple is and that is kind of the inspired point. It's anonymous for a reason. We don't need to know!

Later church tradition is where the name "John" gets associated with this gospel. This is primarily because John, a major figure in the other gospels, is not mentioned in the Gospel of John (except a passing reference to the "sons of Zebedee" in 21:2). In contrast, the beloved disciple, a major figure in the Gospel of John, is not mentioned in the other gospels. If you are looking for which disciple has been replaced by "the beloved disciple" you're likely left with John.

Many have noticed a few problems with this interpretation, however.[1] Many of the events John witnessed that you would expect him to write about are absent, and the beloved disciple does things the other gospels give zero indication John ever did. Notably, the other gospels seemingly imply all the disciples abandoned Jesus in Gethsemane (Mark 14:50) and were absent at the cross, including John. The beloved disciple is there though and actually becomes Mary's primary caretaker. He becomes her own son (John 19:25–27).

Lazarus or John?

An interesting theory put forth by Ben Witherington III, is the "beloved disciple" is actually Lazarus.[2] While John would have been with Jesus from the beginning, the "beloved disciple" is not introduced until after Lazarus is raised. Jesus stayed and reclined with Lazarus after he was raised (John 12:1–2) and large crowds knew they were together (John 12:9). If it's John, why wasn't the beloved disciple present earlier? If it is Lazarus, who wasn't there earlier, it makes a lot of sense to begin mentioning him in John 13, after Lazarus enters the picture.

When Lazarus becomes ill the news brought to Jesus is "Lord, behold, he whom You love is sick" (John 11:3). When Jesus wept at his tomb, the crowds all said, "See how he loved him!" (John 11:36). So Lazarus is introduced in John 11 as a disciple loved by Jesus, or in other words, a beloved disciple. (It may be noteworthy, however, both John 11:3 and 36 use the word phileo for love, but most of the time the beloved disciple is described with agapao. John 20:2 is an exception where the beloved disciple is called phileo just like Lazarus).

The beloved disciple has a personal relationship with the high priest. It would be far more likely a well-known man from Judea, like Lazarus, would know the high priest, rather than a random uneducated fisherman all the way from Galilee (John 18:16).

Finally, there seemed to be an early Christian belief the beloved disciple would never die (John 21:22–23). That belief makes sense if the beloved disciple was somebody Jesus had already raised from the dead. He already defeated death. Then when Jesus says he'll possibly be around "until I come" (John 21:22–23), this cements the belief even more! Granted, it's wrong, but it is at least interesting to ponder how it developed.

Now, am I saying it was Lazarus who wrote the fourth Gospel? Certainly not. I don't know for certain who wrote it. Just like Hebrews. There are good reasons to think it is John, and I usually stick with tradition unless there are overwhelming reasons not to.

For the purposes of this study, we're just going to refer to the author as John. It's just easier that way and has a lot of Christian tradition behind it. There are problems and uncertainties with whoever you choose, which is why we should be cautious about making these choices. Let the author have his way. If he leaves it ambiguous, perhaps so should we.

The Beloved Disciple and Peter

One fascinating fact about the beloved disciple is almost every time he is mentioned, he is connected or, you might even say, compared with Peter, and he always seems to be a step ahead of him (both figuratively and literally).

When he is first introduced, Jesus and the disciples are reclining at a table (not sitting in chairs but lying next to each other around a short table), and Peter wants to know who is going to betray Jesus. Rather than asking Jesus, he asks the beloved disciple who then asks Jesus. The beloved disciple occupies the space in between Peter and Jesus (John 13:23–25). He's physically closer to Jesus and intercedes between Peter and Jesus. That may not be insignificant.

The beloved disciple and Peter both follow Jesus to the court of the high priest after His arrest, but it is the beloved disciple who gets Peter through the gate (John 18:15–16). Peter cannot get there on his own. While inside, it is Peter who denies Jesus three times, but the beloved disciple follows Him all the way to the cross. Again, the beloved disciple is literally closer to Jesus.

It is the beloved disciple, while Jesus is on the cross, who becomes the caretaker of Mary, while Peter is nowhere to be found (John 19:25–27). The beloved disciple becomes part of Jesus' family while Peter denies even knowing Him.

Upon hearing word of the resurrection, it is the beloved disciple and Peter who sprint to the tomb and, keeping with the competition motif, "the other disciple ran ahead faster than Peter and came to the tomb first" (John 20:4). What a funny detail unless it has some spiritual meaning. The beloved disciple is always ahead of Peter in following Jesus.

While at the empty tomb standing together, it is the "other disciple" who "saw and believed" (John 20:8).

After the resurrection, while fishing, the disciples do not recognize the man standing on the shore, but it is "that disciple whom Jesus loved" who says to Peter, "It is the Lord" (John 21:4–7).

The beloved disciple is the first to recognize Jesus and he points Peter to Jesus.

Finally, while Peter is walking with the resurrected Jesus, he is challenged to follow. Follow even to the point of death, even death by crucifixion. Jesus says, "You follow Me!" (John 21:18–19). Peter responds with trepidation by looking around for the beloved disciple, the one who reclined on Jesus' bosom at the supper, and who is already "following" (John 21:20). Peter asks, "What about this man?" (John 21:21). There is a sense Peter has noticed this competition also. He compares himself to the beloved disciple. Jesus tells Peter not to worry about that man, if he's around until the second coming that has nothing to do with you. Peter needs to focus on Peter, or more accurately: Peter needs to focus on Jesus. "You follow Me!" (John 21:22).

We don't know for certain exactly who this beloved disciple is, but he is a follower of Jesus. He is a true disciple. He's an eyewitness, and his writings have impacted the church in immeasurable ways. He excelled in every instance where Peter failed but note that Peter is not told to follow the beloved disciple, nor is he told to stop following Jesus. Don't compare yourself to the disciple next to you, just follow Jesus. That's your call. That's your mission. As wonderful as the beloved disciple appears to be, as faithful as the youth minister, preacher, elder, or scholar may appear to be, you follow Jesus. Make sure, more than anything or anyone else, your loyalty, allegiance, and discipleship is rooted in Christ. That's what He is looking for.

Reflection Questions

1. Why might the beloved disciple have kept his identity secret? What do you think is significant about the description "beloved disciple"? Why would Jesus have chosen him to look after Mary?

2. Do you ever struggle with comparing yourself to others? Why is this problematic in the church? What can you do to overcome this?

1. Mark Allan Powell, *Introducing the New Testament: A Historical, Literary, and Theological Survey* (Grand Rapids: Baker Academic, 2009), 173–177.
2. Ben Witherington III, *What Have They Done with Jesus?: Beyond Strange Theories and Bad History—Why We Can Trust the Bible* (San Francisco: HarperCollins, 2006), 144–47.

REFLECTION 5
COME AND SEE

~

The Fourth Wall

The so-called fourth wall is a dramatic convention in acting. Like the four walls in a bedroom, the stage itself is broken into four walls. The fourth wall separates the actors from the audience and is supposed to serve a purpose similar to a one–way mirror. The audience can see through the wall to what is on the other side, namely, the performance. The actors, however, are not supposed to be able to see through the wall to the audience. To the actors, the fourth wall is fixed and solid, as if there is nothing on the other side.

In several modern television shows it has become common to "break the fourth wall," meaning, the actors address the audience directly as though they are part of the performance. Shows like *The Office* and *Parks and Recreation* do this regularly. Frequently on *The Office* when Michael says something absurd, Jim glances over at the camera/audience. Sometimes, even during scenes, the camera will cut to a character sitting alone to talk to the audience, like an inter– view. In the early '90s, Zack Morris had the ability to freeze time by saying, "Time Out." Then while everyone else was frozen, he would address the audience. This is called "breaking the fourth wall" and it brings the audience into the performance.

To the Reader

At this point, you may be wondering what any of this has to do with the Gospel of John. Well, the fourth gospel likes to break the fourth wall. There are times when the characters are speaking to one another, but it's obvious they are actually, in a profound way, addressing the reader. For example, when Jesus says to Thomas, "Because you have seen Me, have you believed? Blessed are they who did not see, and yet believed" (John 20:29). Thomas believed because he had the privilege of seeing the resurrected Jesus. Those first reading the Gospel of John do not have this same privilege. They must all come to believe without seeing. When Jesus says, "Blessed are those who did not see, and yet believed," you should imagine His head turning to face the camera, Him looking directly at you, breaking the fourth wall to address the reader with these words.

The same thing can be seen with the call to "Follow Me" throughout the gospel. These calls break the fourth wall, not only addressing the character, but the reader also. This gospel ends with Jesus telling Peter, "You follow Me!" (John 21:22). The reader should be struck by this final call. It is not meant only for Peter, but for all who have followed along to the end. For all who have read the signs and heard the testimonies. For all who now believe without having seen. All of us are addressed in this final call, "You follow Me!"

Come and See

With this in mind, I want to reflect upon a phrase that is used several times throughout this gospel: "Come and see" (John 1:39, 46; 4:29; 11:34). When John the Baptist told his disciples that Jesus was "the Lamb of God," they turned from John to begin following Jesus. When they asked Jesus, "Where are You staying?' He said to them, 'Come, and you will see" (John 1:38–39). Sight takes on symbolic meaning throughout the Gospel of John. This phrase serves as an invitation into the life of Jesus.

When Jesus saw Philip, He called him, saying, "Follow Me" (John 1:43). We're not told how, but Philip immediately understands something of the identity of Jesus. In fact, from there he tells Nathanael, "We have found Him of whom Moses in the Law and also the Prophets wrote—Jesus of Nazareth, the son of Joseph" (John 1:45). This is an unprecedented claim and Nathanael remains skeptical. The only thing he knows about Jesus is where He's from, Nazareth, a town of little importance which has never produced anything akin to greatness. Nathanael responds, "Can any good thing come out of Nazareth?" (John 1:46).

The conversation could have ended right there. Nathanael could have remained unconvinced and comfortable in his unbelief, but Philip doesn't let him. Philip comes back with an invitation to investigate, saying, "Come and see" (John 1:46). Come and see if anything good can come from Nazareth. Perhaps this also is an instance of "breaking the fourth wall." Perhaps at this point, as Jesus is introduced to the reader, it is not only Nathanael who needs to come and see, but also us. We are invited to come and see the signs and testimonies. We are invited into the life of Jesus.

Nathanael does come and when he meets Jesus, he sees. He is utterly blown away, proclaiming, "Rabbi, You are the Son of God; You are the King of Israel" (John 1:49). This testimony comes from Jesus saying, "I saw you under the fig tree" (John 1:49). When Jesus notes how easily Nathanael believed in Him, He asks, "Because I said to you that I saw you under the fig tree, do you believe? You will see greater things than these" (John 1:50; note the similarities and differences with John 20:29). If you come you will see amazing things!

Later in John 4:29, after Jesus converses with the woman at the well, she testifies to others about Him, saying, "Come, see a man who told me all the things that I have done." Many who heard her speak came to believe (John 4:39). Then they "came" to Jesus (John 4:40).

After meeting Jesus for themselves they understood that Jesus "is indeed the Savior of the world" (John 4:41–42).

Repeatedly we find the words, "Come and see." Whenever anyone actually does, when they take the challenge, they come and see Jesus as King and Savior (John 1:49; 4:42). Are you willing to come and see Jesus for yourself? John "breaks the fourth wall" to invite you to come and read with an open heart to see who Jesus is. Since you can't see Jesus in the flesh for yourself, take comfort in His words: "Blessed are they who did not see, and yet believed" (John 20:29).

Reflection Questions

1. Do you want to know more about Jesus? What are some things you would like to understand better about Him? What steps will you take to "Come and See" Him? How will you investigate Jesus even further?

2. Why is it important to occasionally "break the fourth wall"? What are the benefits of including the reader in the telling of the story?

REFLECTION 6

YOU FOLLOW ME

~

Following the Leader

We just had our first snow this winter. I've always loved snow, but this year was particularly special. For Oliver, my 17–month–old, it was his first snow ever. He's never been so excited. In one of our games, I shuffled my feet through the snow, making a path, and he ran the best he could, stumbling down the path towards me. I led the way, made the path, and he followed. That's probably the simplest and most literal way I've led Oliver. The much more challenging way to lead is through my words, actions, and example. I'm supposed to be guiding him through life. I hope and pray multiple times every day that he follows well, and I lead him well.

More than anywhere else, I want Oliver (and Levi, our 2nd son) to follow me to the One I'm following. I hope I lead well; I know He leads well. As followers of Jesus, our life's call is to stay on His path and lead others to Him.

When John the Baptist saw Jesus, he testified to two of his disciples, "Behold, the Lamb of God" (John 1:36). The result was "two disciples heard him speak, and they followed Jesus" (John 1:37). As a preacher, this is a summation of my goal every week. I pray people hear what I say and follow Jesus. As a father, as a husband, as a schoolteacher, and as a man, that should be my goal in everything I do.

Following in a Spiritual Gospel

In this passage, when it says they followed Him, they literally started walking behind Jesus. Jesus "turned and saw them following" (John 1:37). The word "follow" in the Gospel of John is theologically loaded. It is a keyword and major theme you need to recognize. I'd suggest marking or highlighting it every time it appears. You have to see it and pay attention to it as you read.

The Gospel of John is bursting at the seams with symbolism, more so even than the other gospels. In early church history, John acquired the reputation of being a spiritual gospel, while the others were more physical. The word "follow" is a good example of why. So much of what is pictured physically and literally has deep spiritual underpinnings the reader must be aware of. It's not just the literal "Oliver walking through the snow" type of following. This is the "Oliver following my actions and example throughout his life" type of following. They are walking behind Jesus, but the meaning is much richer.

Then, the next day, Jesus "found Philip. And Jesus said to him, 'Follow Me'" (John 1:43). Again, this is so much more than walking behind Jesus. This is a call to leave everything and dedicate your life to someone. To be a follower is a dramatic display of discipleship and service. That's how Jesus explains the concept in these three passages:

> Jesus spoke to them, saying, 'I am the Light of the world. Whoever follows Me will not walk in darkness, but will have the light of life (John 8:12).

> When [the shepherd] puts forth all his own, he goes ahead of them, and the sheep follow him because they know his voice. A stranger they simply will not follow, but will flee from him, because they do not know the voice of strangers...My sheep hear My voice, and I know them, and they follow Me (John 10:4–5, 27).

> If anyone serves me, he must follow me; and where I am, there will my servant be also. If anyone serves me, the Father will honor him (John 12:26).

Following Is Hard

Not everyone comprehends this challenging call of following Jesus. When Jesus feeds the 5,000, "a large crowd followed Him, because they saw the signs which He was performing on those who were sick" (John 6:2). They are following because of the signs, and as the story continues, it becomes apparent that by "following" they were merely walking with Him (John 6:26). They were not devoted. They were not giving themselves over to dramatic discipleship. After actually listening to Him, "many of His disciples withdrew and were not walking with Him anymore" (John 6:66). They were followers in the literal sense, but not the deeper spiritual sense.

Peter turns out to be one of the saddest examples of this: "Simon Peter said to Him, 'Lord, where are You going?' Jesus answered, 'Where I go, you cannot follow Me now; but you will follow later.' Peter said to Him, 'Lord, why can I not follow You right now? I will lay down my life for you'" (John 13:36–37). Peter thought he was ready to follow Jesus to death. If he were called to bravely die fighting for the kingdom, he would have; nevertheless, Jesus established a kingdom of nonviolence. To see Jesus willfully taken to be crucified was some–thing Peter couldn't handle. When an army showed up to arrest Jesus, Peter took out his sword, ready to die in the fight (John 18:10–11). Yet after Jesus was arrested, Peter denied three times (John 18:17, 25–27). Peter would follow Jesus, provided Jesus was walking on the path Peter chose.

One of the interesting features of Peter's denials is where they took place. When Jesus was arrested, "Simon Peter was following Jesus, and so was another disciple..." (John 18:15). The other disciple enters the courtyard, but Peter "was standing at the door outside" (John 18:16). Peter can't follow closer. He can only enter the courtyard after the other disciple brings him and that's as far as Peter got. The other disciple follows all the way to the cross (John 19:26, 35), but Peter stops at the courtyard. In that dreadful courtyard on that terrible night, he stopped following and started denying.

A Challenge to All

Following the resurrection, no doubt remembering his denials, Jesus makes Peter declare his love three times (John 21:15–17). Then Jesus challenges Peter to truly become a follower, to live out the call and to give his all. He describes the manner in which Peter will lose his youthful freedom. The time will come when Peter is forced to go where he does not want, spreading his arms in a God–glorifying death (John 21:18). Peter will be a faithful martyr. Jesus concludes this discussion by challenging, "Follow Me" (John 21:19).

Following Jesus means going where you do not want to go. It may mean stretching your arms to be nailed in agony to a cross. After all, that's where Jesus went. To follow Jesus is to give up yourself. Get rid of your map. Don't plan your own path. Throw away your GPS. You are following the car in front wherever it goes. Mountains, valleys, and dangerous roads will not stop you. You are following Jesus. You can only do this by trust. Trust Jesus more than you trust yourself. Trust where He leads and whether you agree or not, whether you see the end or not, follow. "You follow Me."

Reflection Questions

1. What are some things that people commonly follow instead of Jesus? How can those things become harmful? What are some things you should give up for Jesus?

2. Would you rather be in control of your own life? Or turn the keys over to somebody else? Why would you follow anybody to a cross? Why is Jesus worth following?

REFLECTION 7

FEAST DAYS

~

Interpretation and Celebration

John's story of Jesus is largely structured through feasts of the Jews (John 2:13; 5:1; 6:4; 7:2; 10:22; 12:1, 12, 20; 13:1; 19:31, etc.), culminating in the final Passover, where Jesus offers Himself as the Passover Lamb of God. Jesus is supposed to be read in the light of Passover throughout the Gospel of John. Passover provides a good picture of what the Jews wanted from their Messiah: destroy our enemies, give us peace and freedom, and let us be Jews. Let us follow Yahweh and live Torah with autonomy.

Passover is a throwback to Exodus when God led Moses to destroy the Egyptians, give the Torah, and lead his people to freedom. That is the type of Messiah they want. As we will see Jesus has slightly different plans. He fulfills Passover in radically unexpected ways. There are three Passovers in John, each of which are reminders to the reader that something paradigm–shifting is taking place. As huge as the Exodus story is in the Bible, it is merely a tremor compared to the earth–shattering events to come through Jesus. We'll cover the most important third Passover in more detail in Reflection #34.

Throughout John, as each feast occurs, the events recorded during the feasts are to be interpreted as reflecting the feast. We see this clearly in the final Passover where Jesus is sacrificed, without breaking a bone, along with the sacrificial Passover lamb (John 19:31–37). In fact, this is seen in the first and second Passover stories as well.

Consider the second Passover, which is mentioned in John 6:4. What does Jesus do in John 6? He feeds the 5,000 who came out to see Him. What did Moses have to do in the wilderness with the grumbling crowds he was leading out of Egypt? He had to find a way to feed them. God gave Moses bread from heaven to feed the masses. Jesus not only gives bread from heaven, but He is the bread from heaven (John 6:35, 41, 48). In John 6, Jesus fills the Passover roles of Moses who leads and feeds the people, the bread which sustains them, and amazingly, the God who cared for them through it all. Just as Moses led the children of Israel through the sea on dry ground (Exod 14) Jesus walked atop the sea as if it were dry ground (John 6:16–21). Throughout John 6, which is introduced with Passover, just about everything Jesus does is linked directly or indirectly to Passover.

Even in the first Passover when Jesus turns over the tables in the temple and drives out the corrupt money changers (John 2:13–22), important Passover themes emerge. Perhaps in the cleansing of the temple, which had become a source of pride, greed, and power in Jerusalem, Jesus is illustrating that Jerusalem has become a new Egypt. As Egypt was overthrown by the power of God, so Jerusalem and her beloved temple will meet a similar fate in the years to come. Power structures are changing, and God's wrath is coming on a wicked nation. Egypt fell, the temple and Jerusalem will fall, but the body of Jesus will emerge to live on, decisively illustrating the ultimate victory of God over the powers of this world. That's a lot like Passover.

Hanukkah

The point is each of these feasts play a role in the way we read the narrative (see Reflections #31 and #34). One more example can be seen from John 10. Did you know Jesus celebrated Hanukkah? That's the "Feast of the Dedication" in John 10:22. It commemorates a great Jewish victory in their not so distant past. When Syrian king Antiochus IV Epiphanes took control of Judea, he made it his mission to unify those under his rule: same language, same culture, same customs. In essence, like most ancient empires, he wants to create a new Babel. This is referred to as the process of "Hellenization."

This meant ridding the land of unique and questionable religious peculiarities. For most nations, this wouldn't be too difficult. However, Hellenizing the Jews would prove a trying, exhausting, bloody, violent, and ultimately futile mission. The Jews would not give up their peculiar religious practices easily. Remember what the Jews wanted from their Messiah? Destroy the enemies, give them their own kingdom, and let them be Jews! They wanted to keep Torah without some foreign invader getting in the way. That's what Hanukkah is all about.

Antiochus had outlawed sacrifice to the Lord, Sabbath observance, circumcision, and Jewish dietary regulations. He set up altars to pagan gods for the sacrifice of all manner of unclean animals. He took a tribute/bribe from a man named Jason to confirm him as high priest. Jason, in return, would help to Hellenize the Jews, build a Greek gymnasium in Jerusalem, and build a city named after the king, "Antioch." Jason remained high priest until a man named Menelous would give Antiochus an even larger bribe vying to become the new high priest. Imagine Jews having high priests named "Jason" and "Menelous" confirmed by a Greek king to rid Judea of its unique religious practices. Somehow, I don't think that's what Leviticus had in mind for the priesthood. Antiochus offered swine on the altar of the temple. He put an idol to Zeus in the holiest place in the universe, the Holy of Holies in the temple, and "anyone not obeying the king's command was put to death" (1 Maccabees 1:52).

This oppression of the Jews led to an uprising called the Maccabean Revolt. Mattathias and his sons led a revolt against their Greek over-lords and eventually won back their freedom. They attempted to establish the monarchy again called the Hasmonean Dynasty, built a new altar, and rededicated the temple back to Yahweh. When they entered the temple, there was only enough oil for one day, but miraculously, God allowed that oil to burn for eight days while more oil was being prepared. Thus, Hanukkah, or the Festival of Lights, is now traditionally celebrated for eight days and nights with the lighting of a nine-candle menorah (the 9th candle, in the center, is used to light the other eight during each day of celebration). It's that rededication of the temple Jesus is celebrating in Jerusalem in John 10:22.

This is a holiday the Romans wouldn't love. It stirs up reminders of a successful revolt against ruling powers. It's a holiday that encourages courageous acts of rebellion. It's a holiday, perhaps similar to Passover, where God-given victories of the past inspired hope for a better future, and it's on this holiday, at the temple, where Jesus is finally asked the question. No riddles. No games. Stop all figurative language. "If you are the Christ, tell us plainly" (John 10:24). Can you give us freedom again? Can you destroy our enemies? Can you defeat Rome, like Moses over the Egyptians and the Maccabees over the Greeks, can you lead us to victory? Jesus reaches back to Ezekiel 34, a condemnation of the crooked leaders of Israel, to say He will finally be the God-chosen Good Shepherd. He will be the leader Israel long needed. Yes, He is the Christ. No, He is not the Christ they are expecting.

Feasts, Memory, and the Story of God

I can't help but think it's important that Jesus celebrated these feasts. Jesus actively took part in the celebration of Israel's story and in the remembrance of God's history of caring for His people. Some of these feasts were directly commanded in Torah (Passover, Booths, Yom Kippur, etc.) Others came along later as new events unfolded (Feast of

Purim; Esth 9:20–32). Others, like Hanukkah, were not mentioned in Scripture (at least Jewish and Protestant Scripture) but became valuable and important parts of Jewish memory. Jesus did not condemn this, rather He celebrated along with His fellow Jews.

Memory is so important. God's dealings with Pharaoh were in part to make a great story that could be told from generation to generation (Exod 10:1–2). Feasts like Passover were inaugurated so nobody forgot the amazing works of God. These were yearly reminders of God's glory which continued to form new generations of Jew for years to come. It is so important for Christians to have reminders of the story of God. Weekly gatherings, the Lord's Supper, and even events like Easter and Christmas can have a profound impact on the continuing story of God. They provide moments of celebration to tell our children and grandchildren about who Jesus is and what He has done for us. They provide us with a living memory of God. Let's continue to remember, live out, and celebrate the amazing things God has done for us.

Reflection Questions

1. What is the value in celebrating God's story through days and moments of remembrance? (The Lord's Supper? Christmas? Easter? The anniversary of your baptism? etc.) Do you think new celebrations and days of remembrance should be added over time?

2. What things has God done in your life that you want to celebrate and always remember? What are some real ways you can celebrate your faith? What ways can you rejoice and commemorate major moments in the lives of your brothers and sisters?

REFLECTION 8
MISUNDERSTANDING JESUS (PART 1)

~

Talking Past Each Other

Have you ever had a conversation that went nowhere? You spoke about something you cared about, and the other person didn't get it at all? Or they responded in a way that shows they were uninterested or didn't understand? Sometimes communication fails. You mean one thing but something else entirely is heard. As a preacher I speak multiple times every week to hundreds of different people. They are different ages, have different interests, different education levels, and different life stories. Some like sports and some hate sports. Some have seen all the popular movies, some never watch movies. Some people are similar to me and it feels easy and natural to connect with them. Some people take a lot more work.

Have you ever seen the famous Abbott and Costello, "Who's on First?" routine? It's clever, funny, well performed, and entirely accurate. Even important conversations about vital issues can end up as an exercise in bad listening and poor communication.

Misunderstandings happen in friendly conversations, but they really get ramped up in political and religious disputes. Consider the rhetoric that flies around concerning abortion. The pro–life proponent passionately shouts, "Killing babies is evil and murder is wrong!" But somehow no one is persuaded. Why? 1. Pro–choice people already agree murder is wrong but, they don't think abortion is murder. So the passionate shouting is irrelevant. Then, the pro–choice person gets a chance to respond. They passionately shout, "A woman has freedom over her body! My body, my choice!" But somehow, again, no one is persuaded. Why? Pro–life people agree a woman has freedom over her body but, they believe the baby is not part of the mother's body. Both groups stare incredulously at the blindness of the other, raising their voices louder and louder, but the arguments are lost. They are talking past each other, not to each other.

This hindrance to communication is not new. In fact, it's one of the main features of dialogue in the Gospel of John. If two people from the earthly realm can talk past each other, how much more will it happen if one of them is from heaven? That's what John is going to show. Almost every single time Jesus opens his mouth the audience misses the point, sometimes by an embarrassingly wide margin. He speaks of heavenly things, but people only hear the earthly.

The Misunderstandings

After cleansing the temple, Jesus proclaims, "'Destroy this temple and in three days I will raise it up.' The Jews then said, 'It took forty-six years to build this temple, and will you raise it up in three days?' (But He was speaking about the temple of His body)" (John 2:19–21). Jesus makes a dramatic point about His connection to the temple. The temple is the dwelling of God on earth, the meeting place between God and man, and Jesus links it to His body through His death and resurrection. Yet, all the audience hears is, "He thinks he can build a big building in three days?!"

During Jesus' conversation with Nicodemus, He explains, "'Truly, truly, I say to you unless one is born again he cannot see the kingdom of God.' Nicodemus said to Him, 'How can a man be born when he is old? He cannot enter a second time into his mother's womb and be born, can he?'" (John 3:3–4). This miscommunication is intentionally humorous, but also enlightening. The word "again" in verse 3, can literally be translated "from above." In fact, the exact same word is used in John 3:31, "He who comes from above is above all..." Since spiritual birth comes from God (John 1:13), Jesus is saying you need to be born "from above," where God is. It's another way of saying "born of God" (cf. John 1:12). However, the word can also mean "again," thus the confusion. Nicodemus is so earthly–minded the meaning "from above" never even occurs to him. He furrows his brow and ponders how a man can re–enter his mother's womb. Jesus means heavenly rebirth; Nicodemus hears earthly rebirth.

Introducing Himself to the Samaritan woman at the well, Jesus says if she knew who He was, she 'would have asked Him, and He would have given you living water.' She said to Him, 'Sir, You have nothing to draw with and the well is deep; where then do You get that living water?'... Jesus answered and said to her, 'Everyone who drinks of this water will thirst again; but whoever drinks of the water that I give him shall never thirst; but the water that I will give him will become in him a well of water springing up to eternal life.' The woman said to Him, 'Sir, give me this water, so that I will not be thirsty nor come all the way here to draw' (John 4:10–15).

See the miscommunication? Jesus is not just talking about H2O. He is speaking symbolically about something life–giving and spiritual (John 7:37–39). She's thinking about her bucket and long difficult trips to a well. Jesus means heavenly water; she hears earthly water.

Misunderstandings like this happen over and over. Jesus is misunderstood about bread (John 6:26–66), slavery (John 8:32–34), shepherding (John 10:6–7), death (John 11:11–13), Judas (John 13:27–29), returning to the Father (John 14:3–6), death and resurrection (John 16:16–18), His kingdom (John 18:36–37), and about how long the Beloved Disciple would live (John 21:22–23). They are a common occurrence from beginning to end.

A Proposed Explanation

Why does this happen? Perhaps the answer is all the way back in the prologue of John: "The Light shines in the darkness, and the darkness did not comprehend it" (John 1:5). The word "comprehend" can also be translated as "overcome" or "grasp." They did not grasp the plane on which Jesus stood and spoke. "There was the true Light which, coming into the world, enlightens every man. He was in the world, and the world was made through Him, and the world did not know Him. He came to His own, and those who were His own did not receive Him" (John 1:9–11). This introduction to Jesus foreshadows many of these conversations. These conversations evidence the fact that Jesus is Light and the world is darkness. It is really difficult for darkness to receive, understand, and learn from the light.

There is so much more that needs to be said about this, and it will be further explained as we journey through the Gospel of John. For now, our primary explanation, which will be explored more deeply in the next reflection, is Jesus came from heaven as Light and spoke in true, heavenly figures. He used the language of heaven. His audience came from dirt and darkness, understanding only earthly ideas. The way to make the switch from seeing earthly things to heavenly things is to "be born of God" (John 1:12–13; 3:3). Rebirth "from above" reorients you to see and understand Jesus more clearly.

So here is what we need to ask ourselves: Are we really listening? When you're accustomed to a dark room, it hurts when someone turns on the lights. The darkness is comfort and the light is pain. That's one reason Jesus was rejected. The world was comfortable in its darkness, but Jesus exposed it. The lights came on and no one was ready. So, let's rub our eyes and adjust to the change. Let's get comfortable with the light and listen to Jesus. Despite our natural inclinations towards darkness and worldliness, let's bathe ourselves in light and seek a heavenly perspective. That's how Jesus' words will really penetrate our hearts and change our lives.

Reflection Questions

1. How often do you communicate with others about Jesus? Are there certain settings where it is easier to talk about Jesus? What changes can you make to better communicate the message of Jesus to others?

2. Why did Jesus speak in a way that so many people misunderstood? How could Mark 4:10–12, 21–25, 33–34 contribute to this discussion? Do you find it hard to understand Jesus?

REFLECTION 9

MISUNDERSTANDING JESUS (PART 2)

~

So Much Confusion

In the last reflection, we discussed how often people misunderstand Jesus in the Gospel of John. It happens all the time in nearly every conversation. I use highlighters to note certain themes or important ideas in my Bible. John is lit up with pink on nearly every page. That's the color I use when there is some sort of misunderstanding in Jesus' heavenly teaching. It helps me find them quickly when I teach or study through John. I'd encourage you to read the Gospel of John and pay particularly close attention to how often people don't understand what Jesus is saying.

We posited that the real reason for misunderstanding is because Jesus is from heaven and speaks in heavenly figures, while His audience is from the world and hears only worldly ideas. John 9 uses the illustration of light v. blindness (John 9:5, 35–41). Sometimes this same phenomenon is depicted not with people mishearing or understanding Jesus, but with them seeing Him incorrectly! They actually see Him and still don't know who He is (John 5:13; 20:14; 21:4, etc.). Truly, "He was in the world, and the world was made through Him, and the world did not know Him" (John 1:10).

Plato's Allegory of the Cave

Perhaps Plato's famous "Allegory of the Cave" from The Republic can shed an interesting light on this theme. The allegory deals with forms and ideas, enlightenment and ignorance, and it goes something like this: Imagine a deep underground cave with several prisoners, bound and chained in a still, fixed position so they cannot even turn their heads. They can only look directly in front of them to a dark wall. They have been in this situation their entire lives; it's all they know. Behind them a fire is burning, and people and objects pass by the fire, casting a shadow on the wall in front of them. All they can see are shadows. Having been in this situation their entire lives, never able to turn around, would they not think the shadows are reality? They don't know an object is casting the shadow, they think the shadow IS the object. The shadow would be their reality. They would name the shadows, thinking they are true objects. They would even have competitions to see who was smartest by recognizing the shadow the fastest. They'd form their own intellectual hierarchies.

Then imagine one of these prisoners is released from his chains, and he turns back to see the fire. It would hurt his eyes and he'd be confused when he saw the actual objects. Eventually though he could grow accustomed to it. Then, imagine he is pulled up out of the deep underground cave to stand free under the sunlight. His eyes would hurt, and he wouldn't understand. His only peace would be to close his eyes tightly, find darkness, and take comfort in shadows. Yet over time he could grow accustomed to the sunlight too and begin looking around. He could eventually see true objects and eventually see even the sun itself. The light would become natural and comfortable and then he'd understand the wretched state of slavery and misery in that cave.

Imagine now he is taken back to the cave, rechained, and able only to see the shadows on the wall. Now, those limitations would be agony! He would struggle to see in the darkness; his fellow prisoners would compete to name the shadows and he'd be unable. He would descend the intellectual hierarchy. They would think he became an idiot; leaving the cave made him crazy!

The man who becomes enlightened and sees the forms and ideas of reality, understanding the shadows, the fire, and the direct sunlight, Plato would classify this man as the rare "Philosopher-King." He is enlightened and has a duty to lead the people, even the common people who stare only at shadows, but they can't understand. They think the enlightened are crazy. They'll never understand for themselves unless they also leave the cave, unless they can see the light. They arrogantly but incorrectly think they understand, but they only see shadows and miss the truth behind those shadows.

Now, after discussing His role as the Good Shepherd, consider the reaction in John 10:19–20: "A division occurred again among the Jews because of these words. Many of them were saying, 'He has a demon and is insane. Why do you listen to Him?'" Jesus is the enlightened One from Heaven. Jesus is the One who sees true reality. They still stare at shadows. Jesus brings truth from outside the cave, from outside the entire cosmos, but it seems insane. The shadow is on earth, but the truth is in heaven. They may see physical light, photons and electromagnetic radiation, but Jesus is true Light (John 1:9). They can eat bread, but Jesus is true Bread (John 6:32). They may see vines, but Jesus is the true Vine (John 15:1). The earth has light and bread and vines, but those are mere shadows. Jesus is the reality behind each one.

This is why they have a hard time seeing God in Jesus: "He who sent Me is true; and you do not know Him" (John 7:28). God is the source of ultimate truth. Jesus is the "way, the truth, and the life" (John 14:6). Jesus says, "If you continue in My word, then you are truly disciples of Mine; and you will know the truth and the truth will set you free" (John 8:32–33). Jesus gets you out of the cave, into the light, and into the truth. It's hard to see and painful to comprehend, but it's why Jesus came: "'I have come into the world, to testify to the truth.

Everyone who is of the truth hears My voice.' Pilate said to Him, 'What is truth?'" (John 18:37–38). When you accept truth—not the earthly symbol, but the heavenly reality—then you'll be able to hear Jesus' voice.

Heavenly Language and Heavenly Birth

The Philosopher–King Jesus, the wise and enlightened One, is entering the cave to teach and free those who arrogantly stare at shadows. Jesus does this in figurative, heavenly language: "This figure of speech Jesus spoke to them, but they did not understand ..." (John 10:6). Jesus rebukes Nicodemus, saying, "I told you earthly things and you do not believe, how will you believe if I tell you heavenly things?" (John 3:9–12). Jesus clearly distinguishes between "earthly" and "heavenly" language.

But notice the change in how Jesus speaks to His disciples right before His death: "'These things I have spoken to you in figurative language; an hour is coming when I will no longer speak to you in figurative language, but will tell you plainly of the Father...I came forth from the Father and have come down into the world; I am leaving the world again and going to the Father.' His disciples said, 'Lo, now You are speaking plainly and are not using a figure of speech. Now we know that You know all things, and have no need for anyone to question You; by this we believe that You came from God'" (John 16:25, 28–30).

There are some who do come to understand and believe. "But as many as received Him, to them He gave the right to become children of God, even to those who believe in His name, who were born, not of blood nor of the will of the flesh nor of the will of man, but of God" (John 1:13). Everyone is born of blood, flesh, and will, but not everyone is born of God. Those born of earthly things see earthly things, those born of God see the things of God. This is what Nicodemus is told in John 3:3, "unless one is born from above he cannot see the kingdom of God." Those who are reborn see everything in a new way. This rebirth allows you to see the kingdom, which previously could not be seen. This is how you leave the cave. Remember, the Gospel of John was demarcated early on by Clement of Alexandria as "a spiritual Gospel." It speaks spiritually while others speak materially. Jesus and His kingdom both came from Heaven to earth (John 3:13; John 18:36). Spiritual rebirth allows you to see spiritual, heavenly things, rather than just the material and worldly. It allows you to leave darkness and comprehend the Light. John invites you to join in this spiritual rebirth, to be born of water and Spirit, and to both see and enter the kingdom (John 3:3, 5).

Reflection Questions

1. Have you been born of God? What does that mean? What does that feel like? What connection do you see between "rebirth" and baptism?

2. How does spiritual rebirth change the way you see things? How does being "born again" allow you to "see the kingdom"? Are there "kingdom moments" in the world around us that one must be born again to comprehend? How could 1 Corinthians 2:6–16 contribute to this discussion?

REFLECTION 10
READING THE SIGNS

~

Signs, Signs, Everywhere a Sign

The Gospel of John is a collection of signs. This is most obviously true in the first twelve chapters. There are traditionally seven signs in the Gospel of John, although I'd argue the death and resurrection of Jesus is the 8th and culmination of all the others. As John says, in addition to the resurrection, there were "many other signs Jesus also performed... which are not written in this book; but these have been written so that you may believe that Jesus is the Christ, the Son of God; and that believing you may have life in His name" (John 20:30–31). John carefully chose a collection of signs intended to persuade the reader to believe (Reflection #2). When you read through John, remember to associate the word "sign" with the word "believe." That is their stated purpose.

Some of the signs are specifically detailed in the story (John 2:11; 4:54; 6:14; etc.), while others are briefly referenced in passing: "a large crowd followed Him, because they saw the signs which He was performing on those who were sick" (John 6:2), and "many believed in

His name, observing the signs which He was doing" (John 2:23). These signs caused Nicodemus to come up to Jesus at night saying, "Rabbi, we know that You have come from God as a teacher; for no one can do these signs that You do unless God is with him" (John 3:2). What signs did Nicodemus see? We're not told. We just know after cleansing the temple, Jesus highlighted many signs in Jerusalem during Passover (John 2:18, 23). Nicodemus apparently saw these and arrived at some vital conclusions about Jesus, though the specific signs aren't detailed. As John says, if every sign was recorded, "the world itself could not contain the books" (John 21:25).

What is a Sign?

At this point, let us step back and talk about what a sign actually is. If you think it's a miracle, there's a good chance you are missing the point. The King James Version does not help us when it translates the word "sign" as "miracle" in the Gospel of John. In the same way people misunderstand Jesus' teachings (Reflection #8, #9), they also misunderstand Jesus' signs. Jesus would often say physical things, but the true meaning was found on a deeper, heavenly level. To only hear the physical was to miss it entirely. To think Jesus was talking only about the physical temple (John 2:19–21), or physical birth (John 3:4), or physical water from a well (John 4:10–15), or physical bread (John 6:27), or physical sleep (John 11:11–13) is to miss His true point. This is also true of the signs.

A sign is a physical display that points to something else. A sign pointing to California is not California. It's just a sign, but following it leads you to California. That's why it's important to distinguish between a sign and a miracle. The word sign does not fit our modern definition of a miracle. In fact, no word in the New Testament means "a suspension of natural law" or "a supernatural act from God." The words translated as miracle in your Bible are literally the words for "sign" or "power" or "wonder." Each of these words sometimes refers to supernatural events we call miracles, but they can also refer to events that are not miracles. The New Testament doesn't really use a word that exactly correlates to the modern English idea "miracle." Any great act of God, whether miraculous or not, is a power or a wonder. Any symbolic demonstration to teach you something, whether miraculous or not, is a sign.

A sign is a symbolic demonstration which might or might not be miraculous. In John it usually is miraculous, but the physical miracle is intended to teach you a heavenly reality. There is a rich history of signs in the Old Testament. The rainbow after the flood was a sign (Genesis 9:12, 13). It was a physical demonstration of a truth from heaven. Circumcision was a sign (Gen 17:11). Sabbath observance was a sign (Ezek 20:20). Isaiah walked naked for three years as a sign (Isa 20:3). Ezekiel reclined on his left side for 390 days and on his right side 40 days as a sign (Ezek 4:1–8). Signs are an important part of the Hebrew Bible, and to say Jesus performed signs places Him within this great prophetic tradition. When Jesus cleansed the temple, He was asked what the meaning of the sign was (John 2:18). They saw the physical demonstration, but they wanted to know what it meant. That's like seeing Isaiah walk around naked and wondering, "Why? What does it mean?" Jesus' signs mean something.

Signs that Teach

Remember the question they asked, "When the Christ appears, will He do more signs than this man has done?" (John 7:31). When they saw the signs they realized Jesus was a prophet, perhaps like Elijah. He did so many they started questioning if even the Christ (Messiah) would do as many. It hadn't yet become clear that Jesus was the Christ. Shortly after, "Some of the people...were saying, 'This certainly is the Prophet.' Others were saying, 'This is the Christ'" (John 7:40–41). The signs were teaching people the true identity of Jesus.

When you are reading about a signs don't just look at the physical action of Jesus. As amazing as it may be, don't just marvel at the miracle. Instead, search for the spiritual meaning of it. Where is the sign pointing? What does it tell you about the identity of Jesus? This is where things get interesting and fun. Sometimes the text will hint strongly what the spiritual meaning of the sign is. Healing the blind man was clearly illustrating how Jesus, as the Light of the World, gives spiritual sight, but those who reject Jesus, even though they may see physically, are blind to the things of God (John 9).

But some signs do not explicitly tell you what the spiritual meaning is. They leave textual clues that make you wonder. It is into those signs we are challenged to dig a little deeper, to use our Scriptural imaginations and search for what God has left buried for us. This will admittedly be a little more subjective, but I think it's a wonderful exercise in "seeing the kingdom of God" (John 3:3). When you read the signs in John, don't miss the spiritual substance. Think about them, pray about them, ponder them, meditate on them, and look for clues. Read them over and over again, and see what you find. That's what we'll be doing together in this next section.

Reflection Questions

1. What are the benefits of signs in teaching? Why does God communicate through signs? Why did the prophets of the Old Testament use so many strange signs? Are signs still useful in teaching today?

2. What signs have been the most impactful on your understanding of Jesus? What miracles have helped shape how you see Jesus? Why?

REFLECTION 11

WATER INTO WINE

John 2:1–12

The First Sign

The first sign Jesus performed in Cana of Galilee was turning water into wine (John 2:1–11). Jesus just promised Nathanael "You will see greater things than these" (John 1:50) and He's about to start proving it. We must remember when reading not only to see what literally happened, but to search for the spiritual message behind it (Reflection #10). This message might be overtly stated, or it may be left intentionally ambiguous as a challenge for the insightful reader to ponder and meditate. There are usually clues in the text that help guide our thoughts and control our imagination to point us in the proper direction. While the subjective nature of this study shouldn't be pushed too far, it can be a useful exercise, as those who have been born of God, to open our spiritual eyes to glimpse the deeper meaning of the signs. The Gospel of John specifically invites this kind of reflection.

Take, for example, the first sign in John. If you see the "water into wine" sign and solely think about a doctrinal study on the use of alcohol, you have missed the sign. If you focus on the miracle and how it saved a family from social disaster and embarrassment, you've done well and noticed something important. However, you still may have missed the spiritual destination. We certainly want to see the physical demonstration and the social ramifications, but we also must ponder how this spiritually points to the shocking identity of Jesus.

Water into Wine

This is where the fun really starts when studying John: digging into the signs and searching for clues. What could this be pointing towards? What could the spiritual message be? This is when you scour every word and ask yourself, "Why add that detail? Why word it this unique way? That phrase seems odd, why is it there?"

I believe the true spiritual meaning of this sign is summed up in the final phrase: "Everyone serves the good wine first, and when people have drunk freely, then the poor wine. But you have kept the good wine until now" (John 2:10). This is spoken by the master of the feast. This title appears to be an honor given to a trusted and beloved wedding guest. The master of the feast has the responsibility of making everything run smoothly. There is a word of advice given to those called "master of the feast" in the Deuterocanonical book Ecclesiasticus: "If they make you master of the feast, do not exalt yourself; be among them as one of their number. Take care of them first and then sit down; when you have fulfilled all your duties, take your place, so that you may be merry among them and receive a garland for your excellent leadership" (Ecclesiasticus 32:1–2). This man was chosen by the family to make sure the wedding went smoothly. It's such an honor that Ecclesiasticus has to warn the master of the feast not to become arrogant, but to work hard, enjoy the wedding, and receive a garland for his leadership.

The master of the feast in John is losing control of the wedding.

First, the family runs out of wine. Then when more is brought out (he has no idea it was miraculously produced by Jesus), he notices the family served the wrong wine first (John 2:9). They should have used the good stuff first, but they messed up the order. This reversal of social protocol is significant. In fact, I think it's the whole point. And through this point, the sign somehow "manifests His glory, and His disciples believed in Him" (John 2:11). So let's think: how could turning water into wine manifest the glory of Jesus?

Certainly, one way is that it was miraculous. Looking deeper though, notice the small, innocuous detail about the waterpots: "there were six stone waterpots set there for the Jewish custom of purification" (John 2:6). These waterpots are for Jewish customs and purity regulations, the primary conflict causing issues in the ministry of Jesus. These Jewish pots were filled with unsatisfactory, celebration–ruining water. No one gets excited about water at a party. It's only after the water for Jewish purification comes into contact with Jesus that it becomes "good wine" (John 2:10).

Wine as a Blessing from God

In the Bible, wine is often a symbol of God's blessing, a gift to mankind. God brings "forth food from the earth, and wine which makes man's heart glad" (Ps 104:14–15). Abundance of new wine was one of the blessings of the Promised Land (Deut 7:13; 11:14; 33:28).

In Joel, God demonstrates His wrath through a locust plague (Joel 1:4). The "drunkards" and "wine drinkers" (Joel 1:5) mourn because the locusts destroy all the vines (Joel 1:7) and "the new wine dries up" (Joel 1:10). After a call to repentance, God promises to "make up to you the years that the swarming locust has eaten" (Joel 2:25). God restores the "new wine and oil ... the fig tree and the vine have yielded in full ... And the vats will overflow with the new wine" (Joel 2:19, 22, 24).

Wine was part of Jewish celebrations (Deut 14:23–26). If you couldn't bring the tithe of your produce to Jerusalem because the journey was too long, you could sell your produce, and "spend the money for whatever your heart desires; for oxen, or sheep, or wine, or strong drink, or whatever your heart desires; and there you shall eat in the presence of the Lord your God and rejoice" (Deut 14:26). In fact, one of God's curses for disobedience, as in Joel, would be the removal of wine from the land (Deut 28:39, 51; Hos 9:2; Amos 5:11; Zeph 1:13). Wine almost seems an essential element in celebration before God in the Old Testament.

Wine was also a symbol of the Messianic age (Mark 2:22). The book of Amos demonstrates the outpouring of God's wrath on unfaithful Israel. Almost every passage in Amos is a proclamation of judgment, but the final verses, flowing with optimism, look for future blessings from God for "all the nations called by my name" (Amos 9:12; quoted in Acts 15:16–18). In this hopeful passage, God promises to bless His people so "the mountains will drip with sweet wine ... They will plant vineyards and drink their wine" (Amos 9:13–14).

The Meaning of the Sign

Against this backdrop, perhaps this sign is meant to symbolize the time has come for God to bless His people. These waterpots, meant for Jewish purification, were filled with plain water. Apart from Jesus, the wedding is ruined, the celebration is over. With Jesus, the blessing of "good wine" has arrived to save the day! Perhaps it is also significant that the master of the feast, the one in charge of the wedding celebration, is the one who missed the sign entirely. Those in authority are usually the ones who miss what Jesus is doing, but "the servants who drew the water knew" (John 2:9). With Jesus, the Samaritans, the lame, the blind, and the servants are usually several steps ahead of the powerful, wealthy, and healthy leaders.

Jewish customs and titles of honor apart from Jesus do not bring about God's presence and blessing. With the coming of Jesus, a new and glorious age has arrived, a time of rejoicing and blessing from God. Perhaps that is the significance of the breach of custom, "you have kept the good wine until now" (John 2:10). Jesus did not come at the beginning. He came, as the very presence of God, to rescue and bless His people, transforming their water into good wine. In this, the glory of Jesus is made known (John 2:11). Perhaps it is also of note this sign takes place "on the third day" (John 2:1). The "third day" is the day Jesus changes the world forever, ushering in a new Messianic age of hope and life (cf. John 2:19). Jesus' first sign, "water into wine," and His last sign, "Resurrection," each occur on "the third day" and give a hopeless people reason to celebrate.

Is this the precise symbolic meaning of the first sign in Cana of Galilee? I think so, but maybe not. The manner of Jesus' teaching and signs do invite this kind of thinking though. In John 6, Jesus performed the sign of miraculously multiplying bread. The crowds only focused on the bread and their hunger and forgot to look for the spiritual "sign" behind it (John 6:26). Thus, they missed the point. Let's not be like them. In that case, Jesus explained the sign: "I am the bread of life...He who eats my flesh and drinks my blood has eternal life, and I will raise him up on the last day..." (John 6:35, 54–56). In this case, we are left to examine for ourselves, to open our eyes to see the spiritual possibilities. Perhaps in the way Jesus is "the bread of life," He is also "the good wine" who comes along, just in the nick of time, to usher in God's blessings and Messianic Age. Like new wine bursting old wineskins, Jesus brings God's new age bursting into the world. What a great first message for an introductory sign.

Reflection Questions

1. Why do you think the phrase in verse 9: "and he did not know where it came from" is significant? Can you connect it to any themes we've discussed so far (cf. John 1:10)? Why do some seem to recognize Jesus and His works while others miss them entirely?

2. In what ways does the new wine and the new age inaugurated by Jesus give you reason to celebrate? Why is it significant that the water in pots for Jewish customs of purification became good wine after coming to Jesus?

REFLECTION 12
CLEANSING THE TEMPLE

John 2:13–22

Crazy Ol' Prophets

Prophets did strange things to teach people about God. Jesus continues this tradition when He enters the temple in John 2. Jesus entered Jerusalem because "the Passover of the Jews was near" (John 2:13). This is the first of three Passovers (John 6:4; 11:55) in the Gospel of John, which is why it is said Jesus' ministry lasted 3 years. In the other three gospels, sometimes referred to as the Synoptic Gospels, Jesus cleanses the temple also, but John's telling is unique. For instance, in the Synoptics, Jesus cleanses the temple as one of His final acts in Jerusalem leading to His arrest and crucifixion. In John, however, He cleanses the temple right at the beginning. This placement is theologically motivated. I think it's supposed to tell us something rather important about Jesus, something John wants you to know right from the start, to be kept in the reader's mind throughout the rest of the Gospel.

Another unique feature of John's account of Jesus cleansing the temple is the symbolic way Jesus interprets His actions. Right after Jesus drives everyone out of the temple, He is questioned about it. This also happens in the Synoptics (Mark 11:28; Matt 21:23; Luke 20:2). In John, however, the interrogation is quite different. Both the question and His answer are different. Matthew, Mark, and Luke all portray the question as: "By what authority are you doing these things?" But John is all about signs, right? Notice how the question is asked: "What sign do you show us as your authority for doing these things?" (John 2:18). That is the NASB translation. The word "authority" (ἐξουσία), while in the Synoptics, is not actually in John. The translators added that word, but it's not in the Greek. The question is simply: (τί σημεῖον δεικνύεις ἡμῖν ὅτι ταῦτα ποιεῖς;) "What sign do you show us because you do these things?"

Now that question could be taken one of two ways. First, as the NASB translators think, it could be: "What sign will you now show us to prove you had the authority to cleanse the temple?" Or, the question could be more like this: "What sign are we supposed to see from you cleansing the temple?" When a prophet would do some extravagant demonstration like this, there is a meaning attached to it. What is the sign of cleaning the temple? What does it mean? To take the question this way means cleansing the temple was itself a prophetic sign. It was not a miracle, but like the foot washing in John 13, it was a symbolic physical demonstration meant to teach an important spiritual truth. Jesus is then going to explain the spiritual meaning of it.

Jesus answers: "Destroy this temple, and in three days I will raise it up" (John 2:19). The Jews respond in the typical manner. By the term typical, I mean the way everyone always responds to Jesus, they misunderstand Him. They miss the spiritual point and get lost in the physical details. They snort back incredulously, "It took forty–six years to build this temple, and You will raise it up in three days?" (John 2:20). This is when John lets the reader in on Jesus' true meaning. He clarifies the confusion for us, saying, "But He was speaking of the temple of His body" (John 2:21).

The Meaning of the Sign

So what does this all mean? Jesus cleansed the temple as a sign. When Jesus says, "Destroy this temple" He actually means, "destroy My body." When He says, "in three days I will raise it up," He is not talking about constructing a new temple, but His resurrection. In this way, the destruction of Jesus' body parallels the destruction of the temple (which took place in AD 70). While Jesus was raised from the dead three days later, I think the implication may be, to our surprise, the temple will be raised back also. Perhaps the temple will live on, be raised, not as a brick and mortar building, but as the "body of Christ," or the church. The church as God's new living, breathing, temple is a common New Testament picture (1 Cor 3:16; Eph 2:19–22).

The resurrection of Jesus likely caused the disciples to look back on this event. They looked back and remembered this conversation and this sign and it led them to believe. It's also fascinating His disciples believed "the Scripture and the word which Jesus had spoken" (John 2:22). What Scripture did they believe? I think the answer is back in John 2:17, "His disciples remembered that it was written, 'Zeal for Your house will consume me'" (John 2:17; Ps 69:9).

Rereading the Bible

All of the sudden, after the resurrection of Jesus, the disciples believed Psalm 69:9 is about Jesus. Notice the entire verse: "For zeal for Your house has consumed me, And the reproaches of those who reproach You have fallen on me" (Ps 69:9; Rom 15:3). After the resurrection, this Psalm became a key Messianic Psalm.[1] Romans 15:3 also applies this verse to Jesus. In fact, the entire Psalm came to be read about Jesus. Each of these New Testament passages applies parts of Psalm 69 to Jesus: John 2:17; 15:25; 19:28–29; Matthew 27:34; Mark 15:36; Luke 23:36; Romans 11:9–10; 15:3; Acts 1:20. The cleansing of the temple is what opened this passage up to Messianic interpretation.

The cleansing of the temple, coupled with the death and resurrection of Jesus, was a sign the temple will live on as Jesus' body in the church. It also opened the disciples' eyes to believe and to see Jesus throughout Psalm 69—to read it in a new light. Perhaps it also caused the disciples to read other Old Testament passages about the temple differently, since Jesus links His body to the temple. The temple was seen as God's dwelling on earth, but Jesus is the truest form of God dwelling on earth.

Reflection Questions

1. How can the life of Jesus cause us to read the Old Testament differently? Can you think of specific passages in the Old Testament that you read differently because of Jesus? Should Jesus change the way we read the Old Testament? How can He change the meaning of a passage already written before His time?

2. In what ways does the church act as the new temple of God? How is the church both the dwelling of God and the man? What blessings were received at the physical temple? Are those blessings still received in the church today?

---

1. Richard B. Hays, *Echoes of Scripture in the Gospels* (Waco: Baylor University Press, 2017), 310–13.

REFLECTION 13
JESUS AS THE TEMPLE

∽

The Sign in the Temple

In the previous reflection, we examined that odd scene in John 2 where Jesus visits Jerusalem for Passover and enters the temple and starts flipping tables and driving everybody out and stopping all the buying and selling that was common in the Jerusalem temple. After this dramatic demonstration, Jesus explains His actions by saying, "'Destroy this temple, and in three days I will raise it up.' The Jews then said, 'It took forty–six years to build this temple, and will You raise it up in three days?'" (John 2:19–20). That's where the conversation ends. It is ambiguous, and the Jews leave without understanding. The author, however, fills the reader in on the hidden true meaning behind Jesus' words. We are told, "But He was speaking of the temple of His body" (John 2:21).

It's that explanatory note we will investigate in this Reflection. What is meant by "the temple of His body"? In what way is Jesus' body analogous to the Jerusalem temple? In building up to this question it is helpful to start back at the beginning of John, because there have already been a few hints leading us to this conclusion before you even get to this scene in chapter 2.

New Creation in Christ

Going all the way back to the first verses of chapter 1, John begins with a creation account (Reflection #1). The first words in the Gospel are, "In the beginning" (John 1:1). This should immediately take you back to Genesis 1, which begins with these exact same words. Genesis 1 opens by telling about creation, and John does the same thing: "All things came into being through Him, and apart from Him nothing came into being that has come into being" (John 1:3). Genesis 1 tells that on the first day God said, "'Let there be light'; and there was light. God saw that the light was good; and God separated the light from the darkness" (Gen 1:3–4). Genesis has the coming of light and the separation of light and darkness. John says, "In Him was life, and the life was the Light of men. The Light shines in the darkness, and the darkness did not comprehend it" (John 1:5). These strong parallels tell us John is writing with the Genesis creation account in mind. John even begins listing days like the Genesis creation account (John 1:29, 35, 43; 2:1, etc.) He is retelling the creation story Christologically, that is, reading it through the lens of Jesus.

John can't read Genesis 1 the way He used to. It's different now that He knows Jesus. He now sees Jesus in the entire creation event. However, a serious problem arises: "He was in the world, and the world was made through Him, and the world did not know Him. He came to His own, and those who were His own did not receive Him" (John 1:10–11). The darkness rejected the Light which came from God. It's like God said, "Let there be Light" and the world said, "No!" This Light of God is the Word of God.

Where Heaven and Earth Meet

The account takes a very interesting turn in John 1:14, "And the Word became flesh, and dwelt among us, and we saw His glory,

glory as of the only begotten from the Father, full of grace and truth." There are two words in this verse that strongly imply this is meant to be understood as a Temple description. The first is the word "dwell." The One who created heaven and earth has come to dwell among men. Where does God dwell among men? He did in the Garden of Eden. He did in the tabernacle/temple. And He did in the flesh of Jesus. Creation, temple, and the incarnation are all coming together in this verse. In fact, the word "dwell" is not the usual Greek word for "dwell" in the New Testament. It literally means, "tabernacled" (See also in Revelation 7:15; 21:3). It is the verb form of the noun "tabernacle." When God instructs the Israelites on how to build the tabernacle, He begins by saying, "Let them construct a sanctuary for Me, that I may dwell among them ... the tabernacle" (Exodus 25:8, 9).

Secondly, the word "tabernacled" is coupled with the word "glory." When He tabernacled among men, we beheld His "glory." The glory of God was seen in His temple. Remember the depressing progression in Ezekiel 10:4, 18; 11:23 of the glory of God slowing departing from the Jerusalem temple? That was in preparation for the Babylonian destruction of the temple. The dwelling of God was supposed to contain God's glory. When the temple was reconstructed in the days of Zerubbabel, God encouraged and promised, "The latter glory of this house will be greater than the former" (Hag 2:9). John 1:14 pictures Jesus as the new tabernacle/temple of God who shines forth His glory, "glory as of the only begotten from the Father, full of grace and truth."

This tabernacle motif is further hinted at in John 1:51: "Truly, truly, I say to you, you will see the heavens opened and the angels of God ascending and descending on the Son of Man." This passage clearly references back to Genesis 28:12 where Jacob rests his head on a rock and dreams of a ladder going up into heaven with angels ascending and descending upon it. That ladder was the connection between heaven and earth, between God and men. Jesus, the Son of Man, claims to be that ladder. In the Genesis story, Jacob wakes up with a realization. The place he was resting is "none other than the house of

God, and this the gate of heaven" (Gen 28:17). He then names the place Bethel, which literally means House of God.

The temple is the house of God. It is God's dwelling place and the meeting place between God and man. It is like that ladder going from earth to heaven. It is Bethel. And Jesus has taken the role of the temple for Himself. That's why it's not surprising when John tells us, "He was speaking of the temple of His body" (John 2:21). To the careful reader, these dots have already begun to connect. Instead of going to the temple to find God, go to Jesus. Remember, this whole cleansing of the temple takes place during the Passover of the Jews (John 2:13). Instead of going to the temple to find the Passover lamb or forgiveness, go to Jesus. Don't go to the temple to find the glory of God, go to Jesus. Jesus as the eternal divine Word has become flesh, has become the meeting place of God and man and the dwelling place of God on earth.

Reflection Questions

1. How can this idea change the way we read about the temple in the Old Testament? How can the significance of the temple be seen in Jesus? How can the significance of Jesus be seen back in passages about the temple?

2. Why was there no temple in Eden? Why does the church not need a physical temple? Why is there no temple in the New Jerusalem? (See Rev 21:22) Why was the temple a blessing in the history of Israel?

REFLECTION 14
HEALING THE ROYAL OFFICIAL'S SON

John 4:46–54

~

Jesus Knew All Men

John 4:46–54 contains an inspirational account of Jesus healing the son of a royal official in Galilee. We've jumped forward a few chapters, so just to catch up, this is the third in a series of exchanges Jesus has with various individuals. John 2:24–25 sets up these exchanges with an important detail about Jesus: "He knew all men ... He Himself knew what was in man." Immediately following that verse, Jesus proves He knows all men with a series of interactions.

The first is a well–respected man, Nicodemus, a Pharisee and member of the Jewish Sanhedrin Court (John 3:1). Then Jesus meets the polar opposite: a poor, sinful, and disgraced Samaritan woman (John 4:7). An honorable, wealthy, male Jewish leader versus a poor, female Samaritan of ill–repute. You cannot find two more opposite people. Yet Jesus knows both, talks with both, and leads both closer to Him.

The third interaction is with this important royal official in Galilee (John 4:46). Then immediately afterwards Jesus meets up with an ignominious man who spends his time lying by a pool in Jerusalem with the "sick, blind, lame, and withered" (John 5:3). He had been ill for 38 years and was a social outcast (John 5:5). Again, he is quite the opposite of a royal official in Galilee. Yet Jesus knows these people, too. No one is beneath Him and no one is above Him. No matter who He meets, He responds perfectly because "He knew all men...He Himself knew what was in man" (John 2:24–25).

Jesus Enters Cana of Galilee

The reason for skipping ahead to the third of these interactions, the royal official, is because this is the next "sign" in John's collection. John gives a list of carefully selected signs in hopes of bringing people to believe (John 20:30–31). This event is counted as "a second sign that Jesus performed when He had come out of Judea into Galilee" (John 4:54). After witnessing and receiving the benefits of this sign, the royal official "believed and his whole household" (John 4:53). I think John hopes we will, too.

This story begins with Jesus entering Cana of Galilee (John 4:46). This should immediately remind you of Jesus' first sign in Cana, turning water into wine (John 2:11). To ensure you don't miss it, John says, "He came again to Cana of Galilee (where He had made the water wine)" (John 4:46). This is intentional. You are supposed to read this account with the sign at the wedding feast in mind. Both of these signs are in Cana, both produce belief, and both tell us something about Jesus.

Once in Cana, Jesus meets a royal official. This official has heard of Jesus. In fact, many of "the Galileans received Him, having seen all the things that He did in Jerusalem at the feast" (John 4:45), the Passover Jesus went to right after turning water into wine (John 2:12–13). While there, He cleansed the temple, performed many signs (John 2:23), and met Nicodemus (John 3:1). On His way back north to

Galilee, He interacted with a woman in Samaria (John 4:7). Now, He is back in Galilee and reports have spread about His signs. This royal official is in desperate need of one of them. In fact, he is so desperate that he leaves his dying son behind 15 miles away to go find Jesus.

What Did Jesus Do?

Let's examine the actions that make up this sign and then ask the question, "What does this sign mean?" What Jesus did is quite remarkable. He sent a miracle 15 miles away to the city of Capernaum to a deathbed with precision accuracy. This sign transcends time and space. The official wanted Jesus to go back with him to Capernaum to heal his son, but Jesus refused. Jesus wouldn't go and sent him back home alone (John 2:49–50). He simply said, "Go; your son lives" (John 4:50). That would be extremely hard to do. Your son is dying, you know Jesus can heal, you travel all the way to Him to bring Him to your son, but He doesn't come. He gives you just a few words, only a few seconds of His time, and sends you back.

Imagine turning around and walking home, empty–handed, alone. Why did the official do this? Why didn't he stay and beg Jesus to come with him? Because "the man believed the word that Jesus spoke to him" (John 4:50). He believed the word, even though he hadn't seen the sign yet. This is the opposite of what Jesus has just told him, "Unless you (plural) see signs and wonders, you (plural) will not believe" (John 4:48). So many others only believe if they see the signs. Jesus is testing this man. Can you believe, unlike so many others, without seeing?

The official heads back to his son. The next day he is greeted by slaves who tell him the great news that his son is alive and well. He asks them what time His son recovered, and it was the exact moment Jesus uttered the words, "Your son lives." Thus, the official and his whole household believe. This was the second sign Jesus did in Cana of Galilee.

What Does the Sign Mean?

We know what Jesus did; He healed the son. Yet what does it reveal about Jesus? I can't help but think the true spiritual meaning lies in the fact this sign was believed, but not seen. The Galileans were willing to receive Jesus because they had seen His signs in Jerusalem (John 4:45). Either this official heard their testimonies or was in Jerusalem, but he knew about the signs and he believed Jesus could heal His son. That belief led him to walk to Jesus and even more excruciatingly, to walk away from Jesus. Because he trusted. He did not see his son healed. He didn't witness Jesus touch him, hold his hand, or raise him up. Still he believed the testimonies about Jesus, believed the words of Jesus, and was greatly rewarded for it.

This is an example of how all of John's readers are asked to believe in Jesus. Some were told they will see great things (John 1:50). Some saw the glory of Jesus made manifest, like the first time He was in Cana (John 2:11). Some, like Thomas, had the benefit of seeing the resurrected Lord (John 20:27–28). Some will only believe if they see signs (John 4:48), but Jesus wants us, you and me, to believe based on what we haven't seen. Believe the testimonies about Him. Believe the recorded signs. Believe what we read. Believe in what we long to see one day. Remember, "Blessed are they who did not see, but yet believed" (John 20:29).

Reflection Questions

1. This royal official turned the life of his son over to Jesus. What is causing you anxiety? Stress? Heartache? Fear? Can you trust Jesus enough to turn it over to Him? What does it practically look like to turn your anxieties and stress over to Jesus?

2. What ways can you practice trusting Jesus even when you don't see Him? How can you have confidence when you don't know what He

will do? Is that a struggle in your walk with Christ? How does this relate to the idea of following?

REFLECTION 15
HEALING AT BETHESDA

John 5:1–17

∾

Jesus Won't Stop

After a wedding feast in Galilee (John 2:1, 11), Jesus took a trip up (up in elevation, but south on a map) to Jerusalem for Passover, then He came back up to Galilee through Samaria. Jesus impacted people on every stop of this trip: Jerusalem (John 2:23), Samaria (John 4:39–42), and Galilee (John 4:43–45, 53–54). His signs and people's testimonies are causing large numbers to believe in Him, but the journey is over and He's back home.

Rather than relaxing and staying put for a while, Jesus doesn't stop and take time to rest. Another feast was about to take place, so again "Jesus went up to Jerusalem" (John 5:1). Upon entering the city, He meets a man who "had been ill for 38 years" (John 5:5). This man spends his time by a pool of water with the "sick, blind, lame, and withered" (John 5:3). He's an outcast with no social status. Basically, he is the exact opposite of the last guy Jesus just met (John 4:46–54).

Jesus was just in Galilee with a royal official, and now He's back in Jerusalem with the outcasts of society, yet another example of Jesus' care and compassion for all.

This man Jesus meets is in desperate need of healing, and he does believe he can be healed. He has his hope in something, but unlike the royal official, it is not Jesus. His hope is in a pool of water. He spends all day lying by a mystical pool of water. The pool of Bethesda was believed to have mystical healing powers, which is why so many in need of healing surrounded it. This makes it an excellent place for Jesus to visit—an excellent place for His next sign.

The Myth at the Pool

The ill man wants to be made well but complains, "I have no man to put me into the pool when the water is stirred up, but while I am coming, another steps down before me" (John 5:7). This guy has essentially been stuck at a stop sign at a busy intersection for 38 years. Others keep pulling out in front of him, and he can't go. Over and over and over. Every single time the water is stirred up, he tries to get in, but someone beats him to it. I wonder how many times he has been to that pool?

This whole story is bizarre. Why does he think the pool will heal him? What does he mean by the water being "stirred up" (John 5:7)? Why does he need to get in first? Why can't the second person be healed? Or the third? What is so special about this water?

There's an interesting history to this pool which might help answer some of these questions. It will also show why it's so important Jesus healed him without using this water. Prior to the 19th century, some doubted the pool even existed. It had never been discovered and these mystical beliefs seemed so out of place. Then, as so often happens, the reach of archaeology continued to expand and discover more and a pool matching this description was discovered. We now know exactly where it is, and you can visit it today if you find yourself in Jerusalem. Alternatively, if you want to save yourself the plane ticket, you can just google a few hundred photos of it.

The mystical healing powers of this pool were at first believed to come from the gods of Greek mythology. The son of Apollo, Asclepius, was the god of medicine and healing. This pool was at one time dedicated to him as a place of healing, probably by an occupying Roman garrison. It had pagan roots, and while Jews would have rejected the paganism associated with the water, some maintained the idea of its mystical healing power.[1]

There's a textual variant which is not original to the Gospel of John (although it is maintained in the King James and New King James Version and is bracketed in the NASB) which attributes the healing power to an angel which stirred the water (John 5:3b–4). This variant is an attempt to make the mysticism of this pool consistent with Judaism by attributing the healing power to an angel rather than a god. I think this misses the point though. The pool is supposed to be seen as a place of false hope. Jesus is contrasted as the only source of true hope. Healing and wholeness won't come from a magical pool, it comes from Jesus.

This poor soul spent most of his life with an illness that couldn't be cured. Upon seeing him, Jesus asks, "Do you wish to get well?" (John 5:6). The answer might seem obvious, but perhaps it isn't. The healing Jesus offers is an amazing blessing, but not everyone is interested. Some might grow comfortable by the pool of water, putting false hope in a healing they can never truly receive. The man never actually says, "Yes." He simply explains he has no one to help put him in the water (perhaps hoping Jesus will stick around and be that helper). Jesus doesn't put him in the water. Instead He says, "Get up, pick up your pallet and walk" (John 5:8). Jesus entirely ignores the statement about the water and heals him anyway. Jesus heals him without the aid of mystical waters or pagan beliefs.

But It Was Sabbath

Then, a problem arises. The man picks up his pallet and begins to walk, but it's the Sabbath. You're not supposed to carry stuff on the Sabbath, and the Jews begin to rebuke him. They want to know who is responsible for this sacrilege? Who healed him? Incredibly, John tells us, "But the man who was healed did not know who it was" (John 5:13). What a remarkable thing to say! What a remarkable contrast with the royal official in John 4:46–54. The royal official heard of Jesus, sought Him out, and believed. This man had never heard of Jesus, did not seek Him out, and was healed without believing. He believed in a pool, not Jesus. He didn't even know who Jesus was. When Jesus healed him he was still hoping in the water. He hadn't asked for Jesus to heal him and probably had no idea Jesus could. His hope was in the pool when it should have been in the stranger standing right in front of him. Yet he walks away healed.

Later in the story, this man meets up with Jesus in the temple. Jesus tells him, "Behold, you have become well; do not sin anymore, so that nothing worse happens to you" (John 5:14). Jesus likens this man's physical illness with a spiritual illness. Perhaps in this we see the meaning of the sign. Jesus embodies His Father as the Forgiver of sins and spiritual Healer. So many long to be made well, but so few seek the proper source.

Maybe we would all benefit from opening our eyes and trying to see how Jesus could be our solution. Maybe we would all benefit from asking ourselves the question, Do you wish to be made well? Then go to the Source of all healing. Not Asclepius, not an angel who stirs up the water, not wealth, alcohol, or mindless entertainment, but the working and active Son of God (John 5:17). This man soon learned and reported "that it was Jesus who had made him well" (John 5:15). Hopefully, we all can say the same thing.

Reflection Questions

1. What do you need healing from right now? Are there problems you have been trying to solve for many years that seem hopeless? Have you tried any new approaches? Do you want to be made well? Do you believe Jesus can really help?

2. What types of things steal our spiritual health? What types of things offer the false hope of healing and wellness? What types of things can actually help provide healing? How can Jesus be involved in the process of healing?

---

1. Tom Wright, *John for Everyone: Part 1 Chapters 1–10* (Louisville: Westminster John Knox, 2004), 55.

REFLECTION 16
BREAD FROM HEAVEN (PART 1)

John 6:1–71

The Old Testament Jesus

John is familiar with his Old Testament. He's also familiar with the life and identity of Jesus. At interesting points throughout his Gospel these two subjects intertwine in such a way both Jesus and the Hebrew Scriptures are illuminated. For example, how did God provide food for the children of Israel in the wilderness? It was that mysterious manna which came down from heaven which sustained God's people. This was their source of life; they needed it and depended upon it. Think about that for a moment. Something mysterious came from heaven to earth and gave life to God's people. Can you think of anyone who matches that description? John can. When John reads about the manna, he cannot help but see Jesus.

Listen to these words of Jesus:

Truly, truly, I say to you, it is not Moses who has given you the bread out of heaven, but it is My Father who gives you the true bread out of heaven. For the bread of God is that which comes down out of heaven, and gives life to the world...I am the bread of life; he who comes to Me will not hunger, and he who believes in Me will never thirst (John 6:32–35).

Notice the difference between bread and true bread. The bread of Moses is merely a shadow on the cave wall; the true bread is what casts the shadow. The bread of Moses sustained the children of Israel in the wilderness; the true bread sustains us for all eternity.

Jesus or Moses?

This whole discussion is predicated on understanding a sign Jesus performed at the time of Passover (John 6:4). It's not enough just to see the miracle. You must ask what that particular miracle or demonstration is pointing towards. What is the spiritual lesson or purpose of the miracle? The physical miracle in this instance is feeding 5,000 men with just five barley loaves and two fish, but what is the sign?

Prior to this, Jesus had been performing signs for the sick which caused a large crowd to follow Him (John 6:2). Jesus looks out at the crowd and decides to give His disciples a test, asking Philip how they could afford to feed so many (John 6:5–6). It is interesting to see how Philip and the other disciples will respond to the dilemma. Both Andrew and Philip speak up about the situation: Philip says we don't have enough money, and Andrew says we don't have enough food (John 6:7–9). While they both fail the test, they also set Jesus up with the perfect opportunity for His next sign. He took a kid's bread and fish, gave thanks, and miraculously distributed them, and distributed them, and distributed them to the whole crowd. Everyone ate and everyone was filled.

The crowd was so amazed by this sign they came away with an important realization: "This is truly the Prophet who is to come into the world" (John 6:14). This is what the Jews wanted to know about John the Baptist in John 1:21 ("Are you the Prophet?") and they later argue this point again about Jesus in John 7:40 ("This certainly is the Prophet"). But who is this prophet? This is probably a reference back to Deuteronomy 18:15–18 where Moses writes, "The Lord your God will raise up for you a prophet like me from among you." After the death of Moses, Deuteronomy 34:10–12 says, "Since that time no prophet has risen in Israel like Moses, whom the Lord knew face to face, for all the signs and wonders which the Lord sent him to perform in the land of Egypt against Pharaoh ... and for all the mighty power and for all the great terror which Moses performed in the sight of all Israel."

Moses performed signs and God promised another great prophet like Moses would arise. Now Jesus is performing the signs. Perhaps He is that great prophet? Moses used the signs to destroy the Egyptians. Perhaps Jesus can use His signs to destroy the Romans and become king in Israel? Perhaps He can restore the kingdom to Israel and free them from subjugation to the occupying Romans? After all it is Passover! He just proved He can miraculously feed 5,000. Imagine a king whose people will never go hungry. Imagine a king who can feed an entire army with just 5 loaves of bread. As the crowds were ruminating over these things, "Jesus, perceiving that they were intending to come and take Him by force to make Him king, withdrew again to the mountain by Himself alone" (John 6:15). Off to a mountain alone? That kind of sounds like something Moses would do.

Jesus or Bread?

The Jesus/Moses typology is glaring in this passage, but there are numerous other motifs at work.[1] The people want a prophet like Moses and a warrior king to violently overthrow the Egyptians/Babylonians/Romans or whoever is oppressing them. Jesus rejects this role, but takes on another. He takes on the role of God's bread from heaven. Jesus just gave them bread, and for now they want to follow

Him. They missed the sign for the miracle. They missed the message for the meal. Jesus says, "You seek Me, not because you saw signs, but because you ate of the loaves and were filled" (John 6:26).

They are seeking Jesus because they want a meal and He's the kingly Moses–type figure who can give them bread. They cry out, quoting Psalm 78:24, "He gave them bread out of heaven to eat" (John 6:31). They say Moses gave the people bread and so Jesus, the Prophet like Moses, should give them bread. If He does, they will believe (John 6:30–31). In response, Jesus clears up their misreading of Psalm 78 and makes a radical shift in the way we should all read the wilderness narrative.

Jesus explains it was not Moses who gave them bread, but God (John 6:32; Ps 78:21–24). In the wilderness narrative, Jesus isn't just Moses, He's the God–given bread from heaven. Jesus is the Manna and not just Moses. In order to have life, they need the true, God–given source of life which comes from heaven. Moses did not give them life; God gave them life by sending something from Heaven. Rather than coming to eat manna, they need to come to believe Jesus. Jesus wants them to come to Him, for, "I am the bread of life; he who comes to Me will not hunger, and he who believes in Me will never thirst" (John 6:35)

The bread/manna is a symbol and extension of Jesus Himself. This sign illustrates the necessity of believing in Jesus unto eternal life. It is Jesus who sustains and fills you. Rather than manna, Jesus is the way God gives life to the world.

Reflection Questions

1. Why did Jesus provide physical food for people when what they needed was spiritual food? What should the church be supplying? How can we follow the example of Jesus in helping with both physical and spiritual needs? Why are both vital to the mission of Jesus?

2. In what ways can having plenty of "physical" food make you less hungry for "spiritual" food? How can having physical needs help you see Jesus more clearly? How might Hosea 13:4–6 contribute to this discussion?

---

1. See Richard B. Hays, *Echoes of Scripture in the Gospels* (Waco: Baylor University Press, 2017), 320–23

REFLECTION 17
BREAD FROM HEAVEN (PART 2)

John 6:41–58

〜

The Problem of Jesus' Parents

In the previous reflection we noted a rereading of Psalm 78:24 and the Exodus narrative, specifically regarding the manna which came from Heaven. The manna is not the true source of life that comes from God. Jesus is. The link between the two jumps off the page. John reads about the manna but sees Jesus.

There are, however, some issues with this interpretation. The crowd soon points out one of these issues: "the Jews were grumbling about Him, because He said, 'I am the bread that came down out of heaven.' They were saying, 'Is not this Jesus, the son of Joseph, whose father and mother we know? How does He now say, "I have come down out of heaven"?'" (John 6:41–42). Don't miss the Jews are grumbling at Jesus about bread. This should remind each of us of the grumbling at Moses (and God) about manna in the books of Exodus and Numbers. The Passover/Exodus story is being retold with Jesus as the central figure, just as the creation story was retold with Jesus as the central figure in John 1. This is a major stylistic feature of John's storytelling.

The setting for this story is Capernaum, Jesus' hometown. The issue they bring up is they know His parents. It's a little easier to convince a group of distant strangers about your divine origins. But to people who know your parents, well that's gonna be a problem. Jesus doesn't see the problem this same way, however. Jesus sees the problem as their lack of divine education. They need to be taught. They trust in their own minds rather than what God has taught. Don't look to Joseph and Mary to see if Jesus has come from heaven, look to God.

Jesus warns, "No one can come to Me unless the Father who sent Me draws him; and I will raise him up on the last day. It is written in the prophets, 'And they shall all be taught of God.' Everyone who has heard and learned from the Father, comes to Me" (John 6:44–45). To Jesus, the problem is they aren't reading Scripture correctly. When John reads Torah, He sees Jesus nearly everywhere. Jesus says, "For if you believed Moses, you would have believed Me, for he wrote about Me. But if you do not believe his writings, how will you believe My words?" (John 5:39–47).

Jesus' true identity has been screamed out by God in the writings of Moses. It will all culminate in the cross, where Jesus says, "'And I, if I am lifted up from the earth, will draw all men to Myself.' But He was saying this to indicate the kind of death by which He was to die" (John 12:32–33, cf. John 3:14–15). Jesus' adversaries are ignoring Jesus' signs and God's teaching in Scripture. They are ignoring and skipping right past how He teaches and draws you to Christ. They're reading wrong, getting the wrong information, and missing Jesus. They're unwilling to look at Jesus in a new light—in God's light. They are thinking too much about Mary and Joseph and thinking too little about God.

Temporary v. Eternal Life

The second problem is manna only gave temporary life.

> "Truly, truly,
>> I say to you, he who believes has eternal life. I am the bread of life.
>> Your fathers ate the manna in the wilderness, and they died. This is the bread which comes down out of heaven, so that one may eat of it and not die. I am the living bread that came down out of heaven; if anyone eats of this bread, he will live forever ..." (John 6:47–51).

Jesus gives eternal life. Jesus raises you up (John 6:40, 44). In this way, He is dissimilar from the manna in Exodus. Jesus draws a distinction between the "bread out of heaven" and the "true bread out of heaven" in John 6:32. The manna in the wilderness is an excellent picture of Jesus, as it came directly from God to give life to mankind. Yet it's incomplete. All who ate still died. Jesus is not just the "bread," but the "true bread" and the "living bread" (John 6:51).

By adding the word "living," Jesus indicates He will continue being a source of life. He offered the woman at the well "living water ... the water that I give ... will become ... a well of water springing up to eternal life" (John 4:10, 14). About the bread, He says, "Do not work for the food which perishes, but for the food which endures to eternal life, which the Son of Man will give to you" (John 6:27). Jesus offers living water and living bread, both of which lead to eternal life.

Jesus isn't the literal manna in the wilderness. He is an even truer form of that manna. He gives life, not only at the time of consumption, but for all eternity.

Consuming Jesus

So how do we consume this bread? One way John indicates is through coming to Jesus and believing: "I am the bread of life; he who comes to Me will not hunger, and he who believes in Me will never thirst" (John 6:35).

I'd like to suggest another way as well. Jesus, in striking and vivid language, continues by saying, "He who eats My flesh and drinks My blood has eternal life, and I will raise him up on the last day. For My flesh is true food, and My blood is true drink. He who eats My flesh and drinks My blood abides in Me, and I in him" (John 6:54–56). The echoes of Lord's Supper terminology in this passage are just too loud to ignore. I don't think it's possible Christians hearing these words read at the Sunday gathering would miss the connection to the meal they are sharing.

Consider how often John teaches in spiritual terminology with multiple layers of meaning. He says little directly about baptism, but He does speak of new birth in water. The Gospel of John is the only gospel to contain this conversation about eating the flesh and blood of Jesus. It also happens to be the only gospel not to describe Jesus instituting the Lord's Supper. Perhaps this is the spiritual way John teaches about the Lord's Supper. Perhaps through this sign we should learn about our Christian celebration of Jesus.

If so, it's a tremendous word of encouragement about our connection with Christ at the table. If so, our Eucharist is a powerful promise we abide in Him, He abides in us, we have eternal life, and we have hope of resurrection. What a tragedy it would be for us, like Nicodemus, the woman at the well, or the 5,000, to miss the rich and deep meaning of the words of Jesus. These words can add greater depth and hope to our thinking as we gather around the Lord's table.

Wouldn't it be great to hold the bread and wine and remember, "This is the bread which came down out of heaven; not as the fathers ate and died; he who eats this bread will live forever" (John 6:58)

Reflection Questions

1. Why does Jesus intentionally use language so reminiscent of the Lord's Supper? Do you think this passage can add depth to our understanding of the Lord's Supper? If so, how?

2. How did those who saw and even ate Jesus' miraculous bread miss the sign? How can we make sure we don't just know and read about Jesus but make sure His words actually transform us? How can we experience spiritual transformation in the deepest ways?

REFLECTION 18
WALKING ON WATER

John 6:15–21

All Hail King Jesus

Jesus has just done something remarkable (again!). He just miraculously fed 5,000 people with five loaves and two fish. John 6:1–15 is about the sign, and John 6:26–71 is about the sign's meaning and the crowd's response. Stuffed right in the middle, however, is this incredible moment where Jesus defies every human ability and expectation: he physically walks on water.

Feeding the 5,000 got people talking about Jesus. They said, "This is truly the Prophet who is to come into the world" (John 6:14). As previously discussed, this is a likely reference to Deuteronomy 18:15–18 where God promises to raise up a prophet like Moses. When Moses was leading the people, they had bread miraculously provided. When fleeing from Egypt the Red Sea parted and they crossed over on dry land; the sea was no longer an obstacle. When the disciples see Jesus is this prophet like Moses, "they were intending to come and take Him by force to make Him king" (John 6:15). It makes sense they would want a king like Moses. Moses was favored by God, performed mighty signs, destroyed the enemy Egyptians, and gave bread to the people. Again, it's no coincidence this is taking place near the time of Passover (John 6:4).

They believe Jesus can be this type of king. They know He is favored by God, He has already performed mighty signs, and He just gave bread to the people. Perhaps He can also destroy the Romans and establish peace in the land? But as they come to make Jesus king, He does an embarrassingly unkingly thing. He left His people behind, escaped, and ran off to the mountains alone (John 6:15).

Devastated Disciples

Were the disciples wrong? Is He not the prophet like Moses? Is He too cowardly to lead a charge against the Romans? The timing is perfect. He just fed an entire army! A Roman centurion has authority over 100 men (a century). A Roman cohort was generally made up of 5 or 6 centuries, and a Roman legion was made up of 10 cohorts. That means a Roman legion was roughly 5,000 men. Jesus has a legion at His disposal right now. He could destroy the Roman occupying forces and establish Himself as king right now! The successful Jewish Maccabean revolt which gained independence from their Greek oppressors and established the Hasmonean dynasty was relatively recent history for these people. They could do it again. But instead, their Hope, their Prophet, their Leader, Savior, and Messiah, just fled to the mountains and abandoned them.

The daylight began to wane, and evening came. His disciples were still alone, confused, and depressed. Darkness overcame them, and Jesus was still gone. What to do? Is He coming back? They can't just stay there forever. Without waiting any longer, they decide to get in the boat and go back home to Capernaum, leaving Jesus behind on the other side of the sea. As it turns out, this will not be any ordinary seafaring journey. Soon the winds pick up and the waves begin to rise. A storm is brewing, and their lives are in peril. They are too far from land to disembark. They must ride the storm and hope and pray for the best.

Then all of the sudden, while they are struggling with wind and the waves on the sea, crushed with disappointment and lost hope, something appears on the horizon. Something miles away from shore is coming towards them. It can't be another boat. It doesn't look like anything ever seen on the water before. It looks like a human. It is! It's Jesus! He's walking out towards them. And terror grips them.

He shouts to them in a comforting voice with words of assurance, "It is I; do not be afraid" (John 6:20). What a moment. After feeding the 5,000 they saw a connection between Jesus and Moses; Jesus can provide miraculous food just like Moses did! Jesus can be a king! Now again, just as Moses couldn't be stopped by the Red Sea, Jesus makes His way through the Sea of Galilee. Jesus has no need to split the sea because He has no need for dry land, He can walk for miles right on top of the water. He has that much control over the creation around Him, which is why Jesus is so much more than just a prophet like Moses. He controls even the winds and the seas (Ps 107:23–32).

I AM

When Jesus introduces Himself, it is translated as "It is I; do not be afraid" (John 6:20). That translation alters an important aspect of this declaration. The Greek does not say, "It is I," it says, "ἐγώ εἰμι· μὴ φοβεῖσθε" literally, "I Am; do not be afraid." This is the same phrase He utters in John 8:58, "Before Abraham was born, I Am." It's the same phrase he utters in the garden before His arrest: "I Am" (John 18:5–8). It's a direct reference to the divine name of God from Exodus 3:14.

Jesus comes in an unprecedented way to His disciples, not only confirming to them He is like Moses, but so much more, He is the I Am who sent Moses. In his commentary on John, George R. Beasley–Murray describes this as "an event in which he saw Jesus as the revelation of God coming to his disciples in distress—in the second Exodus!"[1] He is so much more than an earthly king who can defeat the Romans. He is so much more than they could have ever expected. He's not just Moses, and He's not just the bread from heaven, He is the God who controls heaven and earth. The God who sent Moses to Pharaoh. The God of the 10 plagues in Egypt. The God who split the Red Sea. The God who sent manna from Heaven. The God of Passover. The God who became flesh and dwelt among men.

So what do they do? "They were willing to receive Him into the boat" (John 6:21). I believe that little sentence may be at the heart of the meaning of this sign. It's not just as simple and straightforward of a description as it seems. John likes to tell stories in a way that brings about theological truths in the story. To "receive Him" is an important phrase and idea in John. From the prologue onward, men are called to receive Jesus and become sons of God: "As many as received Him, to them He gave the right to become children of God, even to those who believe in His name" (John 1:12). As the darkness does not receive the Light, many do not receive Jesus: "I have come in My Father's name, and you do not receive Me" (John 5:43). Jesus tells His disciples during their final night together: "Truly, truly, I say to you, he who receives whomever I send receives Me; and he who receives Me receives Him who sent Me" (John 13:20). The challenge of the Gospel of John is to receive Jesus for who He is.

Jesus was not what His disciples were expecting. He crushed their dreams of an earthly, violent, liberating king, but when He walked on the water, they received Him anyway. When they saw who He truly was, they received Him on those terms. Are we willing to do the same? Can we receive Jesus as He is, rather than just what we want Him to be?

Reflection Questions

1. Do you ever disagree with Jesus? Is there anything He does or teaches that you wish was different? Has Jesus ever disappointed you? Does that make it hard to trust Him? Can you receive Him anyway?

2. In what ways can you think to link the stories of John 6 to the Passover and Exodus narratives? How can your knowledge of Jesus shape the way you read about the wilderness wanderings?

---

1. George R. Beasley-Murray, *John*, Word Biblical Commentary Volume 36 (Waco: Word Books, 1987), 89.

REFLECTION 19
HEALING THE BLIND MAN (PART 1)

John 9:1–5

∿

The Wrong Worldview

"Why do bad things happen to good people?" This is a huge question. It's been asked over and over by people all around the world. Why? Because we find ourselves in a world full of injustice and suffering. Some have attempted to answer this perplexing question by assuming the premise is just incorrect. All bad things are deserved because all people have done bad things. If a man loses his health and job and family, it must be because he did something awful to deserve it. If a country has a famine or hurricane or virus, it must be just punishment for some national sins.

This answer is usually given from good motives. It's an apologetic answer, meaning it's given to defend God. Suffering must have a just cause. It must have an explanation. God cannot be unjust and suffering cannot be gratuitous. God must have sufficient reasons for all the pain in the world. Eliphaz, Bildad, and Zophar shared this type of worldview and they defended God against the attacks of Job. Their main point is God is just! So Job's suffering must be deserved. They weren't great friends to Job, but at least they stood up for God.

Surely God appreciated that, right? Apparently not. In their zeal to explain God and rationalize suffering, they misspoke. They said things about God which were not so (Job 42:7–8).

There are entire religious structures predicated on God's justice being meted out through suffering in the world. If you see someone with a disability, it must be because of some sin in their life or possibly punishment for a grievous sin committed in a previous life. Even at the secular level, when God is removed, many people still assume this to be the inevitable rule of life. When a homeless man is sitting on the ground, in dirty clothes, missing teeth, thin and hungry, many (without knowing him, his experiences, or his story) will immediately assume the worst about his character: "He's just lazy and needs to get a job!" "If you give him money, he'll just spend it on drugs and alcohol." "I heard about someone who just faked being homeless to rip people off, then drove away in a Mercedes at the end of the day."

The Wrong Question

This is the setting of our next great sign of Jesus. Jesus and his disciples are walking along and they see a man who had been born blind. Rather than feeling compassion, seeing his humanity, or trying to find any small way to help, the disciples turn to Jesus and ask whose fault it is: "Rabbi, who sinned, this man or his parents, that he would be born blind?" (John 9:2). That's a heartless question to ask when you see a person in need. "Is this guy awful, or is he just from an awful family?" Notice the logic though. If someone is experiencing suffering, there must have been some grave sin committed. In order for God to be just, there must be some sort of just explanation for this suffering. Someone did something to deserve this.

Jesus rejects this idea outright. His answer is, "he neither sinned nor his parents" (John 9:3). Jesus wants to change the way His disciples think about those in need. He wants to change the way we think about those in need. Rather than seeing the pain in others as evidence of their sin or failures, try instead to see it as an opportunity to glorify God. See it as an opportunity to display and "work the works of God" (John 9:3–4). Perhaps the disciples would have been content to walk right past this man as they debated retributive justice and the theology of individual vs. inherited sin. Jesus won't have it. When you see someone in need, it's not the time to judge and it's not the time to theologize, it's the time to work. It's time for the love of God to make an appearance.

The Light of the World

Jesus emphasizes the need to be busy working (John 9:4). It's because day is here and night is coming. It's hard to work when the lights go out. In John, there is a constant contrast between light and darkness, day and night, sight and blindness. While Jesus is on earth He is bringing light to the world. He is the Sight and the Day and the Light. Jesus says, "I am the Light of the world" (John 9:5). This is how Jesus is first introduced in the prologue: "In Him was life, and the life was the Light of men. The Light shines in the darkness, and the darkness did not comprehend it ... There was the true Light which, coming into the world, enlightens every man" (John 1:4–9). So from the beginning we've known this about Jesus. Now, in John 9, we're about to get some evidence as to what it really means. What does the Light do when a blind man is in need?

Darkness pretends not to see the man. Darkness walks right past him. Darkness judges and wags its head. Darkness treats this man the way the passersby treated Jesus on the cross. They look, they see suffering, and they immediately blame. Jesus will put an end to the darkness. He will shine the light right on this man and many will see it. Jesus will enlighten this man. Jesus will change the definitions of light and darkness and blindness and sight.

At the beginning of this story, the blind man can't see and is assumed to be a sinner. At the end of the story, the blind man sees, believes, and worships (John 9:38). Those who see at the beginning are revealed to be blind; the righteous spiritual leaders are revealed to be sinners. Jesus explains,

> 'For judgment I came into this world, so that those who do not see may see and those who see may become blind.' Those of the Pharisees who were with Him heard these things and said to Him, 'We are not blind too, are we?' Jesus said to them, 'If you were blind, you would have no sin; but since you say, "We see," your sin remains' (John 9:39–41).

This brief dialogue is absolutely loaded with symbolism, mixed metaphor, and layers of meaning. Jesus does not stop to differentiate between literal blindness and spiritual blindness. He leaves the riddle in the air for us to grapple with in our own minds.

In the next reflection we'll look a little deeper into how this role reversing metaphor actually works. For now just consider a possible change of mind. When you see a stranger on the street, what is your first thought? When you see someone in prison, are you quick to judge? How many were guilty of passing by this blind man assuming the worst? How many were guilty of passing by Jesus as He was executed by the Romans and assuming guilt? Would you have been one? What if we saw these as opportunities to be lights in a dark situation to show the love and glory of God instead of the darkness and neglect of the world? I want to suggest we just hold our judgment a bit longer. I want to suggest we proceed with caution before we say, "We see clearly, but you are blind." Sometimes the one who "sees" is the one in darkness, and the Light is coming to the one who is blind.

Reflection Questions

1. What if instead of explaining, justifying, and rationalizing suffering, we learned to practice the Biblical art of lament? Are there

spiritual benefits to lamenting and mourning? Can you weep with those who weep? Can you love God without having all the answers?

2. What should you do when you see others suffering? Do you ever assume the worst? Are we called to judge them or serve them? What are the risks of assuming the best? Is it worse to ignore a person in need or to be taken by a fraud?

REFLECTION 20
HEALING THE BLIND MAN (PART 2)

John 9:1–41

The Gift of Sight

There's not much I hate more than not being able to see. When a person or an object blocks my view, I might stand on my tip toes, turn my head, stretch my neck, or do whatever I can, but sometimes you just miss it. It drives me crazy when I miss it. At the same time, there's not much I enjoy more than seeing. Seeing my wife and kids playing in the yard when I get home from the office. Seeing a beautiful sunrise over the mountains. Seeing a friend. On vacation my favorite things to do are to go somewhere I've never been, eat their local food, hike, and see incredible stuff. There is so much I still want to see.

In John 9 Jesus meets a man who has never seen anything. He's never seen a smile, the stars in the night, a tree, a stream, a friend. He has seen nothing. He was born blind. He couldn't work. He couldn't support a family. He was a beggar. Then, Jesus changed all that. Jesus gave this man a gift no one else could. What indescribable joy and opportunity now lay in front of him. As amazing as that truly is, it's not actually the true point of the event. John doesn't just tell stories for the purpose of learning history. There are layers to his stories: layers of what the characters in the story are experiencing, layers of what the original readers are thinking many years later, and deep spiritual truths from which we are all to glean.

The signs are truly about that deeper spiritual layer. Jesus did an amazing sign by giving sight to this blind man, but to what does it point? What does it actually mean?

I think the true meaning of the sign is seen at the beginning and the end of the event. Before healing the man, Jesus is asked whose fault it was this man was born blind? Jesus responds, "It was neither that this man sinned, nor his parents; but it was so that the works of God might be displayed in him. We must work the works of Him who sent Me as long as it is day; night is coming when no one can work. While I am in the world, I Am the Light of the world" (John 9:3–5). This is how Jesus introduces the sign.

New Creation

When Jesus says, "I am the Light of the World," His point is not He is the sun or His face and appearance are astoundingly, blindingly, bright. Light is used metaphorically to describe spiritual illumination and enlightenment: "There was the true Light which, coming into the world, enlightens every man" (John 1:9). This description, this whole story, is a picture of new creation. It connects strongly with Genesis 1, where God saw darkness over the whole earth, so He said, "Let there be light." In Genesis 1:5, God equates light with day and darkness with night; Jesus does the same in John 9:4–5. Jesus then adds the concepts of sight and blindness to the new creation motif.

Think for a moment about God's original creation. Think about the blissful Garden of Eden. There was no sickness, infirmity, or death. There was no blindness. When Jesus restores this man's sight, He is not only doing a brand–new thing. He is also doing an ancient thing. He is restoring this man to what He was originally created to be. In God's original creation no one was to be blind. Jesus is engaging in new creation. He is giving this man a glimpse (literally) of what life on earth was supposed to be.

Eden seems to be the goal of so much of His ministry. His teaching on divorce goes back to Eden (Mark 10:6–8). His reversal of Adam's sin (Rom 5:18) is a return to Eden. His miraculous healings show people what their lives were supposed to be, what they would have been in Eden. Even resurrection goes back to the ideal in the garden with the tree of life, when there was no death. Sin is responsible for our expulsion from the garden and all the darkness, pain, suffering, and death which are present in the world. That's why the resurrected Jesus is called the "Last Adam" (1 Cor 15:45). It was not because "this man or his parents" sinned that he was born blind, but because we left Eden and the entire world is in darkness. "Men loved darkness rather than the Light" (John 3:19).

This blind man is a picture, an illustration, of what Jesus is doing in the world. He is, in a real way, recreating Eden. He is recreating what God did in Genesis 1. Perhaps this is how Jesus will "work the works of Him who sent Me" (John 9:4). God's work is creation, light, and goodness. By being the Light of the World, and giving sight to the blind, Jesus is doing God's work. This blind man represents the world without Jesus. Giving him sight is a picture of Jesus' ministry, an illustration of His Light which shines in the darkness and enlightens the world.

Role Reversal

However, not all will come to see. The flip side of Jesus' ministry is many who think they see will find out they are blind. There is no sight without Jesus. Anyone who thinks he can see on his own, trusting in his own wisdom or righteousness, is blinding Himself to God's truth. Jesus says, "For judgment I came into this world, so that those who do not see may see, and that those who see may become blind" (John 9:39). The Light is blinding. When the Light entered the world, so did judgment. Darkness cannot remain as it did. Darkness is condemned by the presence of the Light.

This healing really shows the blindness of the Pharisees. An incredible, unprecedented miracle has taken place right in front of them. The blind man is the only one who sees it! "Since the beginning of time it has never been heard that anyone opened the eyes of a person born blind. If this man were not from God, He could do nothing" (John 9:32–33).

The Pharisees had eyes to see this man. They had eyes to see Jesus. They had eyes to see an incredible sign had taken place. Sadly, rather than seeing the Light of the World, they were blinded by it. Some will begin to see everything because of Him. Some will be blinded because of Him. What we must answer is what will the Light of the World do with us?

Thanks be to God He gives sight to the blind!

Reflection Questions

1. In what ways do you think eternal life will be like the Garden of Eden? How is the temple like the Garden of Eden? How is the ministry of Jesus like the Garden of Eden? How are they the same and how are they different?

2. What modern examples can you give where the teachings of Jesus blind some but give sight to others? Are there teachings that would turn people away from Jesus? Are there teachings that could turn those same people to Jesus? How do we balance that in our speech about Jesus?

REFLECTION 21
HEALING THE BLIND MAN (PART 3)

John 9:6–14

Signs Point

You're probably getting tired of hearing it, but signs are meant to point to something. They are not merely miracles but, they are lessons with spiritual application. This sign of healing this blind man is no different. I think the primary lesson is how Jesus, Light of the world, brings vision, color, and clarity to a world of darkness. Those who are blind will now be able to see because of Jesus. Those who "see" will only realize how blind they truly are.

Much can be learned by looking at the actual way Jesus performed signs. Take a moment and read Ezekiel 4. Ezekiel grabs bricks, inscribes cities, lays siege to it, builds an iron wall, lies on his left side 390 days then his right side 40 days, then he makes bread and cooks it over cow dung. Um, what in the world? Why is he doing all of this? It's a sign. It illustrates something. It is supposed to be out of the ordinary. People are supposed to notice and be shocked. That's exactly the type of thing Jesus is doing when He heals the blind man.

Making the Clay

The way Jesus performed the sign is interesting on a number of levels. For one thing, He made clay. He didn't just use His hands to touch the guy's eyes; He spat, kneaded dirt, made clay, and rubbed it on the man's eyes. He could have healed the man by blinking, or shouting "See!" or waving His hands around. He could have done it any number of ways. He didn't have to spit and rub mud on the man, so why do it this way? I believe it was an intentional act to separate the honest from the hard-hearted. It was meant to cause division. Watering the ground and making clay was forbidden on Sabbath. Certainly, the intention of the Law of Moses was not to forbid spitting or healing on the Sabbath, but things had become so rigidly defined that even making a small amount of clay was forbidden by Sabbath tradition.

Does this sound familiar? It should. Recall the events depicted in John 5. Healing the man at the pool of Bethesda did not violate the Sabbath, but when Jesus told him to "take up your bed and walk" (John 5:8), He was just inciting people. Carrying your bed was forbidden on the Sabbath just like making clay was forbidden on the Sabbath. Jesus is purposefully stirring up controversy. Notice the way the story is told, "Now it was Sabbath on the day when Jesus made the clay and opened his eyes" (John 9:14).

This is where you see what people's hearts are really like. Will you care more about spitting on the Sabbath, or a blind man miraculously gaining sight? Some people think, it doesn't matter the man was healed, we know Jesus can't be from God because He just broke the Sabbath. He's a sinner! Others think, it doesn't matter He just broke the Sabbath, He just did something that's never been done before, He healed a man born blind! He's clearly not a sinner! Jesus gives people something to determine who will really, honestly, care about the sign.

Healing from a Distance

It is also interesting that this is another example of Jesus healing from a distance. Just like He saw Nathaniel from a distance (John 1:47–49) and healed the royal official's son from a distance (John 4:51–54), Jesus also heals this man from a distance. Time, space, and distance have no power over Jesus. He was nowhere around when the blind man was healed. In fact, the blind man didn't even know where Jesus was (John 9:12). How could he? He was still blind when he was last with Jesus. By the time he got to the pool, washed, and could see, Jesus was already gone. He had no idea what Jesus looked like until John 9:37 when Jesus says, "You have both seen Him, and He is the one who is talking with you." This is an illustration of Jesus' power over time, distance, and creation.

Washing with Water

Also of note is it took "washing" for the man to see. Washing and water both seem to have symbolic meaning in the Gospel of John. One must be born of "water and Spirit" to enter the kingdom of Heaven (John 3:5). Jesus offers "living water" that leads to eternal life (John 4:10–14). Jesus cries out, "'If anyone is thirsty, let him come to Me and drink. He who believes in Me, as the Scripture said, "From his innermost being will flow rivers of living water."' But this He spoke of the Spirit, whom those who believed in Him were to receive" (John 7:37–39).

Jesus tells Peter, "If I do not wash you, you have no part with Me" (John 13:8). John 13:11 makes it clear He is talking about more than just cleaning dirty feet (even after his feet were washed, Judas was still "unclean"). At His death when His side is pierced, "blood and water" poured out (John 19:34). When this man washed his eyes with water, He regained His sight. When the Light of the world gives you sight through washing with water, there is symbolism taking place. Perhaps this "washing" has a deeper meaning also. Perhaps, like His references to the Lord's Supper (John 6:53–58), He gives glimpses of baptism in symbolic language also.

Pool of Siloam, Sent

The symbolism is even more apparent when you realize he washed in "the pool of Siloam (which is translated, Sent)" (John 9:7). What an interesting name. The idea of being sent is a major theme in the Gospel of John (John 1:6; 3:17; 5:36; 6:29; 7:29; 17:8, 18; 20:21, and many more passages). This whole story is introduced by Jesus saying, "We must work the works of Him who sent Me" (John 9:3). Jesus is the One sent by God. The blind man, without seeing Jesus, goes to wash at the place "Sent," and comes back seeing. Perhaps the pool called "Sent" represents the One who was sent. Perhaps we must follow the example of this blind man if we are to receive sight from the Light of the World. We go to the One sent, we wash in water, and we receive sight. Jesus came so those "who do not see may see." Perhaps this is a similar picture to being "born again with water and Spirit" to "see the kingdom of God" (John 3:3–5). He physically washed so he could physically see. Perhaps we're called to spiritually wash so we can spiritually see.

Reflection Questions

1. Why would Jesus want to intentionally cause division? Why heal on the Sabbath so much? Couldn't Jesus just wait a day or do it a day earlier? Why make mud or ask a man to carry his bed on the Sabbath? Could this be seen as a form of protest?

2. In John, water is used for baptism, new birth, the Holy Spirit, eternal life, sight, footwashing, and is combined with the blood of Jesus on the cross. What ways is water important in our lives? Why is water given such significance in John's Gospel? What use is water in modern Christianity?

REFLECTION 22
HEALING THE BLIND MAN (PART 4)

John 9:6–41

Divisive Jesus

Jesus has always been a divisive figure. People respond to Him with worship and praise, hatred and murder, and everything in–between. John writes, "a division occurred in the crowd because of Him" (John 7:43) and "a division occurred again among the Jews because of these words [of Jesus]" (John 10:19). This happened regularly. When Jesus comes around, expect things to get uncomfortable. That's exactly what happens when He meets the man born blind.

This man was a well–known beggar. He had parents and neighbors and a life. People saw him every day. He only survived on the scraps he could get from others. It's amazing he reached adulthood. Then Jesus changed everything. Jesus spat on the ground, made some mud, sent him to a pool, and he was healed. He came back seeing. When this happened, people talked: his parents, his neighbors, the whole community. This miracle did not go unnoticed.

Division among his Neighbors

You must note, however, not everybody was convinced. The neighbors couldn't agree if this was actually the same man they all once knew. Some were saying, "'Is not this the one who used to sit and beg?' Others were saying, 'This is he,' still others were saying, 'No, but he is like him.' He kept saying, 'I am the one'" (John 9:8–9).

It was such an amazing transformation they couldn't even tell if he was the same person. Perhaps reading this should cause us to ask ourselves a few questions. When we go from blindness to sight after contacting the Light of the World, can people see this change in us? Does it amaze people you are really the same person you used to be? Jesus made this man almost unrecognizable. Jesus changed not only his eyesight, but his whole life and reputation. What change transpired in you when you came to Jesus?

Division among the Pharisees

Now the Pharisees enter the story. They need to make a judgment on the issue. Remember from the last reflection, the primary Sabbath issue is not healing the man, but mixing liquid and dirt to make clay: "It was a Sabbath when Jesus made the clay and opened his eyes" (John 9:14). So when he tells them what happened, the Pharisees respond in different ways, "some of the Pharisees were saying, 'This man is not from God, because He does not keep the Sabbath.' But others were saying, 'How can a man who is a sinner perform such signs?' And there was a division among them" (John 9:16; cf. John 7:43; 10:19). Notice the two types of people. Some thought, He sinned by making the clay, He cannot be from God. Others thought, He healed a blind guy, He cannot be a sinner. Some missed the forest for the trees.

Some were focused more on the mud than the man. Some saw the Sabbath and not the sign.

Division in His Family

Just like the neighbors, the Pharisees wanted to verify this actually was the same man who had been born blind, so they found his parents. It turns out his parents were well aware of three facts: 1. He was their son. 2. He was healed by Jesus. 3. Confessing Jesus will have dire consequences. It will get them kicked out of the synagogue. So while they admit he was their son who was born blind, they refused to admit he was healed by Jesus. They tried to remove themselves from the situation by saying, "ask our son, he is old enough to answer for himself." They put their own son in a difficult spot but not themselves. "His parents said this because they were afraid of the Jews" (John 9:22). Fear kept them from confession.

A Man Comes to Faith

Jealousy, hatred, and fear are all determining factors when people react to Jesus. A noteworthy fact about this whole conflict though is Jesus wasn't even around for it. He rubbed clay on the man's eyes and that's the last we see of Him. After that, the man washes, is healed, doubted by his neighbors, accused by the Pharisees, and betrayed by His parents. He doesn't even know what Jesus looks like. He still hasn't seen Jesus. He doesn't have all the answers to the controversy, but he says, "one thing I do know, that though I was blind, now I see" (John 9:25). He knows a sign took place, and it changed his life. He knows whoever healed him must be a powerful prophet (John 9:17).

The Pharisees claim to be disciples of Moses rather than Jesus (John 9:28). If they were truly disciples of Moses, they would know Jesus because Moses wrote about Him (John 5:46). They trust Moses because God spoke through Moses. It's difficult to trust someone new whom you don't know. In response, the previously blind man offers a profound point: God wouldn't hear Jesus if He were a sinner, but God did hear and do an amazing work through Him. This singular event in human history has never happened before (John 9:32). That's what this blind man knew. That is a powerful proclamation of Jesus.

In disgust, the Pharisees expel him from the synagogue and arrogantly hurl the accusation: "You were born entirely in sins, and you are teaching us?" Remember the question that the disciples asked Jesus when they first saw this man: "Rabbi, who sinned, this man or his parents, that he would be born blind?" (John 9:2). Well, the Pharisees just gave their answer, but notice how different it is from what Jesus said. They see his blindness as an indication that he is a sinner from birth; Jesus sees it as an opportunity to show the works of God. The Pharisees couldn't answer the man and did not help him, but they could disgrace, blame, and silence him. Neither his neighbors nor his parents came to his aid, but Jesus did. Jesus found him (remember, he still doesn't know who Jesus is or what He looks like) and asked: "'Do you believe in the Son of Man?' He answered, 'Who is He Lord, that I may believe in Him?' Jesus said to him, 'You have both seen Him, and He is the one who is talking with you.' And he said, 'Lord, I believe.' And he worshipped Him" (John 9:35–39).

This is the perfect example of what John has been trying to get his readers to do. To "come and see" who Jesus truly is. There are many opinions about Him. Some think He has a demon. Some think He is a blasphemer. Some think He is a sinner who breaks the Sabbath. Some think He is a prophet (John 4:19; 6:14; 9:17), the Lamb of God (John 1:29, 36), and the Savior of the world (John 4:42). Some even come to believe He is God (John 20:28). How do we know which view is correct? Watch the signs, hear the testimonies, be honest, and believe. This blind man may not have known much, but he knew, "though I was blind, now I see" (John 9:25).

Reflection Questions

1. In what ways does fear hold us back from talking about Jesus? Why do we experience this fear? What can we do to overcome this fear?

2. Why are there still so many different views of Jesus in the world? What does the world most need to know about Him? What can we show the world about Him? How could social media be used positively in the mission of Jesus?

REFLECTION 23
RAISING LAZARUS (PART 1)

John 11:1–46

Life and Death

"If life is like a candle bright, death must be the wind. You can close your window tight, but it still comes blowing in" are the lyrics that begin the Moe Bandy song, "Till I'm Too Old to Die Young." Death affects everyone. Every person reading this book has been impacted by death. There are family members you will never know because death stole them away. There are loved ones you will never see again. There are futures you won't be able to experience. If they haven't already, your mom and dad will die. Your friends will die. Your children will die. You will die. We don't know in what order those things will happen. We have a progression that feels more natural to us, but death doesn't always play by our rules. Death doesn't care about your feelings, your hopes, your future, your finances, your importance, or your love. Death is the cruel, heartless enemy.

There are those who make a pact with death. Rome made a pact with death. They used warfare, violence, death, and the cross to punish and torture their enemies. They instilled fear into the hearts of all who opposed them. They used death for their own gain. There is something ironic about a pact with death though. Death always turns against you, too. No Roman emperors are walking around today. Jerusalem even made a pact with death: "We have made a covenant with death, and with Sheol we have an agreement, when the over–whelming whip passes through it will not come to us, for we have made lies our refuge, and in falsehood we have taken shelter" (Isa 28:15). They think they've bought off death by a deal with Assyria; Assyria will save them from death! Yet death turns against them too: "Then your covenant with death will be annulled, and your agreement with Sheol will not stand" (Isa 28:18). Death is no friend.

The Jews want a Messiah who can destroy Rome. They are asking for way too little. They need a Messiah who can destroy death. What power does Rome have without death? What power does any nation have without death? Death is how nations gain power. How do nations gain independence and establish peace? War brings peace. So many think they can control death, bend death to their own will, make death their slave. In reality, every single person and nation is captive and prisoner to death's chilling chains. Who can free us?

"In Him was life, and the life was the Light of men" (John 1:4). By giving sight to the blind man in John 9, Jesus proved He is the Light of the World. Now it's time to prove He is "the resurrection and the life" (John 11:25). A death has wounded Him. His dear friend, a man He loved (John 11:3, 36), has "fallen asleep" (John 11:11–13). Lazarus has died. This death hurts. It hurts Jesus. It hurts Mary and Martha, his sisters. Everyone knows Jesus could have saved him. Jesus healed the nobleman's son merely by speaking a word (John 4:50). Jesus could have gone to see Lazarus before he died, but He didn't (John 11:6). Mary and Martha, both reeling from the loss of their brother, can't believe Jesus didn't come. He didn't even help (John 11:21, 32). They both believe Jesus could have saved him. Why didn't He come? Why didn't He just speak a healing word? Why did Lazarus have to die? Why did death win again?

This Sickness Does Not Lead to Death

Think about this phrase for a moment: "This sickness does not lead to death" (John 11:4). What a remarkable thing to say about a sickness that absolutely leads to death. Within just a few days it leads to death. In fact, if you read carefully, it actually leads to two deaths. Lazarus died from the sickness, but this sickness also leads to Jesus' death in an indirect way. In John 11:8 the disciples are concerned because Jesus wants to go to Judea to see Lazarus. The last few times Jesus went to Judea, "they picked up stones to throw at Him ... The Jews picked up stones again to stone Him" (John 8:59; 10:31). His disciples say, "Rabbi, the Jews were just now seeking to stone You, and are You going there again?" (John 11:8).

Judea is getting dangerous for Jesus. Jesus and His disciples all seem to know what will happen if they show their faces in Judea again. They still decide to go see Lazarus and Thomas says, "Let us also go, so that we may die with Him" (John 11:16). That's a pretty powerful statement from the one we call "Doubting Thomas." This is not just any trip, this is a final trip. In fact, after raising Lazarus, it became so dangerous "Jesus no longer continued to walk publicly among the Jews" (John 11:54). The raising of Lazarus was the last straw; from that day on, the chief priests decided to kill Jesus (John 11:53). Raising Lazarus seals Jesus' fate as that final Passover draws near (John 11:55).

Lazarus's sickness led directly to his death, and indirectly to the death of Jesus. So why does Jesus say, "This sickness does not lead to death"? Because with Jesus, death leads to life. Jesus is the Messiah who can destroy death. He doesn't need to destroy the Romans. He doesn't need warfare. Jesus will make sure death cannot have the final say. The final result of the sickness is not death, but something glorious. The glory of God will be seen (John 11:4, 40). Jesus will prove emphatically He is the resurrection and the life. He will verify the statement "in Him is life" (John 1:4).

Death Loses and Life Wins

Jesus accomplishes this by raising Lazarus. That resurrection is also a sign. It is pointing to something beyond itself. Jesus will not only raise Lazarus, in a few days, He will be resurrected as well. The raising of Lazarus is a climactic sign that points to the singular moment that changed all human history: the resurrection of Jesus. When Lazarus is raised, he comes out of the tomb still wrapped in his burial clothes. This may symbolize that while Lazarus was raised, he was not raised to immortality. He is still wrapped in death. Death is still draped around him and dictates his future. Death is still in his nature. When Jesus was raised, however, the wrappings were off, they were lying on the ground with his facecloth rolled up by itself (John 20:5–7). Death was removed, cast off, and laid aside forever more.

This moment not only shows Jesus holds the power of life for Lazarus and Himself, but it also vindicates the claims made in John 5:28–29: "an hour is coming, in which all who are in the tombs, will hear His voice, and will come forth; those who did the good deeds to a resurrection of life, those who committed the evil deeds to a resurrection of judgment." Martha, Lazarus' sister, knows about this final resurrection. After Lazarus died, Jesus told her, "your brother will rise again" (John 11:23). She heard this as a generic word of comfort; someday there will be a resurrection at the end of time. A nice thought, but not overly comforting when she misses her brother right now. She says, perhaps despairingly, "I know that he will rise again in the resurrection on the last day" (John 11:23). While that is not exactly what Jesus meant, she's not wrong. Jesus will raise Lazarus from the tomb. Twice. Once in John 11 when Jesus says, "Lazarus, come forth" and again, forevermore, on the last day. Because Jesus was raised from the tomb, all who are in the tombs, all who have ever died will be raised to life again.

In Jesus is life: sorrow turned to joy. Death loses and Jesus wins. Life wins. Life is eternal. Life wins both spiritually and physically. Death cannot destroy spiritual life. Through Jesus, life is more powerful than death. "These things have been written so that you may believe that Jesus is the Christ, the Son of God; and that believing you may have life in His name" (John 20:31).

Reflection Questions

1. How can the love of God be seen in this story? How is death used as a tool today? In what ways does Jesus approach death differently than the kingdoms of this world? How can Jesus impact our view of death?

2. How can this passage be of comfort to one suffering the loss of a loved one? What role does grief have in a proper understanding of death? Can you think of Biblical examples of grief?

REFLECTION 24
RAISING LAZARUS (PART 2)

John 11:33–45

Scriptural Tension Regarding Death

Tension exists within our souls when a loved one dies. This is especially true when the deceased is a Christian. We know better things await. We have hope. We have reason not to "grieve as the rest who have no hope" (1 Thess 4:13). Paul writes, "For to me, to live is Christ and to die is gain ... having the desire to depart and be with Christ, for that is very much better" (Phil 1:21–23). Clearly, death produces something valuable and something better for the Christian. Through this hope, we can find some comfort in our misery. We don't need to fear death or live in dread of its cold grip. We know death isn't the end, so we shouldn't act like it is. The misery is still there though. The pain and anger and hurt lingers. We know the good but feel the bad, and that's where the tension lies. For us, and in Scripture, hope and misery walk hand in hand.

It's hard to be positive about death because we know death is an attack on God–given life. Death is a terrible and dreadful enemy. The majority of Scripture does not paint death in any sort of positive light. God says, "I take no pleasure in the death of anyone who dies" (Ezek 18:32). Death only entered the world by sin.

Because Jesus defeated sin on the cross, life necessarily wins again. Sin is the lifeblood of death. When sin is removed, death dies and life wins again. Jesus' death was a victory over sin. Every death is a reminder of this sinful, painful, fallen world, but we hope for something better. For us, and in Scripture, the death of sin and the victory of life walk hand in hand.

Paul calls death an enemy doomed for destruction; "the last enemy that will be destroyed is death" (1 Cor 15:26). At the final resurrection, when our bodies are raised to eternal glory, we can fully appreciate the saying, "Death is swallowed up in victory. O Death, where is your victory? O death, where is your sting?" (1 Cor 15:54–55). When a weakened army is defeated and captured, the ensuing celebration is replete with taunts and ridicule. Paul pictures Christians taunting death at our victory: "Where is your victory now, death? Where is your sting?"

Even those passages that seem to picture death as precious are often misread or misunderstood. Psalm 116:15 says, "precious in the sight of the Lord is the death of His godly ones." This passage has been quoted time and again to comfort those who have lost loved ones. While that's not inappropriate, I think it might be comforting in a different way than it's often used. To act as though death is precious and wonderful to God is hard to square with God taking no pleasure in the death of anyone who dies. It also makes it hard to square with the rest of the psalm which is about God saving someone from death.

Read Psalm 116. Throughout the entire Psalm, death is the enemy God helps us escape: "'O Lord, I pray, deliver my soul!' ... When I was brought low, He saved me ... You have delivered my soul from death, my eyes from tears, my feet from stumbling; I will walk before the Lord in the land of the living" (Ps 116:4–9). That doesn't make death so precious. This passage is not saying death is precious like a wonderful, cherished event, but death is precious like a gemstone, extraordinarily costly or expensive. It could be translated "[costly] in the sight of the Lord is the death of His godly ones" (Ps 116:15). Death matters to God. It is costly and expensive. That's why He saved the psalmist from it. That's why He is destroying death through the resurrection!

Death was not part of God's original plan, and it is not part of His eternal plan. The grand blessing of Scripture is not that we get to die and be with God, but that death is destroyed forever! We get to live and be with God. Death loses and life wins. Death itself will be cast into the lake of fire with all of God's enemies (Rev 20:14). Death dies and goes to hell. Strangely enough, in some way, there can still be glory in death.

Glory in Death

The glory of God: that's what the raising of Lazarus is all about. Lazarus' sickness was "for the glory of God, so that the Son of God may be glorified by it" (John 11:4). So when Jesus tells them to open the tomb and Mary protests (because her brother's rotting dead body stinks with the aroma of death), He responds, "Did I not say to you that if you believe, you will see the glory of God?" (John 11:40). Verse 4 and verse 40 bookend the raising of Lazarus with "glory," and the sickness, death, and resurrection are all illustrating the glory of God.

Interestingly, in John, the word "glory" is often associated with death. When speaking about His own death, Jesus says, "The hour has come for the Son of Man to be glorified" (John 12:23). When telling Peter about his future death by crucifixion, the text says, "Now this He said, signifying by what kind of death he would glorify God" (John 21:19). That is such a strange connection. Death is not how I usually think of glory. It's a terrible invasion on God's good creation.

There are, however, a few ways death does produce glory. When a martyr dies faithfully for the cause of Christ, death produces glory. Jesus through suffering and death was "crowned with glory and honor" (Heb 2:9). When we follow Him to the cross it is a glorious thing. He brings "many sons to glory" (Heb 2:10). Suffering with

Christ is pictured as a glorious moment, not to be despised, but rather celebrated (Matt 5:11–12; Acts 5:41; Phil 1:29; 3:10; 1 Pet 4:12–16).

Death is the endgame of carrying the cross. It's the finish line. The glory seen in the death of Lazarus is not that he got sick, died, and his body began to decay. It's what happened next. Death didn't win. Lazarus was raised back to life, and death became a failure. Death was plundered by the power of Jesus, and that was glorious. Even more glory, however, is seen in the resurrection of Jesus. Lazarus died, then came back to life. Jesus died, and rather than coming back to His old life, He pushed all the way through death to the eternal glory of life on the other side. He experienced all death could accomplish, and walked away more powerful than ever. Jesus will never die again; He is always carrying around His victory and offering it to us.

Jesus Wept

While death is not the end and death does not win, it still hurts. It doesn't mean we should just accept death as natural or somehow "God's will." Death is an affront to the will of God. It is the destination where sin has led us. It is a theft of God–given life and it steals our friends, family, and ultimately each one of us. It lingers over every relationship because we know it will not last. This is why "Jesus wept" (John 11:35). Others saw the depth of His love in that moment. Miraculously, through His despair and sorrow, Jesus produced glory (John 11:40). Death ends in glory and while for now "you will grieve, but your grief will be turned into joy." Have faith. Have hope. Never give up. The victory is coming.

This sign is the greatest of all the signs we have seen so far but it is not the final sign. The final sign is Jesus' own victory over death. It is the culmination of each of these signs, but also the culmination of all the testimonies, all the conversations, the farewell address, and the cross itself. The final sign comes at the end to give perspective, meaning, and remembrance to everything that came before it. Keep reading as we keep building to that earth shattering moment.

Reflection Questions

1. What is the difference between life after death and resurrection? What is the difference between the immortality of the soul and the resurrected body? When you think of death do you usually picture an immaterial soul or a resurrected body? Why is this an important distinction?

2. Why is death so tragic when we know there is always hope? What is the most important thing we can do for someone who has lost a loved one? How can you face death with confidence? Should Christians hate death?

REFLECTION 25
MEETING NICODEMUS

John 3:1–21

❧

The Conversation that Changes Everything

A prominent older man, a respected leader in society and high–ranking religious ruler of the people, stands alone out in the shadows late one night, waiting for a clandestine meeting with a young, controversial, and rebellious new teacher who just came to town. He intends to covertly pass on a dangerous but important bit of information.

Nicodemus: "Good evening, sir. I'm here to inform you that even though you may not see it publicly, you do have some influential and powerful supporters in these parts. Several colleagues and I have seen what you are doing. You're speaking truth, and your signs simply cannot be explained away. You must be a teacher from God because nobody else is doing the types of things you are."

Jesus: "This truth is for you, unless a man is born in a radically new way, he will never be able to really see the powerful reign of God taking place."

Nicodemus: "Rebirth? What, (chortles) you expect him to crawl back into his mother's womb and start life over?

Jesus: "This truth is for you, unless a man is born in a radically new way, unless his whole life begins anew with water and God's Holy Spirit, he will never enter God's powerful reign. Flesh comes from flesh, but spiritual people come from God's Spirit, and there's no way to control God's Spirit. Just like this wind you hear blowing tonight, it blows wherever it wishes. You can't control or predict from where it comes or where it goes, and that's exactly how it is with people who have been reborn from above by God's Spirit."

Nicodemus: "How is this rebirth possible?"

Jesus: "You're a Pharisee and member of the Sanhedrin. I thought you were supposed to be a great teacher of Israel? But you don't understand? Listen closely; this is for you, people know and talk about the things they have seen. Fleshly people talk about fleshly things because that's all they see and all they understand, but I have descended from heaven. I have seen God's powerful reign at its fullest. I am the ultimate authority on the things of God. I am the very presence of God. When I speak of heavenly things, fleshly people do not understand. That's why you need to be born again, born of God and His Spirit, born anew from heaven itself. Otherwise you'll never understand.

"No one who is fleshly has gone up to heaven, but I have. And I've come down out of heaven. I am the Son of Man, the One who comes riding on the clouds of heaven. Just as Moses lifted up that bronze serpent back in the wilderness, so I will be lifted up. Just as those who looked to that serpent were saved from venomous serpents, so anyone who looks to My death will be saved from death. The one who believes in me will be saved from the condemnation of this world and enjoy eternal life, life as it was always intended to be. This is how God's love for the whole world is seen! He sent His only Son that anyone who believes in Him can have life eternal with God Himself.

"I'm not here to judge or condemn the world, the world has already done that on its own. I'm here to bring salvation. When God created the world, there was only darkness, but God said, "Let there be Light!" Something new and remarkable happened in that moment and through Me it's happening again. In a few hours the sun will rise and the darkness will flee. I am like that light. The light of new creation, of a new day, of a new way of life, of new hope, of new birth, but many in the world will just keep trudging along in darkness, hating the light, because it reveals what is truly there. It reveals the sickness, the sin, the dirt, and the death that has taken over. Anyone who lives in my truth comes to the light. That is rebirth, and it becomes clear he is now seeing and living and doing the things that come from God."

("End Scene")

Born Again

"Are you a born–again Christian?" I've been asked this before. It's an interesting question. The phrase "born again" has taken a life of its own in modern evangelical Christianity. When thinking of a person who needs a completely new life, to restart everything, to hit the reset button, it may be tempting to think about those we reach through prison ministry or drug rehabilitation. We hear the phrase "born again" and immediately picture someone whose life is spiraling out of control, who is recklessly destroying their future, but Jesus uses this phrase and pictures someone altogether different. It's not the drug addict who has lost control of his life, it's not the inmate who longs for redemption, it's not even the Samaritan woman who has been married five times that Jesus meets in the next chapter. It's the wealthy, respected, important teacher of Israel. It's the man who has all things in order. His life is the envy of others. He has success and prominence. He has done well since his birth. This is not the person most would think needs to start his life over, but Jesus does. Jesus sees through the success, the power, and the wealth to a man just like any other: a man in need.

Beginning to See

The story of Nicodemus doesn't go as far as I'd like it to. We don't get to see how it ends but we do get to see a little farther than this conversation. This late–night conversation plants a seed which develops a little further in John 7 where Nicodemus defends Jesus, telling the other members of the council to at least meet with Him and talk to Him before condemning Him. His objection is dismissed, but the seed is still germinating.

Following the crucifixion of Jesus, another disciple, a secret one named Joseph, takes the body of Jesus down from the cross to give it a proper burial. This is where Nicodemus shows up, with 100 pounds of myrrh and aloe to prepare and honor the body of Jesus (Some Bibles may say 75 pounds. The Greek text uses the word 100, but a Roman pound weighs about a fourth less than a modern pound, so a literal reading would be 100 pounds but an accurate modern reading would be 75 pounds) 75 pounds! That is a burial for a king, not some crucified rebel. Not some failed Messiah, but a king. Perhaps, Nicodemus is beginning to see. Perhaps as day breaks on that world–changing Sunday morning, Nicodemus will no longer need to meet Jesus in darkness, but will walk in the light of life.

Reflection Questions

1. Have you ever wanted to start over (rebirth)? Why would Jesus tell the wealthy, respected, successful Nicodmeus to start over? How are Jesus' views of "the good life" different than our own?

2. How would you have felt if you had this conversation with Jesus? What would your main takeaways be? Would you feel drawn closer to Him? What would you be internally grappling with as you walked away?

REFLECTION 26
NICODEMUS AT NIGHT

John 3:1–8

❧

By Night

It is not unimportant Nicodemus comes to Jesus "by night." Little details like that are rarely insignificant. They help shape the story. When Nicodemus is mentioned again after the crucifixion, he is described as "Nicodemus, who had first come to Him by night" (John 19:39). That passage links him to Joseph of Arimathea, who is described as "a secret disciple." Joseph was like Nicodemus in many ways; Joseph was a wealthy, powerful man who was also a member of the Sanhedrin and opposed the decision to crucify Jesus (Luke 24:50–51). He was also unwilling to publicly put his faith in Jesus. Nicodemus put his faith in Jesus, but only at night. Joseph put his faith in Jesus, but only in secret. Following the crucifixion, however, they find themselves together, coming forward to honor Jesus as a king, regardless of what the public thinks.

They weren't alone in their secrecy. John 12:42, 43 explains,

"Nevertheless many even of the rulers believed in Him, but because of the Pharisees they were not confessing Him, for fear that they would be put out of the synagogue; for they loved the approval of men rather than the approval of God."

Their silence is explained by two things: what they feared and what they loved. They feared reprimand. They feared expulsion from the synagogue, which would include loss of status, respect, and community. This is the same thing the blind man's parents feared (John 9:23). This is the same thing many in the early church feared, and, thus they clung to passages that were reminders not to be motivated by fear, but love. Not love for the approval of men; that love makes you a slave, encompasses you with fear, and keeps you silent about Jesus. They needed love for the approval of God. No hatred, persecution, or fear could ever take that from you. Perhaps the cross was exactly what Nicodemus and Joseph needed to move beyond fear and begin to show their love of Christ openly.

Born from Above

One of the famous misunderstandings in the Gospel of John centers on the phrase γεννηθῇ ἄνωθεν, "be born again." The multiple meanings of the word ἄνωθεν become the main source of confusion. The word could mean "again" which is certainly how Nicodemus hears it. However, the word could also mean "from above" or "from heaven" which I think is how Jesus actually means it. In John 3:31, Jesus says, "He who comes from above is above all...He who comes from heaven is above all." Guess what that phrase "from above" is in Greek: ἄνωθεν. It's the exact same word. There is a theme in John about ascending and descending, up and down, above and below. Jesus comes from above, from heaven, so He brings a heavenly perspective to all his teaching. Those who come from below fail to grasp it.

If I told you earthly things and you do not believe, how will you believe if I tell you heavenly things? No one has ascended into heaven, but He who descended from heaven, the Son of Man (John 3:12–13).

There is a difference between earthly things and heavenly things spoken by Jesus. The misunderstandings in John occur when people hear the earthly thing instead of the heavenly. That's why Nicodemus doesn't hear the heavenly message about being born of God from above. He hears the earthly message about crawling back into his mother's womb. To be born from above is the same thing as being born "not of blood nor of the will of the flesh nor of the will of man, but of God" (John 1:13). God is above; God is Spirit (John 4:24). The one who is born from above, and is born of water and Spirit, is born of God.

Being born from above is synonymous with being born of God and the Spirit, but surprisingly also water. Water doesn't seem to fit well with these other descriptions. Water is not God, Spirit, or from above. Water is not divine but is a created substance down below. Yet water does take on a significant spiritual role in the Gospel of John. Immediately following this conversation with Nicodemus water is linked with baptism (John 3:22–23). The phrase "because there was much water there" (John 3:23) seems like a peculiar detail to add, which means it probably shouldn't be glossed over. There is no way the early church doesn't see baptism when they read John 3:5. In fact, we know they saw teaching about baptism in this text: "John 3:5 is the most commonly used baptismal text in the second century."

[1]Water is also connected to eternal life (John 4:10–14), sight for the blind (John 9:7), washing that gives you a part with Jesus (John 13:8), and the blood of Jesus (John 19:34). Most significantly for this passage, it is linked directly to the Holy Spirit:

Jesus stood and cried out, saying, 'If anyone is thirsty, let him come to Me and drink. He who believes in Me, as the Scripture said, "From his innermost being will flow rivers of living water."' But this He spoke of the Spirit, whom those who believed in Him were to receive; for the Spirit was not yet given, because Jesus was not yet glorified (John 7:37–39).

Spirit and Wind

Jesus then uses another word that has multiple meanings: πνεῦμα. This word means "wind" or "Spirit," and Jesus employs both meanings in the same verse! "The wind blows where it wishes and you hear the sound of it, but do not know where it comes from and where it is going; so is everyone who is born of the Spirit" (John 3:8).

Imagine Jesus and Nicodemus talking late into the evening on a gusty night. They can hear the wind but cannot predict where it has come from or where it will end up, nor can they control it. Nicodemus is a man used to authority: making decisions, having control, running his own life. Jesus telling him to be born of the Spirit is telling him to give up control. You have as much control over the Spirit as you do the wind.

Author's Note: We should always be a little cautious when some teacher or preacher tries to tell us exactly what the Spirit can and cannot do or will and will not do. There is a lot of ambiguity to the work of the Spirit in the Bible, and I believe that's intentional. To truly grasp the Spirit is like nailing down the wind.

Reflection Questions

1. What do you think "born of water and Spirit" could mean? How does this relate to being "born from above"? How could this help you to "see" and "enter" the kingdom?

2. In what ways do people try to control or limit God's Spirit? Are you uncomfortable when you hear people talk about the Holy Spirit? Why is it so tempting to deny the activity of the Spirit in the world? Why is "wind" a good illustration of the Spirit?

---

1. Everett Ferguson, *Baptism in the Early Church: History, Theology, and Liturgy in the First Five Centuries* (Grand Rapids: Eerdmans, 2009), 218.

REFLECTION 27
NICODEMUS AND SNAKES

John 3:9–21

Snakes and the Cross

Snakes and humans seem to be natural enemies. Snakes are creepy and make good companions for a villain (see Voldemort from the *Harry Potter* book series). They certainly aren't the hero of the story. That's why Numbers 21 and John 3 work together in a fantastically ironic and beautiful way.

Jesus draws an incredible parallel between a snake and the crucifixion (John 3:14–15). If you remember Numbers 21, the children of Israel begin to complain against God ... again. This is a constant problem after the Exodus. They long to go back to Egypt. They desire to return to slavery where they were miserable, cried and wept for deliverance, hopelessly labored without end, and had their children murdered and thrown into the Nile. You know, the good ol' days. During the complaining in Numbers 21, a plague of venomous serpents swarmed the camp and people started dying. They cried out to God, and He heard them and prepared a means of salvation. Moses was to fashion a serpent made of bronze, put it high on a pole, and all who were bitten could look up to the bronze serpent and miraculously be saved. God did not, by the way, rescue them by removing the snakes. Instead, he allowed them to coexist with the snakes, but gave them a means of deliverance through it.

The serpent on a pole has long been a symbol of healing power, from Moses to Asclepius, the god mentioned in Reflection #15, to Hermes, and even to the modern field of medicine. Jesus sees this symbol from Numbers 21 as the prefiguration of a different kind of healing. Just like that rod with the bronze serpent was lifted up, so will the Son of Man be lifted up. Ironically, serpents were the cause of death in Numbers 21, but a serpent lifted high was the means of salvation. In our lives, death is the problem we all face, but a death lifted high is the means of salvation. It is to this beautiful life–giving death of Jesus that we must all look.

Just like those venomous snakes still existed to bite and spread death in Numbers 21, so sin and its lethal bite still exist in our world. Thankfully, a means of salvation exists right alongside. This sacrificial means of salvation is the clearest image of the love of God that can be seen: "For God so loved the world, that He gave his only begotten Son, that whoever believes in Him will not perish, but will have eternal life" (John 3:16).

Before the bronze serpent was made, the people were already bitten and dying. The bronze serpent had one purpose, to bring about salvation. Condemnation was already part of the story. So it is with the coming of Jesus. The world condemned itself on its own without Jesus' help. He came not to condemn, but to provide a way out of condemnation (John 3:17–18) to the hope of eternal life and salvation. He came as a focal point of deliverance and the love of God.

Light and Darkness

The conversation with Nicodemus shifts again to a major talking point in the Gospel of John: light and darkness. In John, "night," "darkness," and "blindness," are all representative of a spiritual condition without Christ. Jesus came as a Light to shine in the darkness (John 1:4–5, 9). He twice describes Himself as the "Light of the World" (John 8:12; 9:5). The first time is a call to leave darkness and to have "the Light of Life." The second is a description of his role in the world right before He heals a blind man. Giving sight to the blind, one who sees only darkness, is done by the Light of the World. Those who are in darkness need this light. Those who are blind need this light. Nicodemus, who came to Jesus "at night," needed this light.

In Genesis 1, light is the first thing God sends to the world of chaotic water and darkness. In John 1, Light is what God sends to the chaotic world of sin and darkness. Jesus came to enlighten the world, not to condemn it. Tragically the world preferred darkness. Imagine in Genesis 1, the world rejecting God's act of creation. In John we see the world actively rejecting God's work of New Creation. Some get on board though. Some actually are born from above. Some see the kingdom as it truly is. Some come out of darkness into His marvelous Light. Some, Mr. Nicodemus, find eternal life.

Summarizing the Conversation

This conversation between Jesus and Nicodemus has a lot of twists and turns, but I think the key to it all is in the first words Jesus says: "Unless one is born from above, he cannot see the kingdom of God" (John 3:3). Jesus is bringing a kingdom. This kingdom is "not of this world" (John 18:36). It's easy enough to see a worldly kingdom. The Roman Empire was so visible no one could miss it; Jesus' kingdom can be missed if you don't look carefully.

Remember when Jesus is arrested, beaten, and paraded before the Jews with a purple robe and a crown of thorns on His head? He stood there, alone, bloodied in weakness and anguish while Pilate said, "Behold, your King!" That's a kingdom moment. Most people who look don't see the sacrificial love of God, don't see the Light of the world, and certainly don't see a king. They see weakness and failure and a fool getting what He deserves. They see a false Messiah, a failed rebellion, a criminal who lost to the mighty Roman Empire. The kingdom of God is appearing right in front of them, and they walk by wagging their heads.

But those who have been born from above have eyes that see. They see the kingdom and they behold their King. I wish I knew more, but the story of Nicodemus ends with a "perhaps." Perhaps Nicodemus and Joseph of Arimathea give Jesus the burial worthy of a king (John 19:38–42) because their eyes have been opened. Perhaps birth from above is causing them to see things they previously missed. Perhaps an entirely new life awaits them. Perhaps the same could be said of you. Perhaps.

Reflection Questions

1. Why didn't God just remove the serpents? Why command Moses to fashion a bronze serpent for them to look at? According to 2 Kings 18:4, it actually became an idol. What is the benefit of that serpent? Why would this serve as a good illustration of Jesus?

2. What would have hindered Nicodemus from becoming a follower? What would have convinced him? Do you think Nicodemus became a Christian and follower of Jesus? Why or why not?

REFLECTION 28
THE SAMARITAN WOMAN AT THE WELL

John 4:1–26

◈

Samaritans Were the Wrong Race

Jesus is traveling north (or "down" in elevation) from Judea to Galilee, and apparently "He had to pass through Samaria" (John 4:4). Why He had to is not stated. In fact, it may have been rather uncharacteristic for many Jews to pass through Samaria. While this would have been the direct route to Galilee from Judea (as Samaria was geographically in–between the two), we know there were routes taken from Judea to Galilee that bypassed Samaria altogether. It's impossible to know how common it was, but hostile attitudes towards the Samaritans and the increased likelihood of meeting attackers created a custom of avoiding Samaria as much as possible. There is some evidence of Jews traveling east to the Jordan Valley, traveling along the river past Samaria, then turning west to enter Galilee or Judea. John, in fact, is clear to point out to his readers, "Jews have no dealings with

Samaritans" (John 4:9). Yet Jesus doesn't do this. Perhaps, He "had to" go that way because there was an appointment He just couldn't pass up.

Overshadowing this meeting is a long history of animosity between Jews and Samaritans. Samaria, once the capital city of Northern Israel, fell in 722 BC to the Assyrians. Many of the nobles and wealthy inhabitants were removed and exiled, while foreigners from other conquered lands along with Assyrians began to repopulate the land. The remaining Jews intermarried with these foreigners and Assyrians and came to be known as impure half–breeds. This racial prejudice remained in the days of Jesus.

Samaritans Were the Wrong Religion

There were also religious disagreements which contributed to the animosity. The Samaritans rejected Jerusalem and its temple as God's chosen place of worship, instead preferring the temple built around 400 BC on Mount Gerizim. They only accepted the Pentateuch as Sacred Scripture (not the rest of the Hebrew Scriptures), and in various places changes were made to suit their theology. Notice, as an example, the last of the 10 commandments in the Samaritan Pentateuch:

> "It shall be when your God will bring you to the Canaanite land, which you are going to inherit, you shall set yourself up great stones, and plaster them with plaster, and you shall write on them all the words of this law. It shall be, when you are passed over the Jordan, that you shall set up these stones, which I command you this day, in Mount Gerizim. There shall you build an altar to Yahweh your God, an altar of stones: you shall lift up no iron tool on them. You shall build the altar of Yahweh your God of uncut stones; and you shall offer burnt offerings thereon to Yahweh your God: and you shall sacrifice peace–offerings, and shall eat there; and you shall rejoice before Yahweh your God" (Exod 20:17).

Needless to say, that's not quite the way our book of Exodus reads.

Samaritans Were the Wrong Nationality

If racial prejudice and religious disagreements weren't enough, Jews and Samaritans had a history of warfare and violence that kept the hatred running hot. I have an old Jewish coin in my office with the name and title of John Hyrcanus inscribed on the front (the Jews did not engrave faces on their coins, as they were not to make graven images), and a double cornucopia on the back.

John Hyrcanus was a Hasmonean ruler and high priest of the Jews during the 2nd century BC. The Hasmonean dynasty was a short-lived attempt to reclaim an independent kingdom after the successful Maccabean revolt against the Seleucid Empire. Hyrcanus led several military campaigns, one of which was into Samaria. After conquering, enslaving, and forcing Jewish customs on many of his defeated foes, Hyrcanus made his way to Gerizim and destroyed the Samaritan temple. Yahweh only had one temple and it was to be in Jerusalem! Well, these types of accounts in the recent national past didn't endear Jews to Samaritans or Samaritans to Jews.

Samaritans Were Unclean

The prejudice and disagreements and violent histories lead to statements like this one found in the Jewish Mishnah, Niddah 4.1,

> "The daughters of the Samaritans are [deemed unclean as] mensturants from the cradle; and the Samaritans convey unclean-ness to what lies beneath them in like degree as [he that has a flux conveys uncleanness] to what lies above him, since they have connexon with menstruants."

Or consider this lovely comparison,

"Places of uncleanness that belong to Samaritans convey uncleanness by overshadowing, since they bury abortions there. R. Judah says: They did not bury them but only threw them away, and the wild animals dragged them off" (m. Nid. 7.4).

The idea is Samaritans, particularly women, are unclean, and anyone who comes into contact with them is unclean like a woman constantly menstruating from birth (Leviticus 15:19–33). These sentiments provide a helpful backdrop to the conversation Jesus has with this Samaritan woman.

But Not to Jesus

This is why she is so aghast when Jesus, clearly a Jewish male, sits at a well in Samaria and begins to speak to her. He not only speaks, but asks her for a favor. He asks her to touch her bucket, fill it with water, and hand it to Him so He can press His lips to it and drink. The thought would be horrifying and disgusting to most Jewish men, especially considering not only that her national and religious life render her unclean, but failures in her personal life do as well. Her past and reputation, which Jesus mysteriously knows all about, would keep all men away except for the most unscrupulous who may want to take advantage of a "loose" woman for their own gratification. She is living with a man to whom she is not married, and she has already had 5 husbands! Her reputation alone would repulse the honorable, pure, clean, holy men of the day. This highly inappropriate conversation should never take place. And she knows it.

All of this baggage lies behind her statements, "How is it that you, being a Jew, ask me for a drink since I am a Samaritan woman?" (John 4:9). Or "I have no husband" (with her thoughts probably being, and let's drop it). Or again, her mention of the irreconcilable theological dispute, "Our fathers worshiped in this mountain [Gerizim], and you people say that in Jerusalem is the place where men ought to worship" (John 4:20). These are conversation stoppers, but they don't deter Jesus.

Jesus doesn't let her get away that easily. He doesn't let status, history, purity, clean or unclean, prejudice, sexism, racism, nationalism or any other –ism, any ideology, or any cultural baggage get in the way of seeing a woman. A person. A human with intrinsic value who is in need of something only He can provide. We haven't really even discussed their conversation yet, but the fact it took place tells us something about Jesus, something the world is still in desperate need of. Racism and prejudice continue to divide and harm. They knock people into the dust and hold them there with the ferocity of a lion. To give up the grip is to give up privilege. To loosen the grip is to loosen control. It is to let power and comfort slip through the fingers. It is always met with resistance, sometimes with violence, murder, and warfare. But Jesus willingly treats this woman with dignity, compassion, and value. He gives her a platform and an opportunity to be heard, and as our example, He listens. This marvelous example would do wonders to facilitate racial peace and reconciliation in our modern world.

There are a million reasons to hate, but really only one reason to love. To reach out. To be kind. It's because we were all created with God–given value. No matter who we are, where we're from, what we look like, or even what we have done, our failures do not define us. Our mistakes don't need to be the end of our story. Jesus is still there. He still reaches out. He still offers "living water" that leads to eternal life. He's still sitting at the well.

Reflection Questions

1. How does racism develop, and what can Christians do about it? In what ways does racism go subtly undetected? Have you ever felt superiority over other races? Have you ever judged individuals or groups of people based on skin? How can Jesus be your example in dealing with people different than you?

2. How does nationalism develop, and what can Christians do about it? In what ways does nationalism harm the mission of the church? Have you ever felt superiority over other nationalities? Have you ever judged individuals or groups of people based on their nationality? How can Jesus be your example in dealing with foreigners?

REFLECTION 29
MEETING GOD AT THE WELL

John 4:7–45

∽

Jesus v. the Patriarchs

Is Jesus greater than Jacob? As a well–versed Christian hopefully, you answer "Yes." But hopefully you also recognize how inconceivable or even scandalous this idea would have been to a Jew or Samaritan in the first century. Jacob is one of the great patriarchs. Jacob, a.k.a. Israel, is the patriarch from whom God's people are named. The names Abraham, Isaac, and Jacob just roll off the tongue when you think of the fathers of Judaism. Even Samaritans revered Jacob. This question is asked by a Samaritan woman standing right by Jacob's Well (John 4:12). Jesus didn't have a well. He wasn't a father of Judaism. He wasn't revered by the Samaritans. He was just a thirsty guy who met a woman at a well.

Yet, while there, He offered this woman something much more valuable than Jacob ever could. Jacob offered water for a day or two or however long it took for her water pot to run out. Jesus offered water from which she would never thirst again.

Wouldn't that be amazing? Working with a church, we get a lot of requests. We've given people water and food, filled their cars with gas, and provided places to stay. We've paid bills, provided transportation, and furnished homes. Then, after a short time, they are hungry and thirsty again. They run out of gas. Their nights at the hotel run out. The bill is due again next month. It's not that those things aren't important, but frustratingly, they do not last. Jesus is offering something Jacob cannot. Jesus offers life, living water.

"You are not greater than our father Jacob, are You?"

This question gets at the heart of an important issue explored in the Gospel of John: is Jesus greater even than the Hebrew patriarchs? This question is asked again a few chapters later about Abraham: "Surely you are not greater than our father Abraham ...?" (John 8:53). Even if you don't know Greek, just look at these two sentences and compare what the words look like:

μὴ σὺ μείζων εἶ τοῦ πατρὸς ἡμῶν Ἰακώβ (John 4:12)

μὴ σὺ μείζων εἶ τοῦ πατρὸς ἡμῶν Ἀβραάμ (John 8:53)

It's the exact same question, asked the exact same way, except the names Jacob and Abraham are switched, and the answer is the same for both. Jesus can offer life which the deceased Jacob and Abraham cannot (John 8:51–59). A notable detail in John 4 is the woman brings a water–pot to Jacob's Well, but after meeting Jesus, she leaves her water–pot behind (John 4:28–29). She came for the water Jacob offers, but found greater value in the water Jesus offers. Yes, Jesus is greater than Jacob. Jesus' water leads to eternal life. Jesus is eternal life.

God, Women, and Wells

It's likely no accident this whole conversation takes place with a woman at Jacob's Well. A woman at a well is an ancient and important biblical image, especially as it relates to the patriarchs. It was at a well Jacob met Rachel, the love of his life (Gen 29:1–12). It was at a well Jacob's mom, Rebekah, was found before she married Isaac (Gen 24). Even after the patriarchs, it was at a well Moses met his wife Zipporah (Exod 2).

Perhaps most relevant of all, however, it was at a well a desperate woman, mistreated and cast out of her master's household, met God. In a fascinating and ironic twist, she gave God a name. Hagar, after being used by Abraham and Sarah, was discarded and found herself at a well. She was still pregnant and the Angel of the Lord rescued her, promising her child would survive and even become a great nation. When everyone else had turned away from her, God looked directly at her. Hagar then "called the name of the Lord who spoke to her, 'You are a God who sees', for she said, 'Have I even remained alive here after seeing Him?'" (Gen 16:13). Hagar, the abused foreign slave, gave God the name El–Roi (You are a God who sees). Similarly, in John 4 it was a foreign woman at a well who was seen by God, saw God, and went and told others to "come and see" also (John 4:29).

Later, Hagar is cast away again, when she already has her son. She knows they will die, abandoned and alone. This child with her master was her only shot at having value in her world. It was her only chance to matter, perhaps to be more than just a foreign servant to a beautiful, wealthy woman who seemed to have it all (Sarah). Hagar's only advantage over Sarah was she could bear a child. Once Sarah did the same, however, Hagar no longer had any use. She was sent away. She carries her child out, alone in the heat, with no shelter, no hope, and soon no water. She recognizes her child, her only son, her only companion, her only love, is going to die. I cannot imagine what it felt like to be in this state, but she does the only thing she can bear. She lays her child down in the bushes to die and she walks away, far enough so she can die without hearing his screams. There is no hope.[1]

But the God who sees is also the God who hears. He hears the child's cries. God again meets Hagar and tells her to pick up the child.

Then the God who sees opens her eyes so she can see also. She sees a fresh well of water, a place of hope, a place of life, a place of salvation where God gives exactly what she needs. She and her son are saved by God at a well.

Meeting God at the Well

These Genesis accounts provide some striking similarities to what the Samaritan woman experiences at Jacob's well: a desperate woman who needs water but also needs life and hope. Just like God saw Hagar when no one else did, Jesus saw this woman. Hagar and the Samaritan woman, both foreigners, both outsiders, both insignificant in the world's eyes, both mistreated and abused—both met God at a well. A God who sees. A God who hears. A God who gives life.

Is Jesus greater than Jacob? Jacob built a well of water, but Jesus gives living water, from which one will never thirst again. Jacob met a woman at a well and took her for a wife. Jesus meets a woman at a well and offers her eternal life. God in the person of Jesus is far greater than Jacob, Abraham, or anyone else you put Him up against. He is not too great though to see a desperate woman. A Samaritan. A sinner. A person. When God meets you at the well, salvation is near.

Reflection Questions

1. How can the name "You are a God who sees" shape our understanding of God? Why is it so important that He saw Hagar? In what ways is Hagar similar to the woman at the well? Why does God care for people who usually go unseen? How can it shape what we do and what we know about God?

2. Why does John tell us she "left her water pot" and went and told men about Jesus? Is it important that she left her water pot? How is it significant that a woman with a bad reputation was instrumental in

bringing a whole city to Jesus? How is Acts 8:4–8 relevant to this study?

---

1. A beautiful and memorable description of these events can be found in Rachel Held Evans, *Inspired: Slaying Giants, Walking on Water, and Loving the Bible Again* (Nashville: Nelson, 2018), 29–33.

REFLECTION 30
EQUALITY WITH GOD

John 5:16–47

God and the Sabbath

When Jesus healed the man at the pool of Bethesda (Reflection #15) it created quite a stir. Not because of His miracle and not because of His sign, but because the day of the week. Jesus did this work on the Sabbath. How dare He show compassion on God's day of rest! "For this reason the Jews were persecuting Jesus, because He was doing these things on the Sabbath" (John 5:16).

Why did God give the Sabbath? The Sabbath is rooted in the imitation of God in creation (Exod 20:8–11). God created the world and rested on the 7th day. The Sabbath is a reminder that rest is of God. Do not spend every day working, making money, fixing up your house, etc. Instead, slow down, remember God, and rest. It is a healthy and life–giving exercise. The Sabbath is also rooted in the memory and imitation of God through the Exodus. The Egyptians forced the Jews to work constantly, with no rest, all day, every day. Their lives were miserable.

When God became their king and overthrew the Egyptians, He promised rest. He also wanted them to give rest to others:

> The Sabbath day is a Sabbath of the Lord your God; in it you shall not do any work, you or your son or your daughter or your male servant or your female servant or your ox or your donkey or any of your cattle or your sojourner who stays with you, so that your male servant and your female servant may rest as well as you. You shall remember that you were a slave in the land of Egypt, and the Lord your God brought you out of there by a mighty hand and by an outstretched arm; therefore the Lord your God commanded you to observe the Sabbath day (Deuteronomy 5:14–15).

Your family, your servants, and even the animals get rest when God is king.

When Jesus frees the man at Bethesda from his physical bondage and suffering on the Sabbath, He is not violating Moses' command. He is honoring and imitating God. Jesus does what God does, even on the Sabbath: "My Father is working until now, and I Myself am working" (John 5:17). Will Jesus work on the Sabbath? Yes—when that work is healing, saving, and helping. Because that's what His Father does.

Equality with God

Did you catch that? Not only did Jesus break the Sabbath, He justified it by saying God is His Father and He does whatever God does. If God works on Sabbath, Jesus works on Sabbath. This goes too far for those listening to Jesus: "For this reason therefore the Jews were seeking all the more to kill Him, because He was not only breaking the Sabbath, but also was calling God His own Father, making Himself equal with God" (John 5:18). It is a double accusation: Jesus broke the Sabbath and said He was equal to God. No one can claim equality with God, especially after just sinning and breaking Sabbath!

Jesus gives an amazing response to this accusation. He doesn't deny it. He explains it. He illustrates it. He doesn't back down and say, "No, no, you misunderstood. I'm not equal to God." Instead He gives them a list of ways He is equal to God (John 5:19–30). He already mentioned work: God works on the Sabbath so Jesus will also (John 5:16–17). Where did Jesus learn to do this work? In life, sons grow up to learn and imitate their fathers. Professionally, this was way more common back in Jesus' day, but it still happens now. Jesus was a carpenter because Joseph was a carpenter. Jesus healed on the Sabbath because God heals on the Sabbath. The Father loves Jesus and "shows Him all the things that He Himself is doing" (John 5:20). You can see the works of God by looking at Jesus.

Jesus also does other things only God can do. "Just as the Father raises the dead and gives them life, even so the Son gives life to whom He wishes" (John 5:21). Jesus, just like God, has become the source of life. This will be illustrated vividly in the raising of Lazarus and when Jesus says: "I am the resurrection and the life" (John 11:25) and "I am the way, and the truth, and the life" (John 14:6). All the way back in the prologue, John writes, "In Him was life, and the life was the Light of me" (John 1:4). Giving life is another way Jesus shows His equality with His Father.

Like the Father, Jesus has become the judge (John 5:22; John 12:48). In fact, God has given His judgment to His Son, "so that all will honor the Son even as they honor the Father" (John 5:23). Judgment and honor show equality between Jesus and His Father. As judge, Jesus gives life to all who hear Him (John 5:24; 6:68; 10:27–28) and believe in God. They escape condemnation and enter into life; that is Jesus' call. Like a father passes on the family business to a son, God has given judgment to Jesus.

John 5:25–30 is a vivid image of what it's like for the Son to have life, authority, and judgment which come from God.

An hour is coming, in which all who are in the tombs will hear His voice, and will come forth; those who did the good deeds to a resurrection of life, those who committed the evil deeds to a resurrection of judgment (John 5:28–29).

There is no clearer image of Jesus doing God's work, giving life, and judging mankind than in the final resurrection. All will be raised, even the wicked, and will face judgment. All of this authority has been given from Father to Son. So yes, Jesus also has the authority to heal a man on the Sabbath. And yes, as God's Son, Jesus is equal with His Father.

The Witnesses

Jesus doesn't end His argument there. He has done the works of God and shows His equality with God, but he proves it with witnesses. Who is trustworthy and can verify those claims Jesus just made? Who can testify Jesus is equal with God? Jesus will not simply testify about Himself (John 5:31); He will use the testimony of four others.

The first witness is John the Baptist (John 5:33–35). He's also the first witness in John's Gospel; sent by God as a witness to testify about the Light (John 1:6–7). John was not the Light of the world (John 1:8), but He did shine some light, like a lamp burning and shining (John 5:33–35). While the people were willing to rejoice "for a little while" at his work, there are still greater witnesses to come.

The second to bear witness are the works of Jesus (John 5:36). If you want to know the identity of Jesus, look at what He does. Having already observed many of His signs, what do they tell you about Him? His works prove He is from the Father.

The third witness is the Father Himself (John 5:37–38). God bears witness to the true identity of Jesus. Yet because they rejected Jesus, they can't hear the Father. His word is not in them because they rejected His Logos.

The fourth and final witness is Scripture (John 5:39–47). Searching Scripture is a wonderful thing, but it is not the words on the page that bring eternal life. The words on the page testify to Jesus, and He brings eternal life. They overlook Him for the Scriptures. Then they don't actually believe Scripture because they testify of Jesus (John 5:39). Moses wrote about Jesus (John 5:46). To find where Moses wrote about Jesus, don't look up the word "Jesus" in the Pentateuch. Look to the creation in Genesis 1. Look to Joseph's ladder. Look to the Exodus. Look to the Passover. Look to manna from heaven. Look to the bronze serpent Moses lifted high. Look to the tabernacle and temple. Jesus ends the discussion with a final question: "But if you will not believe his writings, how will you believe My words?" (John 5:47).

Reflection Questions

1. How is Scripture related to eternal life? Does the Bible give life or does Jesus give life? How does the Bible lead one to Jesus? If a person did not have a Bible, how could they become a follower of Jesus?

2. How will Jesus judge those in the final resurrection? According to the text, on what basis will Jesus render His judgment? How will this event show Jesus is equal to God, gives life, dispenses judgment, and is worthy of honor?

REFLECTION 31

BEFORE ABRAHAM WAS, I AM

John 7:1–8:59

The Unbelievers

One of the most contentious and difficult sections of the Gospel of John centers around a conflict in Jerusalem at the Feast of Booths (Sukkot). This particular feast was both a celebration of harvest and a reminder of sleeping in "booths" or tents upon leaving Egypt (Lev 23:34–44; Deut 16:13–15). Like Passover, Purim, and the Feast of Dedication (Reflections #7 and #34), the Feast of Booths also looked back to times of victory over oppression. The Feast of Booths, while rooted in the Exodus narrative, actually focused specifically on the less than glamorous time period of camping out in the wilderness, the time between Egypt and the Promised Land. They had escaped slavery but they were still awaiting the rest of their salvation. The Promised Land, sworn to their fathers, was so close they could taste it, but we know how the story goes. They were in those tents far longer than they ever expected: forty years of wilderness wanderings because they refused to trust what God was accomplishing right before their eyes. "They were not able to enter because of disbelief" (Heb 3:19).

As we'll see in this section of John, this problem continues into the time of Jesus. Jesus, like Moses, has just miraculously fed the people bread from God (John 6:32–35), has just crossed the sea (John 6:16–21), and was just recognized as the Prophet (John 6:14) and the Holy One of God (John 6:69). During the feast He even shouts out an offer of water to any who will drink (John 7:37–39). He is doing amazing things in front of everybody, but He is still met with stubborn disbelief. This includes his own family, for even His "brothers were not believing in Him" (John 7:5).

When Jesus goes to the Feast in Jerusalem, He must do so in secret, because any time He goes to Jerusalem His life is on the line. This section begins by saying "the Jews were seeking to kill Him" (John 7:1) and ends with them furiously grabbing stones (John 8:59). It's amazing; Jesus just miraculously fed the 5,000, performed incredible signs, and yet when He arrived at the feast, "There was much grumbling among the crowds concerning Him" (John 7:12). Wow, grumbling at the Feast of Booths. That's interesting. This word "grumbling" (γογγυσμός), in the Septuagint, is used in Exodus 16:7, which is right after God gave them "bread from heaven" (Exod 16:4). In Exodus, after the Passover and the escape from Egypt, right after they passed through the Red Sea (Exod 14), they begin to grumble about water (Exod 15:24) and food (Exod 16:2, 8, 12).

When the Israelites thought they were grumbling against Moses, Moses clarifies, "Your grumblings are not against us but against the LORD" (Exod 16:8). Jesus just fed the people, crossed on the sea, and is with the Jews at the Feast of Booths remembering the wilderness wanderings, and they are again grumbling and not believing. They say things like "He leads the people astray" (John 7:12) and "You have a demon!" (John 7:20). Leading the people astray kind of sounds like the old accusation hurled against Moses (Exodus 14:11; Numbers 14:1–4; 21:5). They argue Christ can't come from where Jesus is from (John 7:27, 41, 52; remember John 1:46). They shout, "Your testimony is not true" (John 8:13) and "Do we not rightly say that You are a Samaritan and have a demon?" (John 8:48). These are not mere grumbles against a man. They are grumbles against God. Ironically, they are speaking blasphemy which is the very thing they want to stone Jesus for doing.

The Believers

But let's not overstate their failures. Some actually do believe. Remember Nicodemus? He reappears in this section. In John 7:50–51, he defends Jesus to his peers, saying they ought not judge Him without first going to hear from Him. Hearing from Jesus is exactly what Nicodemus did back in John 3, but his argument is ignored because Jesus is from Galilee. Nicodemus, along with many others, is starting to believe: "many of the crowd believed in Him; and they were saying, 'When the Christ comes, He will not perform more signs than those which this man has, will He?'" (John 7:31). Some were saying "Certainly this is the Prophet" and others "This is the Christ" (John 7:40–41). In fact, the more Jesus teaches, the more people begin to believe, "As He spoke these things, many came to believe in Him (John 8:30).

No matter how many reject Jesus, blaspheme Him, and even try to kill Him, there are always some who believe. They cannot help but be drawn in by who He is and what He is doing. In John 8:31, Jesus talks to "those who believed Him." He promises "if you continue in My word, then you are truly disciples of Mine; and you will know the truth, and the truth will make you free" (John 8:31–32). This becomes another one of those common misunderstandings. They take Jesus to be talking about freedom from literal slavery, and their response is a bit befuddling: "We are Abraham's descendants and have never been enslaved to anyone, how is it that You say, 'You will become free?'" (John 8:33). Excuse me? Abraham's descendants have never been enslaved to anyone? You are currently at the Feast of Booths! You were living in booths because you were escaping slavery. Jesus, as the new Moses, is offering freedom from slavery again! An even better freedom. Where you won't be stuck in tents but will have eternal life!

"Truly, I say to you, everyone who commits sin is a slave to sin. The slave does not remain in the house forever; the son does remain forever. So if the Son makes you free, you will be free indeed" (John 8:34–36). Jesus, as God's Son, offers freedom from sin's enslaving power, to be eternally free. Instead of taking hold of this great freedom, however, they just turn it into an argument.

The Blasphemy

It is imperative to say: be careful as you read this next section. Tragically, passages within John 8:37–59 have been used in antisemitic rhetoric and to incite hatred and violence against Jews because of some of the strong language. Bear in mind, Jesus is a Jew. Many of the Jews have believed in Him. And poor decisions made by some Jews 2000 years ago should not lead to hatred or distrust of Jews living today. In fact, it shouldn't even be met with hatred against those Jews, because it wasn't by Jesus. True imitation of Jesus would never lead us to violence, hatred, or antisemitism. It would lead us to loving self–sacrifice for those with whom we disagree. True imitation of Jesus leads us to the cross. Never forget that.

Having said that, in this section, the insults fly and violence ensues. Jesus says to those before Him, by their actions they have rejected God as their Father and instead their father has become the devil. They are trying to kill God's Son; they are rejecting His grace, forgiveness, and kingdom. They are murderers and liars who are doing the work of the devil. In response they call Jesus a demon and Samaritan. They scoff that Jesus can offer eternal life because the faithful of the past have already died. Those who listened to Abraham died. Abraham himself died. If one dies after listening to Abraham, the father of their faith, how can an insignificant man from Nazareth give life? "You are not greater than our father Abraham, who died? The prophets died too; whom do you make yourself out to be?" (John 8:53). That question gets to the heart of the Gospel of John.

Who does Jesus make Himself out to be? Is He greater than Jacob? (John 4:12) Is He greater than Abraham? (John 8:53). Is He greater than the prophets? Is He even greater than Moses? Jesus' answer shows that each one of these questions drastically and embarrassingly undershoot. Jesus, the man not yet 40 years old, has seen Abraham. In fact, Jesus declares, "Before Abraham was, I AM" (John 8:58). I AM. This statement is not intended to be bad grammar but another allusion back to the divine revelation of the identity of God to Moses (Exod 3:14; 6:2–3). The God who appeared to Abraham, Jacob, and Moses has now appeared again. The great and indescribable I AM is here.

For the first time, they pick up stones to kill Jesus. They will try this again at the Feast of Dedication in John 10:31. They believe His blasphemy must be punished. Hatred and animosity toward Jesus are heating up every time He opens His mouth, especially around Jerusalem. With each passing feast day Jesus is getting closer and closer to the cross.

Reflection Questions

1. In what ways can the truth of Jesus make us free? In what ways are all people slaves and in need of freedom? How does sin enslave? How can you relate the ministry of Jesus to the Exodus out of Egypt?

2. How are feast days shaping the story of the Gospel of John? Why is it important to know about the Jewish feast days? What do these feasts tell us about Jesus?

REFLECTION 32
FINALLY, A GOOD SHEPHERD

John 10:1–19

He Knows the Sheep by Name

Jesus just healed a blind man. Unsurprisingly to the reader of John, the reaction to this amazing moment was not great. In fact, a division arose in the crowds concerning Jesus (John 9:16). There seems to be a pattern here. While some couldn't deny the signs, many of the Pharisees did not believe in Jesus. They kicked the blind man out of the synagogue. They are seeing the works of God before their very eyes, but they are blind to it. Jesus even says this is why He came, so the blind could have sight but the Pharisees become blind: "that those who do not see may see, and that those who see may become blind" (John 9:39). It is these blind ones Jesus is talking to when John 10 begins. Ignore the chapter break; this is a continuation of the same conversation.

Jesus makes a contrast between different kinds of leaders. There are some who try to lead sheep without knowing the sheep. Some are thieves and robbers who try to break in and steal the sheep (John 10:1). And some are strangers who the sheep simply will not follow (John 10:5). Then there is the shepherd—the leader who goes through the door, calls the sheep by name, and leads them out. The sheep follow this shepherd because they know his voice. And he knows his sheep. He knows them by name.

Who are you most likely to follow? The leader you've never met? The one who doesn't even know your name? Or the leader who knows you and cares for you? I think this passage serves as a wonderful reminder to those desiring to be leaders and shepherds. Know and love people. The Pharisees just threw a man out of a synagogue because Jesus healed him (John 9:30–34). That isn't leadership. They are no shepherds. They try to lead God's people, but they are not going through the door. They try to lead God's people but are unwilling to know God's people. They themselves are blind to the things of God.

Good shepherds and leaders enter through the door. They lead the sheep through the door, and because of their relationship with the sheep, the sheep know and follow them. Shepherds, if you have not intentionally led, encouraged, taught, and guided the church towards Christ, you are failing at your God–given call. Shepherds, if the church does not feel comfortable going to you with struggles and questions, something is terribly off. Shepherds, if you are better at kicking people out of the synagogue than leading them through sin, darkness, and danger to the arms of the Savior, you have devastatingly missed the mark. Shepherds, know your sheep, be available, communicate, and love. Shepherds, enter through the Door.

I Am the Door

But what does it mean to enter through the door? What door? In one of those famous "I Am" statements, Jesus declares, "I Am the door of the sheep" and "I Am the door" (John 10:7, 9). A converging of ideas takes place in this passage. On the one hand, the Pharisees, who are supposed to be leaders and shepherds of God's people, are pitiful shepherds. They won't go to the sheep through the door, because they reject the Door. Jesus is the way to lead God's people. All spiritual leaders who try to lead without Jesus are thieves and robbers of God's sheep. They are stealing sheep from God. They break in and take the sheep by force. The only way God wants shepherds getting to His sheep is through Jesus. This lesson is both for shepherds and the sheep. If you want to be God's sheep, you need to enter through the Door. Through Jesus. That is where salvation is found (John 10:9). Both sheep and shepherds must meet through Jesus.

Those shepherds who try to lead while bypassing Jesus, like the blind Pharisees He is talking to, have actually only come "to steal and kill and destroy; I came that they may have life, and have it abundantly" (John 10:10). They are stealing God's sheep and leading them towards death and destruction, away from eternal life provided through Jesus. Jesus brings life and Jesus is life (John 11:25; 14:6). This is not some vague ethereal life for some unknown future day. This is life right now. Jesus is bringing life abundantly, but you must walk through the Door to experience it.

I Am the Good Shepherd

Jesus has just contrasted robbers, thieves, and strangers with the shepherd. The shepherd enters to lead the sheep through Him. As the illustration continues, Jesus switches His role in the metaphor. He was the Door through which shepherds and sheep met. Now He takes up the role of the Shepherd Himself: not just any shepherd but the Good Shepherd. Not every shepherd is good. If you are going to lead God's flock, Jesus is your example of what a good shepherd is all about. He also adds another contrast between the Good Shepherd and the hired hands. Hired hands don't really care for the sheep but are paid to do a job.

What separates the Good Shepherd from the hired hands? The wolf. When the wolf comes, hired hands flee but the Shepherd lays down His life for the sheep. The true difference is not just what they do when adversity comes, but the reason they do it. The hired hand flees because he "is not concerned about the sheep" (John 10:13). The Good Shepherd stays and lays down His life because "I know My own and My own know Me" (John 10:13–15). He actually knows and loves His sheep. He knows them by name.

The cross was not just about some job Jesus was paid to do. The cross wasn't about bravery or what Jesus was forced to do. It wasn't about what man did to Jesus but what Jesus did for man. "I lay down My life ... No one has taken it away from Me, but I lay it down on My own initiative. I have authority to lay it down, and I have authority to take it up again" (John 10:17–18). Jesus could have avoided the cross. He could have behaved like a hired hand, but He suffered and bled and died of his own initiative, because He loved His sheep. He loves us.

He loves us so much, in fact, He wants more of us. "I have other sheep, which are not of this fold; I must bring them also, and they will hear My voice; and they will become one flock with one shepherd" (John 10:16). Jesus being the Good Shepherd was about love for and the unification of all mankind. That they would be one flock, recognized by love (John 13:34–35), and through unity change the world (John 17:22–23). Jesus died that through His love Jews and Gentiles could be reconciled together in one flock. I think the same is true for any man–made division and social, racial, or national barrier we have concocted. The love of the cross is strong enough to bring enemies together, let's make sure we are not standing in the way of it.

Reflection Questions

1. In what ways is Jesus the "door" to the sheep? What can you learn about leadership and shepherding through this illustration? How can one incorporate Jesus more fully into their view of leadership?

2. What are the important differences between the robber (John 10:1), the stranger (John 10:5), the hired hand (John 10:12), and the Good Shepherd? Can you think of examples of each in the Gospel of John? Can you think of times you have been each in your walk with God?

REFLECTION 33
I AND THE FATHER ARE ONE

John 10:19–31

More Division

People just don't know what to make of Jesus. He doesn't fit anyone's paradigm. He is frustratingly unpredictable and never conforms to expectations. If He would just heal someone on a Tuesday, it'd make Him a lot easier to figure out. That way everyone could be happy, and perhaps greater numbers, with less controversy and hysteria, could see Him as the Messiah. The problem is people want Him to be their vision of the Messiah. They want to tame Him or control Him. They want a Messiah to satisfy their agendas. They want a kingdom, freedom, victory over enemies, and maybe a little wealth. They want a seat at the world table to keep their customs: Sabbaths, circumcision, food regulations, Torah, privilege for the sons of Abraham, and the Supremacy of Yahweh.

But Jesus is way too subversive. Every time He does something amazing, a seemingly unnecessary controversy comes with it. He meets with Jewish leaders secretly at night but meets with a Samaritan woman openly in broad daylight (John 3, 4). He goes to Jerusalem to celebrate feasts, but He flips tables while He's there (John 2:13ff). He'll teach truth, but He'll do so in riddles or parables to puzzle His listeners and wage a war within their own hearts. He heals a man who can't walk, but tells him to pick up his bed and carry it on the Sabbath (John 5:9–10). He'll give sight to the blind, but He'll make mud to do it, again, on the Sabbath (John 9:13–15).

Every time Jesus does anything, arguments arise (John 6:40–44; 9:15–16; 10:19–21). "This is the Prophet!" "This is the Christ!" "The Christ cannot come from Galilee." "This man is not from God!" "How can a man who is a sinner perform such signs?" "He has a demon and is insane!" "A demon cannot open the eyes of the blind!" And on and on the shouts and arguments go. What position are they taking? What position are you taking? I think there is a reason these arguments keep popping up. You, as the reader, are supposed to begin taking a side. Whose side are you on?

To get their answers, they finally just ask Him. They choose a fitting feast day (refresh yourself on Reflection #7 to see why), and they want an answer. "How long will you keep us in suspense? If you are the Christ, tell us plainly?" (John 10:22–24).

God, David, and Ezekiel 34

To answer this question, Jesus appeals to His works (John 10:25). They have already made it plain who He is. He's given sight to the blind and food to the hungry. He's healed the sick and lame and fended off the wolves. He's done the work of a leader. He's done the work of a Good Shepherd. Their unbelief is evidence they are not His sheep (John 10:26). His sheep have been paying attention, they hear and they follow, and Jesus knows every one of them (John 10:27; 10:4, 5). And He, as the source of life (John 1:4; 11:25; 14:6), gives them eternal life. He protects His sheep now and forever. The eternal Shepherd of eternal life; the truly Good Shepherd.

Israel has seen its fair share of bad shepherds. The Pharisees

Jesus has been talking to are among them. Ezekiel 34 dives deep in discussing the wicked shepherds of Israel, "Son of man, Prophesy against the shepherds of Israel ... Behold, I am against the shepherds" (Ezek 34:2, 10). These shepherds feed themselves, Jesus feeds the 5,000. "Those who are sickly you have not strengthened, the diseased you have not healed, the broken you have not bound up, the scattered you have not brought back, nor have you sought for the lost" (Ezek 34:4). The sheep were scattered and dominated by wild beasts (the Babylonians) because they were abused, neglected, and led astray by worthless shepherds. As a result, God promises to take His sheep back from the worthless, lazy, self–indulgent shepherds (Ezek 34:10).

God Will Be Their Shepherd!

> I Myself will search for My sheep and seek them out ... I will care for My sheep ... I will bring them out from the peoples ... I will feed them ... I will feed my flock and lead them to rest ... I will seek the lost, bring back the scattered, bind up the broken and strengthen the sick ... (Ezek 34:11–16).

These promises of the love and devotion of God to His lost, scattered, injured, and hungry sheep don't end here. He continues,

> I will set over them one shepherd, My servant David, and he will feed them; he will feed them himself and be their shepherd. And I, the LORD, will be their God, and My servant David will be prince among them; I the LORD have spoken (Ezek 34:23–25).

So God will be their shepherd, but He'll also be their God and raise another to be their shepherd.

Two Shepherds or One?

God both sees Himself and some future servant called "David" as those who will shepherd His people. This is clearly not King David, who is long dead by the time Ezekiel is written, but some future David. A future shepherd who will initiate a "covenant of peace" between God and His people (Ezek 34:25). I can't help but think this is the prophecy Jesus sees Himself fulfilling. Notice, as the shepherd, Jesus says "no one will snatch them out of My hand ... and no one is able to snatch them out of My Father's hand" (John 10:28–29). This promise of divine protection is offered by the twin shepherds, the Father and the future David. Their hands are equally strong. Their hands equally can protect against any enemy. How is that possible? "I and the Father are one" (John 10:30).

Ezekiel 34 ends with the words, "As for you, My sheep, the sheep of My pasture, you are men, and I am your God" (Ezek 34:31). God is the Good Shepherd. Jesus gives those standing near Him the same message. "I am the Good Shepherd ... I and the Father are one." Jesus is their shepherd because He is their God. This is a shocking statement. So shocking that for those who don't believe, it merits a death sentence for blasphemy: "the Jews picked up stones again to stone Him" (John 10:31). Notice the word "again." That's a call back to John 8:59, just moments before Jesus gave sight to the blind man. Jesus had just said, "before Abraham was, I AM" and stones were picked up.

This alarming truth of the identity of Jesus is His most controversial claim. Nothing about Jesus will cause more division than this. It is also the grounds for all He says and does in the Gospel of John. It is His source of authority. So divisive and polarizing is it that the reader is left with only two options: grab a stone and beat Jesus down to the earth, or fall on the earth yourself in worship.[1]

Reflection Questions

1. How do Jesus' works testify about Him (John 10:25; 5:36)? What do our works testify about us? What do our works testify about Jesus? If you did one thing tomorrow that made Jesus look good, what would it be?

2. Bad shepherds are those who fatten themselves while their sheep starve and become prey. Can you think of examples of this type of leadership? Do you ever fatten yourself while others go hungry? Do you use privilege for power? What qualities make for a good, God-like shepherd?

---

1. See Richard B. Hays, *Echoes of Scripture in the Gospels* (Waco: Baylor University Press, 2017), 318–20.

REFLECTION 34
PASSOVER

John 2:13; 6:4; 11:55; 12:1, 23; 13:1

∾

So Many Feasts

"Now before the Feast of the Passover, Jesus knowing that His hour had come that He would depart out of the world to the Father ..." (John 13:1). Jesus' "hour" has finally come, and Passover is the major indication. In fact, Passover has repeatedly been a major factor in the progression of the Gospel of John. In fact, just about everything in the Gospel of John has been paced and focused on various feast days and Jewish celebrations. Let's just walk through John together to bring us to John 13, the final Passover.

John 2 begins at a wedding in Cana of Galilee where Jesus turns water into wine. In John 2:13 we are introduced to the first Passover in John. This required a trip to Jerusalem and is where Jesus flipped the tables and cleansed the temple. While in Jerusalem, he met Nicodemus at night and began teaching and baptizing many in Judea (John 3:22; 4:1–3). Upon returning to Galilee, Jesus passes through

Samaria and meets the woman at the well before finally making it back to Cana of Galilee to heal a nobleman's son (John 4:46–54). He doesn't appear to stay long though because "a feast of the Jews" began to take place in Jerusalem, so Jesus traveled back. He heals a man at the pool of Bethesda and gets into a lengthy argument with the leaders in Jerusalem. Jesus makes a quick trip back up to Galilee (John 6:1) when it is about time for the second Passover (John 6:4). Jesus feeds the 5,000, walks on water, gets into another argument that leads to chapter 7 which begins with "the feast of the Jews, the Feast of Booths, was near" (John 7:1–2).

Notice chapters 2–4 are about Jesus' travels to and from the first Passover, then the next three chapters begin with a series of feast days! In chapter 7 Jesus, after arguing with his unbelieving brothers, travels to Jerusalem again, which has become an exceedingly dangerous area for Him (John 7:1), and gets into another argument. This argument leads to an attempt on His life (John 8:58). So Jesus escapes the stoning and runs into a blind man, heals him, and again gets into an argument (John 9–10:21).

John 10:22, right in the heart of Jesus' discussion about the Good Shepherd, tells the reader, "At that time the Feast of the Dedication took place at Jerusalem." For this feast, Jesus is again in Jerusalem at the temple, again gets into an argument, and they again try to kill Him (John 10:31). Jesus leaves Judea to go beyond the Jordan, and many there come to believe in Him (John 10:40–42). The sickness and death of His dear friend Lazarus brings Him back to Judea, to Bethany near Jerusalem, where He raises Lazarus and more people want to kill Him (John 11:53), and the third Passover is approaching (John 11:55; 12:1). Jesus makes His final, triumphant entrance into Jerusalem in John 12:12–26. It is this final trip to Jerusalem, this third Passover, where Jesus knows His hour has come (John 12:23, 27; 13:1). The Passover and the Crucifixion are at hand.

Jesus as the Passover Lamb

That Jesus' death coincides with Passover should not come as a surprise. Remember all the way back to one of the first testimonies we have about Jesus: "Behold the Lamb of God who takes away the sin of the world!" (John 1:29) and "Behold the Lamb of God!" (John 1:36). John the Baptist, the first character witness to testify to the identity of Jesus, calls Him the Lamb of God. The reader by this point knows Jesus is the embodiment of God Himself, but we never abandoned the idea Jesus is also in some way, God's Lamb. Jews bring their lambs to the priest to be offered for forgiveness. If God is going to make an offering for forgiveness, what does He use? He uses Himself. No one else needs to die for God to forgive the world; He will take on the role of the Lamb for Himself.

This image of Jesus as Lamb of God sacrificed for the forgiveness of the whole world is maintained throughout the Gospel of John. Even on the cross, it is vividly portrayed.

> Then the Jews, because it was the day of preparation, so that the bodies would not remain on the cross on the Sabbath (for the Sabbath was a high day), they asked Pilate that their legs might be broken, and that they might be taken away (John 19:31).

As the Passover lamb is being killed in preparation for the Passover, so the Lamb of God is being prepared as well.

This connection is made vividly clear by what happens to the legs of Jesus. Breaking the legs of a criminal on the cross is a way of speeding up the crucifixion. Their legs can no longer lift them up to draw in air, they slump down low, their lungs deflate, and they suffocate in their own misery. They break the legs of the two criminals on either side of Jesus, but when they get to Jesus, "He was already dead, they did not break His legs ... For these things came to pass to fulfill the Scripture, 'Not a bone of Him shall be broken'" (John 19:33, 36). Now, I challenge you, read the Old Testament and find a prediction that the Messiah would never break a bone. It's not in there. So what passage does John quote? What Scripture does this fulfill? Exodus 12:46 and Numbers 9:12 give you your answer. (Psalm 34:20 shares this language, but careful reading shows it is also not a direct prediction of the Messiah.) These are not predictions about the Messiah, but prescriptions on how to prepare the Passover lamb. You are to do so without breaking any bones. How on earth does Jesus' death on a cross fulfill a 1,400 year old Jewish recipe for cooking lamb? Because Jesus is what that lamb had been pointing to the entire time. Jesus is truly God's Passover Lamb.[1]

Why Passover?

A final thought that strikes me as I reflect upon this passage is—why Passover? Especially if this Lamb "takes away the sins of the world," why did Jesus die on Passover? Why not Yom Kippur, the Day of Atonement? The day where the sins of Israel were atoned for by the blood of the goat? Remember there are two goats, one symbolizes the removal of sin from the land while the other sheds its blood for the purification of the people? Doesn't that look a little bit like Jesus and Barabbas put before the people (John 18:39–40)? Granted, they make the wrong choice, but still, that definitely has Day of Atonement vibes. It seems like the sin–cleansing blood of Jesus who died for our forgiveness would fit well with the Day of Atonement. Why Passover?

I think the answer is seen in what Passover is all about, the over-throw of the wicked, oppressive, and dark powers that have enslaved God's people. Jesus has been hinting at this: "You will know the truth and the truth will make you free ... everyone who commits sin is a slave to sin" (John 8:32, 34). Sin is the new Egypt. Jesus is the new Moses. And the cross is the new Passover. The powers of darkness, the chains of sin, and authority of the spiritual rulers who hold this world captive, the Satan, the new Pharaoh, called three times "the ruler of this world" (John 12:31; 14:30; 16:11), will be overthrown. When Jesus is "lifted up from the earth" He will draw "all men" to Himself. In that moment, God is glorified and the "ruler of this world" is overthrown (John 12:28, 31–33). Jesus comes to save His people as the

Lamb, the Moses, and the God of Israel. He leads the greatest Exodus the world has ever seen; the only Exodus in which the rest of the world has hope. Jesus is the New Passover.

Reflection Questions

1. Why did Jesus go to this Passover knowing what it meant for Him? Why would Jesus willingly put Himself in harm's way? Are you ever willing to put yourself in harm's way for others?

2. Why is Passover such an important celebration for thinking about the cross? How does Jesus conquer our enemies and lead us to freedom through His death? How can this cause us to read the book of Exodus differently?

---

1. Richard B. Hays, *Echoes of Scripture in the Gospels* (Waco: Baylor University Press, 2017), 313–17.

REFLECTION 35
WASHING FEET—THE INCARNATION

John 13:1–14

Sacrificial Love

Nobody likes a demotion. No player likes to lose their starting status. People don't generally like to go backwards, make less money, get less than they deserve, or work hard for nothing. However, sometimes people do. They may be under appreciated. They may work hard but be incompetent or be under–performing. Or maybe, they chose to do less, make less, or "be" less at some job, because their priorities are changing. Some willingly take demotions, less pay, fewer responsibilities, and work fewer hours so they could do more of what they care about—spend time with their family, travel, read, or simply enjoy life and leisure more.

Taking a "demotion" is something virtually nobody wants, unless they want something else more. It has to be for something important. Jesus willingly took less than He deserved. In a way that none of us will ever be able to understand or grasp, He took less than He deserved. He didn't do it for nothing. There was something important to Him, motivating Him to take less than He deserved ... love.

Love motivated Jesus. A level and depth of love the world has never seen before. After washing the disciple's feet, Jesus says,

> A new commandment I give to you, that you love one another: just as I have loved you, you also are to love one another. By this all people will know that you are my disciples, if you have love for one another (John 13:34–35).

This "new commandment" is to love just as Jesus loved. An active, sacrificial, service–oriented love; a love that can change the world.

Incarnation vs Exaltation

Christology is a theological term which describes a field of study focused on the origin, nature, and personhood of Jesus. Christology addresses topics like the Hypostatic Union (the nature of the union of Jesus' humanity and divinity), Aryanism, Adoptionism, etc. In New Testament scholarship, various books are described as having a High Christology if Jesus is pictured as divine and equal to God (like John), or as having a Low Christology if Jesus is pictured as merely human (often said of Mark and Luke), Richard Hays's book *Reading Backwards: Figural Christology and the Fourfold Gospel Witness* presents an excellent case that all four Gospels picture Jesus as divine and the embodiment of the God of Israel.[1]

Adoptionism is a form of Exaltation Christology which advocates Jesus was born simply as a man, but was adopted to become divine (usually at His baptism or resurrection). He was exalted to divinity. This is the idea of promotion. Jesus was faithful to God and was promoted because of it. The Gospel of John does not teach an Exaltation Christology. John teaches quite the opposite, an Incarnation Christology, this is the idea Jesus was already divine. "The Word was with God and was God" (John 1:1), but came to earth to become human. He became incarnate, enfleshed, "the Word became flesh and tabernacled among us" (John 1:14). This would be a demotion, a willing, self–sacrificial demotion.

Jesus' life was about willful demotion for the sake of love. The incarnation itself is a complete act of self–giving love. The cross is the most vivid, heart–wrenching, and powerful picture of self–giving love that has ever been seen. In–between those two events were 33 years of life, a life spent in selflessness, kindness, service, and sacrifice. Paul, while possibly quoting an early Christian hymn, writes about the incarnation, life, and death of Jesus in this way:

> though he was in the form of God, did not count equality with God a thing to be grasped, but emptied himself, taking the form of a servant, being born in the likeness of men. And being found in human form, he humbled himself by becoming obedient to the point of death, even death on a cross (Phil 2:5–8).

Demoted to Slavery

As Jesus was preparing to depart from His disciples, as He was preparing for his impending execution on the Roman cross, He gave them a unique and beautiful display of willful demotion. He got down on his hands and knees, took a rag, took upon Himself the job of a slave, and with their feet in His hands, began to wash. Jesus washed their feet. The Word who was with God and was God washed their feet. God washed man's feet. Dirty man. Sinful man. Man who would soon abandon Him. Man who would soon deny Him. Man who would soon betray Him. God loving took the dirty foot of Judas, a traitor and thief, a son of perdition, and scrubbed it clean.

Jesus is God. Jesus is Lord and Teacher and Master. Yet He was not above becoming the slave who washed men's feet. Just like the signs of Jesus are meant to teach important and valuable lessons, so is this. When He finished washing their feet, He asked,

Do you understand what I have done to you? You call me Teacher and Lord, and you are right, for so I am. If I then, your Lord and Teacher; have washed your feet, you also ought to wash one another's feet. For I have given you an example, that you also should do just as I have done to you (John 13:12–15).

That concluding challenge from Jesus sounds a lot like what He says later in this chapter "you love one another; just as I have loved you" (John 13:34). Love, serve, and wash one another, because Jesus loves, serves, and washes us. Jesus, as Lord and Teacher, was not above any task. Nothing was too demeaning. Nothing was too lowly or dirty for Him. So, what jobs are beneath you? What are you unwilling to do because, "that's not my responsibility"? Are you willing to take a demotion? If we ever feel too proud, too educated, too wealthy, too important, too clean, too smart, or too busy to get on our hands and knees and wash a dirty foot, clean a dirty floor, or work on some lowly unglorifying task, perhaps we need to remember the love, service, and humility of Jesus. Remember the incarnation and the cross. Remember the dirty feet in–between.

Reflection Questions

1. Why is a healthy understanding of Christology and the deity of Jesus so crucial to the Christian life? In what practical ways does it matter that Jesus is equal with God? How does this affect our worship and prayer life?

2. Have you ever literally washed feet? How would you feel doing that? Are there any reasons to practice this today? Do you think there could be any beneficial lessons learned? Are there other, perhaps more modern ways we can practice this same lesson?

---

1. Richard B. Hays, *Reading Backwards: Figural Christology and the Fourfold Gospel Witness* (Waco: Baylor University Press, 2014).

REFLECTION 36
WASHING FEET—LET GO AND LET GOD

John 13:1–14

≈

How to See God

As we noted in the previous reflection, the Gospel of John teaches an Incarnation Christology, meaning Jesus existed as God prior to becoming human flesh. The Logos was with God and was God and created all things with God. So anything you see Jesus doing, you see God doing. He is not merely teaching you about God, He is showing you God. One of the problems we sometimes run into is we have concepts of who God is and we try to fit Jesus into those concepts. I think a better approach is to forget everything you thought you knew about God. Then look at Jesus. Learn God from Jesus and fit everything else into that.

"No one has seen God at any time; the only begotten God who is in the bosom of the Father, He has explained Him" (John 1:18).

This passage is saying we haven't seen God, so if you want to get to know Him, if you want to see Him, look at Jesus. He has explained or literally exegeted Him. This is why, when Philip tells Jesus, "Show us the Father, and it is enough." Jesus responds by saying, "Have I been so long with you, and yet you have not come to know Me, Philip? He who has seen Me has seen the Father; how can you say, 'Show us the Father'? Do you not believe that I am in the Father, and the Father is in Me ... Believe Me that I am in the Father and the Father is in Me." (John 14:8–11). Or, consider the unfathomable claim, "I and the Father are One" (John 10:30).

If your view of God is inconsistent with the life and teachings of Jesus, then change your view of God. If you read passages that depict God differently than Jesus, then change the way you read those passages. A remarkable aspect of early Christianity is how Jesus entirely changed the way the church viewed God and the way they read the Old Testament. Paul says Christians can now read with "unveiled faces" (2 Cor 3:14–16). Luke says Jesus opened His disciples' minds to "understand the Scriptures" (Luke 24:44–45, 27). John, after Jesus cleansed the temple and quoted Psalm 69:9, says it wasn't until after the resurrection "His disciples remembered that He said this; and they believed the Scripture and the word which Jesus had spoken" (John 2:22).

So when you see Jesus doing something, you're learning about God. You're watching God. When Jesus washes feet, you're learning God washes feet.

Why Wash Feet?

In 1st century Palestine, foot–washing had a practical and beneficial purpose. In fact, it still does in many parts of the world. It's both an ancient and modern blessing. All the way back in Genesis 18, Abraham had 3 visitors (one of whom was the Lord) and made sure they got rest, food, and foot–washings (Gen 18:4–5). Walking on old dusty roads in worn–down sandals, unable to hop in a car, sit in a cushioned seat, or wear cotton socks and Sonoma shoes (that's my brand!), there was little more pleasurable or comforting than to arrive at your destination, have a young servant come over, remove your sandals, take a bowl of clean water and a towel, and rub your feet clean.

Why wash feet? It was a kindness of genuine practical value. What about today? It can still be a kindness, however, it is also a powerful symbol. A symbol that reinforces the mindset of servitude we are to have towards one another. When the Pope washes feet at a juvenile detention center outside of Rome, it illustrates something important. In the same way a sermon (hopefully) encourages you to take a message and go apply it, foot–washing can be a call to go out and find ways to serve.

Two important reasons stand out as to why Jesus did this. The whole passage begins by saying "Jesus knowing that His hour had come that He would depart out of this world to the Father, having loved His own who were in the world, He loved them to the end" (John 13:1). Jesus washed His disciples' feet, quite simply, because He loved them. We know He loved "the beloved disciple." But He also loved Thomas, and Andrew, and Philip. He loved Peter and in this same chapter predicts he will deny Him (John 13:38). He loved Judas who, as we will observe in more depth in the next reflection, would get up immediately following the foot–washing and betray Him. Jesus loved them, every unworthy one of them, and served them.

The second reason is stated right after the foot–washing, when Jesus is explaining Himself. "If I then, the Lord and the Teacher, washed your feet, you also ought to wash one another's feet. For I gave you an example that you also should do as I did to you" (John 13:14–15).

The disciples are going to have some important roles in the church. People will know them. They will have authority and respect. They need to remember what it is all about. Ministry is not ever about becoming famous, getting praise, or feeling important. It is about foot–washing. It is about kindness and service and following the example of Jesus.

Let God Wash Your Feet

Putting all of this together, remember Jesus is how we see God. Jesus' love led Him to humbly take on the role of a servant, usually a low-ranking female servant, and benevolently wash the feet of His disciples. That's the kind of God who loves us. That's the kind of God we serve. As we imitate Jesus and follow His example, we're showing that God to the world.

When Jesus started to wash Peter's feet, Peter protested, "Never shall You wash my feet!" (John 13:8). Peter had a social hierarchical structure in mind. The Lord shall never be a servant to me! This may have been humility on Peter's part, but it was misguided. So often we want to reject an offer of kindness. We feel uncomfortable. Unworthy. That's the wrong response. Accept people's kindness, and then give it to others. Instead of rejecting or negating kindness, multiply it! Accept the love of God given to you, and give it to others! Let God wash your feet, then go wash somebody else's.

Reflection Questions

1. Why is it so hard to accept generosity from others? Does pride play a role? Why is it good to allow people to serve you?

2. Does it change your view of God that He would wash feet? If Jesus came to visit you, would you let Him wash your feet? Clean your bathroom? Do your dishes? In what ways can we imitate God by serving others?

REFLECTION 37
WASHING JUDAS'S FEET

John 13:1–14

Judas Was There ...

The story of Jesus washing His disciples' feet is a magnificent look into Jesus' whole worldview, a picture of what His ministry was all about. It's a glimpse of the humility and love that ultimately takes Him to the cross. It's a call and challenge to each of His disciples to lay down pride, status, and social hierarchies and submissively and humbly love. Love with kindness. Love with service. Love with action. "Love one another, even as I have loved you" (John 13:34).

But even more than that, it is a call to love and serve all. Even the sinful. The greedy. The unlovable. Those who have mistreated you. Or will mistreat you. Love even your enemies. Love and expect nothing in return. Serve without repayment. Be kind no matter what. That's what the cross is all about: Giving up everything for sinful humanity. Most of whom will not really care. Most of whom will not return that sacrificial love. Foot–washing and the cross closely mirror each other.

That's why Jesus washed Judas's feet. He was living out His own radical teaching. Read and really meditate on these words:

> I say to you who hear, Love your enemies, do good to those who hate you, bless those who curse you, pray for those who abuse you. To one who strikes you on the cheek, offer the other also, and from one who takes away your cloak do not withhold your tunic either. Give to everyone who begs from you, and from one who takes away your goods do not demand them back. And as you wish that others would do to you, do so to them.
>
> If you love those who love you, what benefit is that to you? For even sinners love those who love them. And if you do good to those who do good to you, what benefit is that to you? For even sinners do the same. And if you lend to those from whom you expect to receive, what credit is that to you? Even sinners lend to sinners, to get back the same amount. But love your enemies, and do good, and lend, expecting nothing in return, and your reward will be great, and you will be sons of the Most High, for he is kind to the ungrateful and the evil. Be merciful, even as your Father is merciful (Luke 6:27–36).

Judas was there. Judas had his feet washed just like everybody else. He wasn't skipped. He wasn't rejected. Even though he would not respond with kindness. It would not soften his heart. He wouldn't change his ways. Jesus still loved and served him. Because that's what Jesus does. That who Jesus is. And that's our challenge to imitate.

Washing Judas' Feet

The more I read John 13 the more I see Judas's feet are actually a focal point of the whole story. Notice how it begins: "During supper, the devil having already put into the heart of Judas Iscariot, the son of Simon to betray Him, Jesus … got up from supper, and laid aside His garments; and taking a towel, He girded Himself. Then He poured water into the basin, and began to wash the disciples' feet" (John 13:2–5). The whole story begins by focusing everyone's attention on the unclean heart of Judas.

Now, notice how this story ends:

> When Jesus had said this, He became troubled in spirit, and testified and said, 'Truly, truly I say to you, that one of you will betray Me ... After the morsel, Satan then entered into [Judas] ... So after receiving the morsel he went out immediately; and it was night" (John 13:21–30).

Immediately following the foot–washing, Judas leaves the meal to go betray Jesus. It is one of his last interactions with Jesus. It's sandwiched between Satan putting the sin into Judas' heart, then Satan actually entering fully into him. Not only is Judas in the beginning and end of the story, he's right in the middle of it.

When Jesus is washing their feet, Peter shouts, "Never shall You wash my feet!" (John 13:8). Jesus' response is remarkable:

> 'If I do not wash you, you have no part with Me ... He who has bathed needs only to wash his feet, but is completely clean; and you are clean, but not all of you.' For He knew the one who was betraying Him; for this reason He said, 'Not all of you' (John 13:8–10).

Right in the middle, Jesus makes a brief comment about Judas, then continues washing their feet.

Judas is at the beginning, middle, and end of the foot–washing narrative. That probably means we should reflect on him as we read.

Judas Betrayed Jesus with Clean Feet

Jesus' kind act of service did nothing to stop Judas. It did not change his heart or mind. In fact, things escalated from there almost immediately. It's wonderful to believe kindness can change people. It can and it has and it does. But not always. Judas's feet were cleansed, but his heart wasn't. Judas betrayed Jesus with clean feet and a filthy heart.

Earlier in John, this reality is foreshadowed in another foot–washing scene. Mary washes Jesus' feet with an expensive perfume, but Judas objects, saying she should have sold the perfume to provide for the poor. Then John gives the reader a little insider information: "He said this not because he was concerned about the poor, but because he was a thief, and as he had the money box, he used to pilfer what was put into it" (John 12:3–6). These two foot–washing scenes fill in a lot of details about Judas, and none of them are good.

While reading John 13, it's important to notice the comparison taking place. On the one hand you have Judas. He has been following Jesus for years now. He has seen incredible things: the hungry fed, the blind given sight, the lame healed, and the poor blessed. He has seen the signs, but has rejected their significance. He may like Jesus, but he loves money more, and he serves himself above all. On the other hand you have Jesus, the polar opposite. He was humble, self–less, and generous. He freely took upon Himself the job of a slave. He cared more about His disciples' feet than His own pride, status, or self–importance. Money, power, or fame didn't motivate Jesus. Self–giving love. That's who Jesus was. That's what Judas rejected. And that's what we are all challenged to embody.

Reflection Questions

1. Do you have a Judas in your life? Do you have someone who has betrayed you? Been cruel and hurtful? How does this foot washing challenge you to treat them?

2. Jesus accepts foot–washing and offers foot–washing; in what ways can we follow that example? What are ways we can make the church a community of giving and receiving? How can Acts 4:32–37 relate to this idea?

REFLECTION 38
MORE THAN CLEAN FEET

Washing Feet

If you've been reading these reflections up to this point, it may be starting to sound like a broken record, but when reading the Gospel of John you must look for meanings beneath the surface. There are things that physically, literally happen, but there are also hints and clues towards deeper layers the reader is supposed to pursue. Jesus literally got on His hands and knees, literally took water and a towel, and literally washed at least twenty–four feet. This took time and effort. It was done with care. It was an act of service He wanted His disciples to experience and imitate.

I've seen a preacher scrub vomit out of the church carpet where a little girl got sick. I've seen Christians open up their home on Thanksgiving to the homeless for a warm family meal. I've seen disciples give rides to the elderly, repaint widow's houses, rake leaves, change light bulbs, fix appliances, repair cars, hold hands, pray, and physically wash those who cannot wash themselves. I've seen the message of foot–washing lived out in the daily life of the church. While it's possible to emphasize the failings and misconduct of the church, it's essential to remember the good, kind, servants. We must remember the foot–washers (1 Tim 5:10).

That message and challenge must be seen in John 13. It must be lived out. At the same time, there is more going on here. Is it possible there is more than just a message of service? More than a literal foot washing? Perhaps a message about a different kind of washing that Jesus provides?

Symbolic Language and Foot–Washing

Read closely this exchange between Jesus and Peter:

> He came to Simon Peter, who said to him, 'Lord, do you wash my feet?' Jesus answered him, 'What I am doing you do not understand now, but afterward you will understand.' Peter said to him, 'You shall never wash my feet.' Jesus answered him, 'If I do not wash you, you have no share with me.' Simon Peter said to him, 'Lord, not my feet only but also my hands and my head!' Jesus said to him, 'The one who has bathed does not need to wash, except for his feet, but is completely clean. And you are clean, but not every one of you.' For he knew who was to betray him; that was why he said, 'Not all of you are clean' (John 13:6–11).

There are a few clues alerting the careful reader to something deeper happening here. Notice first, when Jesus says, "What I am doing you do not understand now, but afterward you will understand." What does this mean? There is something missed at that moment only to be recognized by looking backwards. You know the expression, hindsight is always 20/20? Sometimes removing yourself by time from an event can help you see the event much more clearly. After the cross perhaps the disciples will look back on the foot–washing and see it in a whole new way.

John sometimes lets the reader know about events that were not fully understood until some later point in time. Remember Jesus cleansing the temple? In this action Jesus profoundly links His body to the temple, but it's a connection no one seems to understand. Even the disciples. However John, the narrator, lets the reader know, "when He was raised from the dead, His disciples remembered that He said this; and they believed the Scripture and the word which Jesus had spoken" (John 2:22). Only by looking backwards were they able to understand and believe.

So when Jesus tells Peter "afterward you will understand," the reader should begin looking for something that might be missed during the foot–washing but that will come to light later.

A Share with Jesus

The second phrase we should notice is, "If I do not wash you, you have no share with Me." The word "share" means to be or have a part of something bigger. It is used for parts of clothing, parts of the body, parts of a land, etc. In order to have a part, or a share, with Jesus, He must wash you. Peter, always one to go overboard (once literally), then jumps to the conclusion that the foot–washing is not enough. He tells Jesus to wash his hands and head also. He definitely wants to have a share with Jesus. Knowing this, Jesus reassures him, "The one who has bathed does not need to wash, expect for his feet, but is completely clean. And you are clean, but not every one of you."

Do you believe that? Literally? If you wash only your feet, will you be completely clean? Try it for a few weeks and see how the rest of you smells. Practically, hygienically, it won't work. The tone is changing here from literal water and washing to something else— some sort of washing that makes you completely clean and gives you a part with Jesus.

Hearing this and thinking physically (as is common in John), Peter misunderstands. He demands more than the washing Jesus provides, but is told what Jesus does is sufficient to make you completely clean. Just sit back and let Jesus lead. Let Him administer the washing. See what He does. At the end, rest assured, you will be completely clean.

Not All of You Are Clean?

Notice third the phrase, "but not all of you [are clean]." This is about Judas (v. 11). This is the dead giveaway we are no longer talking about literal foot–washing. Jesus didn't skip Judas's feet or do a sloppy job or use dirty water. Judas's feet were as clean as everyone else's. His heart wasn't. Jesus masterfully transforms the conversation into a discussion about cleansing of sin, of impurity, a washing that gives you a share with Him. Judas received a washing, but walked away without ever really being clean.

Water is almost always used symbolically in the Gospel of John (see Reflection #21). It is linked with baptism (John 3:5, 22–23), eternal life (John 4:14), the Holy Spirit (John 3:5, 7:37–39), sight (John 9:7), and the blood of Jesus (John 19:34). I think the foot–washing is no different. The text hints towards a deeper and symbolic washing provided by Jesus, a washing that makes one completely clean and gives you a share with Jesus. Perhaps while reading this, it's appropriate not only to ask ourselves questions about humility and service to others, but also about baptism, the Holy Spirit, forgiveness, and eternal life. Have you been washed by Jesus?

Reflection Questions

1. Do you think there could be a deeper meaning hidden within this passage? Could "washing" take on a symbolic meaning related to baptism or receiving the Holy Spirit?

2. Why wasn't Judas clean? He had his feet washed like everybody else. He saw the signs and heard the testimonies like everybody else. He actually spent time with God. Why wasn't he transformed? How can we make sure we follow Jesus and not Judas?

REFLECTION 39

IN MY FATHER'S HOUSE

John 13:36–14:4

Bad News for the Disciples

Jesus just gave His disciples some troubling news: He is going away, they cannot follow, and they are not quite as faithful as they think they are (John 13:36–38). Peter argues. He believes he's willing to pay the ultimate sacrifice for Jesus. He believes he would lay down his life for his Lord. And you know what? I believe him. I believe Peter would willingly die for Jesus, provided it happened on his own terms. It's not too long before Peter whips out a sword to take on an entire band of Roman soldiers (possibly a cohort [600 soldiers] or a maniple [200 soldiers]) and Jewish police (John 18:3–11). Peter was willing to gloriously die fighting in a battle he could never win, unless the Messiah intervened, which I'm sure he was hoping would happen. There is a major difference between losing a fight, and willingly, lovingly giving up your life for somebody else. When the fight doesn't happen, Peter's faithfulness plummets. Rather than faithfully following Jesus to death, Peter denies Him three times. And Jesus knew it would happen.

I imagine those words were hard to hear. I imagine the mood in the room was tense and uncomfortable. Jesus had just washed their feet, but ended that demonstration by saying one of them would betray Him. He had commanded them to love one another, but then predicted they would abandon and deny Him. Chapter 14 begins with Jesus changing the whole tone of the discussion. He knows just the thing that should cure their troubled hearts.

Faith and a Troubled Heart

"Do not let your heart be troubled; believe in God, believe also in Me" (John 14:1). The word "believe" (πιστεύετε) is repeated twice in this verse, but it presents an interesting dilemma for the translator. It can either be a 2nd person imperative or 2nd person indicative. It's written the exact same either way, and usually context is what tells you how to translate it. However, the context here isn't quite so clear. For the latter usage, it's clearly a command to believe in Jesus, but the first usage could go either way. This could be an indicative statement "you believe in God" or it could be an imperative command "Believe in God!" Most translations seem to go with a double command: "Believe in God, believe also in Me," and then they add a footnote at the bottom of the page for clarification. I think I'd actually prefer to translate it, "You believe in God; believe also in Me." As one statement and one command. In the way they already believe in God, now it's time to fully believe in and trust Jesus. Trust Him as you trust God. In just a few verses He's going to boldly state, "He who has seen Me has seen the Father" (John 14:9). If you're going to trust the Father, you better likewise trust Jesus also.

Regardless of which way you translate that phrase, you're also left with the dilemma of the "troubled heart." Jesus Himself has already been battling a troubled heart in this story. It actually becomes a major theme in this farewell discourse. At the death of Lazarus, Jesus was "deeply moved in spirit and troubled" (John 11:33). Upon the realization His hour had come, He lamented, "Now My soul has become troubled" (John 12:27). When facing the reality one of those closest to Him would actually betray Him, "He became troubled in spirit" (John 13:21). In spite of this (or possibly because of this) He implores His disciples twice, "Do not let your heart be troubled" (John 14:1, 27). The reality is, a troubled heart is the natural response to the events that are brewing. The Lord is going to be rejected, betrayed, denied, mocked, beaten, tortured, and crucified. The disciples will lose faith. Jesus will suffer. Darkness will take over. Your heart should be troubled a little bit. These words of Jesus don't have the desired impact, as He soon admits, "sorrow has filled your hearts" (John 16:6). This sorrow He promises will be short lived: "you too have grief now; but I will see you again, and your heart will rejoice, and no one will take your joy away from you" (John 16:22).

My Father's House

Jesus is going away. He will not be with the disciples much longer. They need to believe. They need to have faith. They need to trust. He is not abandoning them. He's actually going to prepare a place for them. They will be together again. "In the house of My Father there are many rooms; and if not, would I have told you that I go to prepare a place for you? And if I go and prepare a place for you, I will come again and receive you to Myself, in order that where I Myself Am, there you may be also" (John 14:2–3). This is a beautiful passage that combines several images into a vivid collage of God's plans for us.

Image #1: God's Mansion. The King James Version has done modern readers no favors with the translation "In my Father's house are many mansions." Things are further complicated by songs like "Mansion Over the Hilltop" and "Mansion, Robe and Crown." Here's the bad news. This passage doesn't promise you a mansion. Really, it doesn't even make sense to have mansions inside of a house anyway. What this passage is promising, and it's way better, is we get a place inside God's mansion. Rather than my own mansion down the road from God, I actually get a room in God's mansion. And it's prepared by Jesus. Let not your heart be troubled.

Image #2: Temple. The word I translated above as "room" is only used twice in the New Testament. One time is right here where we get a room in God's house. The other time is just a little later in this same chapter where Jesus says, "If anyone loves Me, he will keep My word; and My Father will love him, and We will come to him and make Our abode with him" (John 14:23). God makes His abode with us (John 14:27) and gives us an abode with Him (John 14:2–3). This abode/room is in "God's house." Read the Old Testament. Read the Gospels. What place is almost singularly referred to as God's house? It's the temple. The temple on earth will not last. Jesus already demonstrated its destruction in John 2. However, God still has a house and rather than being barred and distanced from the holiness inside the temple, we are invited and welcomed into it. There is a place prepared just for us. Just as God abides with us, we get to abide with Him, in His Holy temple. Let not your heart be troubled.

Image #3: Marriage and Family. In Jewish families, the house and the property were usually passed on from generation to generation. Rather than a child turning 18 and moving off to college and then out on their own somewhere far away, Jewish families usually stayed together. Like, multiple generations under one roof, together. When the families arranged for their son to marry another families' daughter, she would leave her generational family home, and join the family of her husband. She would leave her father's house and be added to her husband's house. In order for this to happen, the son would need to prepare a place at his father's house for him and his new bride to live. So during the betrothal, he would prepare this place for her to then move in and become part of the family. Jesus is borrowing this beautiful image and applying it to His followers. He is preparing our room in His Father's house. We will become part of His family, now and forever. He has chosen us. Prepared a place for us. And lovingly accepted us as His own. Let not your heart be troubled.

Reflection Questions

1. Would you rather have your own mansion or a room in God's mansion? In what ways could this image be impactful on those in poverty or who have no family? What is so comforting about the idea of closeness and family with God?

2. How can faith in God and Jesus soothe a troubled heart? Why is this so hard to do? Read Psalms 42 and 43 and meditate on how to "hope in God" when your heart is troubled.

REFLECTION 40
THE WAY, THE TRUTH, AND THE LIFE

John 14:5–7

How Do We Know the Way?

I hate being lost. In my lifetime there have been some dramatic changes in how one travels from one place to another. For those older than me, the changes are even more dramatic. When I first started driving, maps were on the way out. There was a time or two when I actually had to unfold a massive roadmap (one I could never fold back properly) and find where I was and trace the roads with my finger to where I needed to be. You could even get a highlighter or a pen to mark down your proposed path so you could find your way quickly.

Soon though, I started using this wonderful website called Mapquest. When driving from Denver to Texas, or through the Rocky Mountains to find some park or some church to preach for, I would just get on Mapquest and print out a map with clear step by step directions for how to reach my destination.

Now, I put just about zero thought into directions. I just need an address. Put it in the phone, and it does all the heavy lifting for you. The GPS lady tracks you wherever you are and in the moment tells you exactly where you need to go. Sometimes she can be a little bossy, but she's pretty good at her job. Road unexpectedly closed? No problem, she can find an alternate route in seconds. You can get out on the road and start driving before you even know what turns you will eventually need to take. A lot of people, myself included, put a lot of trust on our phones to lead us home.

Jesus is going ... somewhere. And no one can follow Him (John 13:36). His disciples are still puzzled about where and how to get there. Jesus tells them He is going to His Father's house and "that they know the way where I am going" (John 14:3). Do they really? The Gospel of John repeatedly shows people misunderstanding Jesus. I am curious exactly what His disciples are thinking here. Thomas asks, "Lord, we do not know where You are going. How do we know the way?" (John 14:5). I wonder if he is waiting for directions to Jesus' father's house. Is he looking for a road leading to Nazareth? Where is the map? Where is the road? How do we get there?

I Am the Way, and the Truth, and the Life

Jesus' response makes it clear Thomas is asking the wrong question. "How do we know the way?" Jesus IS the way! You don't need a map, directions, or a road. You need Jesus. Follow Him. The word translated "way" (ὁδός) is the standard word for "road" (Acts 8:36; 9:17). It is a path, a road, a way. It came to be used in a special way to refer to the early Christian movement. The word "Christianity" is never used in the Bible. Instead, the preferred moniker was "The Road" or "The Way" (Acts 9:2; 19:23, etc.). Acts 18:26 uses the phrase "the way of God" to describe a proper understanding of baptism. So the word comes to be used in a number of important ways, but I think perhaps the most important for understanding Jesus' meaning is found all the way back in the book of Isaiah.

Isaiah paints the picture of a remarkable trip home. Imagine being in slavery, in bondage, in subjugation in a foreign land by cruel pagan leaders. Israel found themselves in this situation on a number of occasions. The two that overshadow all the rest in the Old Testament are Egyptian slavery and Babylonian captivity. Both of those tumultuous times in Israelite history saw God's people in utter misery. Yet both of those tumultuous times came to an end. The people were freed, and what stood in between slavery and home was a wilderness, a desert. From Egypt it took 40 years of aimless wandering to make it to the promised land. The return from Babylon will go much more smoothly, better than the Exodus from Egypt. That is the picture Isaiah paints on numerous occasions.

> The wilderness and the desert will be glad, And the Arabah will rejoice and blossom ... encourage the exhausted, and strengthen the feeble ...'Take courage, fear not. Behold, your God will come with vengeance; The recompense of God will come, but He will save you.' Then the eyes of the blind will be opened And the ears of the deaf will be unstopped. Then the lame will leap like deer, And the tongue of the mute will shout for joy. For waters will break forth in the wilderness ... A highway will be there, a roadway, And it will be called the Highway of Holiness ... (Isa 35:1–8).

Compare this journey through the wilderness with the sin–fraught death–plagued 40 years in the book of Numbers. There is rejoicing, strengthening, and salvation from God. The blind see, the deaf hear, and the lame walk. Waters cover the wilderness and a highway appears. The Greek word ὁδός, "the way," appears three times in the Septuagint translation of this passage. The idea of a smooth highway prepared through wilderness, or a new path through the sea, and a more glorious Exodus is repeated by Isaiah over and over again (Isa 40:3–5; 43:16–21; 51:10–14; 52:1–12; 55:12–13). "The Way" is the road from slavery to home. It is a path from lies to truth. It is a path that leads from death to life. Jesus is that way.

Exclusively Open for All

This passage in the Gospel of John ends with one of Jesus' most radical claims. It is claims like this that made Christianity a target for Roman persecution. It is claims like this that make Christianity unpopular to so many today. It is claims like this that offend and anger pluralistic societies. Nevertheless, it is claims like this that Christians must be willing to accept. Jesus is the road or highway, that leads to God. There is no other. "No one comes to the Father but through Me" (John 14:6).

In keeping with the highway illustration, if I want to go from New Orleans to Dallas, I can't take any highway I want. I can't go any direction I choose. Although I have the freedom to get on any road I want, they won't all take me where I want to go. The path to God is exclusively found in Jesus, but it is free for anyone who wants on the road. No matter what color you are, what language you speak, or what your nationality is, you are welcome on the road. No matter what sins you've committed in your past, how much money you have, how thin or fat, ugly or beautiful, educated or ignorant, everyone is welcome on that road. You cannot be too old, and no one is too young. It is the most open, inclusive, and welcoming road in the world. It is open for anyone and everyone. You just need to be on it. The way to the Father is for everyone.

Reflection Questions

1. Would you consider Christianity to be mostly exclusive or inclusive? In what ways is it surprisingly inclusive? In what ways is it surprisingly exclusive? In your life and church, are you inclusive where you ought to be and exclusive where you ought to be?

2. How does John 14:6 relate to John 10:9 and John 11:25? How do John 1:9; 6:32; 8:31–32; 15:1; 18:37–38 shape the idea that Jesus is "the truth"?

REFLECTION 41

I AM THE TRUE VINE

John 15:1–17

I Am the Vine

There are traditionally seven "I Am" statements made by Jesus in the Gospel of John. He uses the expression ἐγώ εἰμι "I Am" more than just these times, and sometimes you can't even tell that's the expression because of the way it's translated (John 6:20; 8:24; 13:13, etc). These seven statements have a particularly powerful impact in revealing the true identity of Jesus:

> *I Am the bread of life (John 6:35, 48)*
> *I Am the light of the world (John 8:12; 9:5)*
> *I Am the door (John 10:7, 9)*
> *I Am the good shepherd (John 10:11, 14)*
> *I Am the resurrection and the life (John 11:25)*
> *I Am the way, the truth, and the life (John 14:6)*
> *I Am the true vine (John 15:1–11)*

This final "I Am" statement comes right in the heart of Jesus' farewell address to His disciples. "I am the true vine" (John 15:1). That word "true" is what separates Jesus from all the competition. There are other literal vines you can see in any vineyard, but they are merely shadows, simple illustrations of who the true vine is. They have branches, they bear fruit, and there is a vinedresser who prunes and cares for them, but the life of the fruit and branches is found in the vine. So it is with Jesus. In this statement Jesus gives roles to every part of this process. Remember how Jesus provides the best wine (John 2)? All that begins right here.

Jesus is the true vine. His Father is the vinedresser. His disciples are the branches stemming off from that vine. They go out and bear fruit. Notice John 17:20, "I do not ask on behalf of these alone, but for all those also who believe in Me through their word." In this passage Jesus (the vine) prays to the Father (the vinedresser) for His disciples (the branches) but also all who believe (the fruit) in Him (the Vine) through their (the branches) word. He is praying for the fruit. The phrase "bear fruit" or "bear much fruit" is used 7 times in this short section (John 15:2, 4–5, 8, 16). The fruit has no life without the branches and the branches have no life without the vine.

The Vine

The life of the kingdom flows through the Messiah. Nothing survives without Him. That's why He is the vine. As invaluable as Scripture is, Scripture is not the vine. The Bible is nothing without Jesus. Before the New Testament was written, there was a church. Before the books were canonized and bound together, there was a church. Before mass printing was available, there was a church. Most people who have been part of the church from the beginning until now have never owned a Bible, and even if they did, they couldn't read it or study it. Production, literacy and translation are essential to the Bible's transformative power. Not so with Jesus. As long as Jesus is the Son of God, there is life and hope. Scripture stems from the Vine and the branches, but it is not the Vine.

The church is also not the vine. Again, the church stems from the vine. Without the Messiah, the church has no vitality or power. The church is the "body" of Christ, but without Christ, the church becomes an empty shell. No theology or doctrine, no ministry or minister, no sermon or book, no congregation, eldership, or seminary has any life without Jesus. He gives life to all we are and all we do. He is the foundation of the church, the Bible, and every ministry we could ever dream up. We are the fruit that comes from Him. Never ever mistake the fruit or the branches for the Vine.

Abiding in Him

In order for the branches to have life and bear fruit, they must remain connected at their root to the vine. This connection to the vine is referred to with the word "abiding." This word is used ten times in this little section (John 15:4–7, 9–10, 16). Take a grape, remove it from the branch, set it on the ground by the vine, and what happens? It rots and dies. Take a branch, cut if off the vine, set it on the ground by the vine, and what happens? It withers and dies. Why? "The branch cannot bear fruit of itself unless it abides in the vine, so neither can you unless you abide in Me ... he who abides in Me and I in him, he bears much fruit, for apart from Me you can do nothing" (John 15:5–6).

To abide in Jesus, in this passage, seems to include several things: Jesus abiding in You (John 15:5), His words abiding in you (John 15:7), and abiding in His love (John 15:10). Jesus explains, "If you keep My commandments, you will abide in My love" (John 15:10). What are the commandments Jesus is talking about? This is where context matters so much. Jesus discusses His commandments quite a bit in this section of Scripture. All those commandments seem to center on love for one another. In fact, Jesus says just a few sentences later: "This is My commandment, that you love one another just as I have loved you ... You are My friends if you do what I command you ... This I command you, that you love one another" (John 15:12, 14, 17). After dining with the disciples and washing their feet, Jesus gave them a new commandment:

> A new commandment I give to you, that you love one another even as I have loved you, that you also love one another. By this all men will know that you are My disciples, if you have love for one another (John 13:34–35).

If you want to abide in Jesus, listen to His words and obey His commandments. Those words and commandments are that you love one another. Truly and deeply. Christian unity and mutual love matters. It's how you abide on the vine and how you bear fruit for Him. Loveless churches do not remain on the Vine or bear fruit for the kingdom.

The Vinedresser

Actively working through this whole process is God, the vinedresser. This is not God's first time to be portrayed as One who tends a vineyard. Isaiah 5 details God as the owner of a vineyard who prepared it, built for it, cultivated it, and "expected it to produce good grapes" (Isa 5:2, 4). The vineyard was Israel and He cultivated it expecting it to produce grapes of "justice" and "righteousness." Instead, it only produced "bloodshed" and "a cry of distress" (Isaiah 5:7). In Hebrew, this is an intentional play on words, the word "justice" sounds strikingly similar to the word "bloodshed" (mishpat; mispach) and the word "righteousness" is almost identical to the word "a cry of distress" (tsĕdaqah; tsa`aqah) (Isaiah 5:7). The point is God planted Israel to produce something valuable for the world, but upon closer inspection, it was producing something worthless.

Jesus grabs this image and takes for Himself the role of Israel.[1] He will bear good fruit, He will produce justice and righteousness, and His Father will prune and tend along the way. To the branch that does not "abide in Him" or "bear good fruit," the vinedresser "takes it away," "he is thrown away as a branch and dries up," and they are cast "into the fire and they are burned" (John 15:2, 6). The branches that do bear good fruit are not cut off or ripped away, rather, they are pruned (John 15:2). There are parts of them that are cut away and they become healthier and purer for it. John 15:2 and 3 contain an intentional play on words with "prune" (καθαίρει—kathairei) and "clean" (καθαροί—katharoi).[2] The disciples are those who have been made clean by the words of Jesus (well, not all of them—John 13:10–11). God cleanses you through pruning, cutting away your imperfections, so you grow, flourish, and produce healthy fruit. And God Himself is glorified as you do so (John 15:8).

Reflection Questions

1. What is the most important thing we can do to bear fruit for God? What does "bearing fruit" actually look like? What is the fruit? Who is the ultimate source of the fruit we bear?

2. In what ways does God prune us and clean us? Has God ever pruned your life? Can this be a difficult process? Can it make us healthier?

---

1. Richard B. Hays, *Echoes of Scripture in the Gospels* (Waco: Baylor University Press, 2017), 335–43.
2. Tom Wright, *John for Everyone: Part 2 Chapters 11–21* (Louisville: Westminster John Knox, 2004), 69–70.

REFLECTION 42

YOU ARE MY FRIENDS

John 15:12–17

Friends and Commandments

"Your are my friends if you do what I command you" (John 15:14). Now, I'm not going to lie, I find that to be a humorous standard of friendship. I cannot imagine offering friendship to somebody based on whether or not they dutifully obey whatever command I make up. I imagine I wouldn't have too many friends. Just picture your first day at a new job—some polite looking person sits down next to you, looks you squarely in the eye, and says, "If you obey everything I tell you to do, I'll let you be my friend." Wouldn't that strike you as kind of odd?

It should. Something odd is happening here. This is not the way we view friendship at all. On the one hand, modern views of friendship do vary significantly from the way the word is used in many ancient contexts. Ancient friendships can be a bit odd to modern readers. Friendship often seemed to be less about simple recreation and mutual interests and more about common goals and mutual benefit. In Roman society you wouldn't want to offer friendship to someone in a lower class than you; it would be of no benefit. Friendship was often about climbing the social ladder or making alliances.

Detailing the trial and their mutual condemnation of Jesus, Luke 23:12 says, "Now Herod and Pilate became friends with one another that very day; for before they had been enemies with each other." The idea is less about them camping together, laughing and telling old stories around the fire, and more about their new political alliance (see 1 Maccabees 8:11–12, 17, 20). The same is true just later in John when the Jews tell Pilate: "If you release this Man, you are no friend of Caesar" (John 19:12). Pilate can't keep a political alliance or "friendship" with Caesar if he allows someone else to go around calling himself a king.

David and Jonathan, members of opposing households formed an alliance with each other. It was an alliance rooted in love for each other, but it certainly had political overtones. They should have been enemies, as Jonathan's dad was king, and Jonathan may have been next in line to inherit the throne, but some meddling prophet, Samuel, chose David instead, a shepherd boy from an insignificant family. Rather than greed and passion for self promotion, Jonathan makes an alliance with David out of respect for God and love for man. In response, David, after Jonathan's death, sees to the care of Jonathan's crippled son Mephibosheth. Friendship does not necessarily mean both parties are on equal footing, David as king would have been able to give commands for even his friends to obey. Yet it does mean trust, loyalty and allegiance.

Perhaps along similar lines, Jesus' extension of friendship is clearly not shared among equals, but is about alliance and loyalty. If you view friendship as merely pleasant and fun relationships among equals, this passage won't sit well with you. Where does Jesus get the nerve to offer friendship only if they obey whatever it is He says? Well, for one, He is the Lord God of the universe. So that changes things a bit. Repeatedly, over and over again, it is so important to read

John in light of the deity of Jesus. John begins with the deity of Jesus intentionally. "In the beginning was the Word, and the Word was with God, and the Word was God" (John 1:1). If that is not true then the saying about Jesus is true: "He has a demon and is insane" (John 10:20). Jesus does not speak the way a mere man speaks. Nor should He.

However, I think there is more going on here also. If you read it as the divine Jesus ordering His "friends" around and only offering friendship to those who obey Him, it sounds more like slavery than friendship. This passage needs to be read with the idea of alliance and the deity of Jesus firmly established, but this passage must also be read in light of what the commandment is. This is not the same as a master commanding a slave. This is not the same as a mighty nation bossing around a smaller nation in the name of an alliance. This is not God bossing around His slaves. This command isn't something a slave master would give. What is Jesus commanding? Somehow, and this is the most important point, obeying this command makes you a friend rather than a slave.

No Longer Slaves

When I think of obeying commands, I think of slavery more than I think of friendship. I don't generally give commands to my friends. They don't give commands to me. Slaves are given commands, though. Slaves must follow commands or face dire consequences. Jesus, as the embodied God of Israel, has every right to give commands. Yet, somehow His commands have the exact opposite effect of a slave master's commands. His commands make you His friend.

"No longer do I call you slaves, for the slave does not know what his master is doing; but I have called you friends, for all things that I have heard from My Father I have made known to you." (John 15:15). I can think of two vital distinctions between Jesus' commands and a slave owner's. The first He mentions in this verse. The slave owner does not explain himself. After all "a slave is no greater than his master" (John 13:16; 15:20). The slave has no idea why he is following a given command. He doesn't know his master's ultimate plans or goals, and the slave's master doesn't sit down around a meal, wash his slave's feet, and tell the slave all of his plans. Jesus is no slave master, and this is not blind mechanical obedience to purposeless or selfish commands. Though He could and has every right to, He does not treat these disciples as slaves. They are friends. So He has this meal and He tells them His plans.

The second distinction is made right before verse 15. Let's look back and see what the command actually is: "This is My commandment, that you love one another, just as I have loved you" (John 15:12; see also 13:34–35 and 15:17). Three times Jesus explains His command is to "love one another." His command is not to go dig a ditch because the master has plans. His command is not to build the master a bigger barn so he can store up for a rainy day. His command is not to pick wheat, plow a field, or wash his feet. His command is to follow His example of love.

Just as I Have Loved You

"Just as I have loved you" is in John 13:34 and John 15:12. This love is seen most explicitly in the life of Jesus through service (like foot-washing) but also in the death of Jesus on the cross. "Greater love has no one than this, that one lay down his life for his friends" (John 15:13). To love one another, just as Jesus loves, is to die for one another. "We know love by this, that He laid down His life for us; and we ought to lay down our lives for the brethren" (1 John 3:16).

This is a hard command. Perhaps the hardest in all of Scripture. Not every brother is easy to love. Not every disciple acts as he should or embodies the love of Jesus. It's hard to love those who don't love you in return, to love "just as I have loved you." Jesus died on the cross not just for those who are easy to love. Not just for those who return His love. Jesus died for me at my best moments and my worst moments. He died for me when I'm kind and when I'm selfish. He died for me when I obey and thrive and when I sin and fail. No human is always right, and certainly no human is always righteous. However, we're called to love in the way of Jesus anyway—Jesus who washed Judas's feet and died for ungodly men. Can you love one another when you are hurt? When you're wronged? When you're abandoned? When you're betrayed? When you're denied? Can you strive to love like Jesus? That's the challenge of friendship with Christ.

Reflection Questions

1. Why is our friendship with Jesus based on obeying His commands? What are His commands? How do they strengthen our friendship?

2. Why is love the greatest way to show we are disciples of Jesus? How does love for each other help us bear fruit for Christ? How does it help us abide in Christ?

REFLECTION 43

PERSECUTION AND RELIGIOUS VIOLENCE

John 16:1–4

Preparing the Disciples

Being a disciple of Jesus will cost you everything. Many literally gave their lives in service to Jesus. Jesus didn't hide this. He didn't try to misrepresent, soften, or sugarcoat it. Jesus plainly prepared His disciples for the fate that lay before them. Jesus told them the world hates them (John 15:19). Jesus told them to expect hatred, exclusion, persecution, and even death. He did not want it to catch them by surprise, but for them to have already prepared in their hearts to face it. To endure it. To overcome it.

> I have said all these things to you to keep you from falling away. They will put you out of the synagogues. Indeed, the hour is coming when whoever kills you will think he is offering service to God. And they will do these things because they have not known the Father,

nor Me. But I have said these things to you, that when their hour comes you may remember that I told them to you (John 16:1–4).

Paul, Zeal, and Violence

Can you imagine that? "Whoever kills you will think he is offering sacrifice to God." Jesus' disciples will need to be prepared to die for God because many believe they are called to kill for God. They think this because they don't know the Father or Jesus. It doesn't take long looking into the teachings of Jesus to know His followers are never, ever called to kill for the sake of the kingdom. In fact, Jesus demands the opposite. He says "My kingdom is not of this world. If my kingdom were of this world, my servants would have been fighting, that I might not be delivered over to the Jews" (John 18:36). Nonviolence in extreme circumstances is a telltale sign of the Kingdom of God. When Peter draws and uses his sword in the garden, he is relying on an old way of solving problems, a way not fit for Jesus' kingdom. When Jesus heals that man and tells Peter to put away his sword, He uses a new way of solving problems. Jesus proclaims a nonviolent kingdom.

But some who don't truly know God have missed this. Many world religions have seen violence as a tool for their advancement, protection, and purity. A familiar example of a man who thought this way is a guy named Saul/Paul. The guy who wrote most of the books in our New Testament. Like Jesus said, he believed his violence against God's people was an act of service to God.

Prior to Jesus, Paul describes himself as "a persecutor of the church" (Phil 3:6). A zealot was one whose religious convictions lead to violence. They would kill for the faith. To be zealous often had violent consequences, and there is a long tradition of this in Judaism. The prime example of this is Phinehas in Numbers 25:6–13. He was "zealous for His God" when he saw an Israelite man flaunting his fornication with a Midianite woman. He grabbed a weapon, followed them into the tent and, with one thrust of a spear, pierced them both through the stomach. He put an end to the fornication and was celebrated as a hero for turning back God's wrath. There were many who followed in the tradition of Phinehas.

A fascinating account of this tradition of violent zeal is seen in Mattathias (1 Maccabees) when Greek officials attempted to force the Jews to blaspheme God and offer pagan sacrifices. Mattathias was offered gold and silver and gifts for him and his sons if he would use his influence to help the Greeks Hellenize the Jews (1 Maccabees 2:17–18). Mattathias refused, to put it mildly. When the Greek officials threatened violence to coerce the Jews to sacrifice, a willing Jewish man came forward. He was going to give in. Now read this next paragraph carefully:

> When Mattathias saw it, he burned with zeal and his heart was stirred. He gave vent to righteous anger; he ran and killed him upon the altar. At the same time he killed the king's officer who was forcing them to sacrifice, and he tore down the altar. Thus he burned with zeal for the law, as Phinehas did against Zimri the son of Salu. Then Mattathias cried out in the city with a loud voice, 'Let every one who is zealous for the law and supports the covenant come with me!' (1 Maccabees 2:24–27).

Paul is one who would have followed Mattathias. He would have been right with Phinehas. Paul saw Christianity as a perversion needing to be snuffed out. He would be blessed as a righteous hero, a zealous devotee of Yahweh. This is what Paul means when he writes, "as to zeal, a persecutor of the church" (Phil 3:6). That's why he was "breathing threats and murder against the disciples of the Lord" (Acts 9:1) and why he says, "being zealous for God ... I persecuted this Way to the death, binding and putting both men and women in prison" (Acts 22:3–4). Paul laments, "I used to persecute the church of God beyond measure and tried to destroy it ... being more extremely zealous for my ancestral traditions" (Gal 1:13–14).

Knowing Jesus and God

Paul loved God. He was zealous for God, and this was one way he showed it. However, according to these words of Jesus, he didn't really know God. Those who act in religious violence do so because they misunderstand God. When Paul met Jesus, everything changed. When he came to know Jesus, he finally came to know the Father. Jesus is our clearest picture of who the Father actually is. Jesus is how we come to know God. When Paul met Jesus, not only did he give up violence against Christians, he became a Christian. He not only became a Christian, he suffered and died as a Christian. He not only suffered and died as a Christian, but he never again advocated violence against his enemies, tried to persecute heretics, or kill so he may live. Knowing Jesus and the Father changed his views of violence and sacrifice, of faithfulness and zeal, of life and love.

Paul, who used violence and death as a tool against those with whom he disagreed is the same man who wrote these words: "Bless those who persecute you, bless and do not curse ... repay no one evil for evil ... If possible, so far as it depends on you, live peaceably with all men ... never avenge yourselves, but leave it to the wrath of God, for it is written, 'Vengeance is Mine, I will repay, says the Lord.' On the contrary, if your enemy is hungry, feed him; if he is thirsty, give him something to drink ... Do not be overcome by evil, but overcome evil with good (Rom 12:14–21).

Sincere conversion to Christ ought to motivate each of us to give up the world's methods of solving problems and to look with trust and boldness at the ways of Jesus. The ways of His kingdom, His life, His love, and His cross. When you come to know Jesus everything changes.

Reflection Questions

1. How can a commitment to nonviolence help reflect God into the world? Why do many religions use violence as a form of punishment

or even evangelism? How important is nonviolence to the Christian cause?

2. Why love the world when the world hates you? Why practice peace when the world is so violent? Why suffer for Christ when you don't deserve it?

REFLECTION 44
THE HOLY SPIRIT AND THE WORLD

John 16:5–11

The Holy Spirit in John

As Jesus prepares His disciples for His departure, in the critical conversation detailed in John 13–17, He covers many topics. Central to this discussion, to this preparation, is an idea He keeps coming back to: when I leave, you will not be alone and there is a Helper, a Comforter, an Advocate, the Holy Spirit, who will be with you.

Jesus does not leave His disciples alone in this dangerous, cruel, and violent world. The Spirit "will be with you forever" (John 14:16), "He abides with you and will be with you" (John 14:17). "He will teach you all things, and bring to your remembrance all that I said to you" (John 14:26). "He will disclose to you what is to come" (John 16:13). The Spirit has been central not only in these defining chapters, but the Spirit has been central to the entire message of the Gospel of John. The Spirit has been an ever present wind blowing across, through, and between these words and pages from the beginning. Jesus' offer has been on the table from the beginning,

> If anyone is thirsty, let him come to Me and drink. He who believes in Me, as the Scripture said, 'From his innermost being will flow rivers of living water.' But this He spoke of the Spirit, whom those who believed in Him were to receive; for the Spirit was not yet given, because Jesus was not yet glorified (John 7:37–39).

When Jesus is glorified (a beautiful yet paradoxical way of envisioning martyrdom—John 21:18, 19), the Spirit will be given to His disciples. This is described in dramatic fashion in John 20:21–22: "Jesus said to them again, 'Peace be with you; as the Father has sent Me, I also send you.' And when He said this, He breathed on them and said to them, 'Receive the Holy Spirit. If you forgive the sins of any, their sins have been forgiven them; if you retain the sins of any, they have been retained.'"

From beginning to end the Spirit has been present and active. From the Spirit descending upon Jesus at his baptism (John 1:32–33), through His discussion with Nicodemus (John 3:5–8), His promises of living water (John 4:10–11; 7:37–39), and His assurances of comfort and truth before His crucifixion (John 14:17, 26; 15:26; 16:13), up even until the resurrected Jesus actually breathes the Spirit upon His disciples (John 20:21–22), God has been promising to give His life–giving Spirit (John 6:63) "without measure" (John 3:34).

So, What Will The Holy Spirit Do?

We know it's a comfort and a blessing and an assurance, to be sure, but what will the Spirit actually do? I don't want to be the one found trying to describe things I can't fully grasp. I can't control or predict the wind and I'm under no illusion I can contain, control, or predict the moving of the Spirit (John 3:8). I can only see and hear where it has gone. And I'm okay with that. I'm comforted by that. What I do know is He is alive and well. He moves and transforms and gives life. I love reading the words of Jesus regarding the impact the Spirit will make on the world. Consider these words carefully:

> But I tell you the truth, it is to your advantage that I go away; for if I do not go away, the Helper will not come to you; but if I go, I will send Him to you. And He, when He comes, will convict the world concerning sin and righteousness and judgment; concerning sin, because they do not believe in Me; and concerning righteousness, because I go to the Father and you no longer see Me; and concerning judgment, because the ruler of this world has been judged (John 16:7–11).

I simply cannot imagine. I can't imagine saying there is something advantageous about Jesus going away. If I were standing in the presence of the Lord Jesus and was told it would be good for Him to leave so something else could come, I'm just not sure I would believe it. What could be better? What could fill that gap? Perhaps here we should all rethink how much value we place on the Holy Spirit. It's easy for us to kind of forget about Him. To relegate Him to the back of our minds and only scarcely mention His presence and power with hushed tones, fearful we might accidentally give Him too much credit for something. Unlike us, Jesus isn't afraid to credit the Spirit with convicting the whole world.

Convicting the World

We're told the Spirit will convict the world on three great accounts: sin, righteousness, and judgment. This means the world will be put on trial for the way it has responded to Jesus and His followers, and the Spirit is our advocate. He will defend us and prosecute the world. Jesus and His followers will be proven innocent; the world will be found guilty.

Guilty of sin because the world has not believed in Jesus. In all Johannine literature, that seems to be the primary way the word "sin" is used. Not so much to talk about moral failures or misgivings, but the sin of rejecting Jesus. "Except you believe that I Am, you will die in your sins" (John 8:24). The primary sin leading to all other sins is disbelief in Jesus.

Of righteousness (justice which may be a better translation here), because Jesus goes to be with the Father and we no longer see Him. Jesus is going to be found guilty at His trial and executed. The world so often sees justice in the execution of a criminal. The world sees Jesus die on the cross and thinks, "Justice has been served." But what they don't see is His glorification and exaltation to the Father. True justice is seen in the absence of Jesus, because He has been vindicated by the Father. The world has so often missed true justice and the Spirit will convict it for such.

Finally, of judgment "because the ruler of this world has been judged." That expression "ruler of this world" has now been repeated 3 times (John 12:31; 14:30; 16:11). One might think the "ruler" of the world is God, but that's not how John describes it. Things are changing. Through the death and resurrection, vindication, exaltation, and glorification of Jesus, through the kingdom of God and the coming of the Spirit, Satan has been weighed, measured, and found wanting. The ruler of this world has been judged by the true Judge.

In the presence of the Spirit we rejoice God has vindicated us through Jesus and found the world guilty. As a Spirit–filled community of believers, we can live with confidence God is on our side. The world may hate us, persecute us, or even kill us, but through the Spirit the world and its forces of darkness will not prevail. They have been cast down. Victory is ours.

Reflection Questions

1. In what ways is the Holy Spirit vital to your life as a Christian? How often do you think about the Holy Spirit? How often do you actively and purposefully rely on the Holy Spirit?

2. What role does the Holy Spirit play in convicting the world? What role does Scripture play? What role does the church play? What role do you play? In what ways can all of these work together?

REFLECTION 45
GRIEF WILL BE TURNED INTO JOY

John 16:16–22

∾

Finish Lines

Finish lines are important. I don't know of any sane person who would begin a race without one. How long will you go? How hard do you run? A person doesn't run the 100 meter sprint the same way he runs a 26.2 mile marathon. Knowing how to run a race is really important. It reminds me of the day back in high school when I became a track star. I was a football player and was in our off–season workout program. Unless they were playing a different sport, off–season football players were also enrolled in track and weightlifting even if they didn't compete. It was all about the extra workout time. One day when our workout was ending, a friend and I were approached by one of our coaches. He asked if we'd be interested in running in a track meet. Or, rather, he told us we'd be running in a track meet. It was all last minute. We had no time to practice for the event (I didn't even know what the event would be), they just needed some fill-ins. Neither of us had ever run track before but we were happy to participate. We said, "Yes, sir!"

We arrived at the meet, still not knowing what we would be running, still having not practiced at all, but ready for anything. Now, I don't know if you're aware of this or not, but track meets take approximately forever, and neither of us had anything to do for what seemed like 85 hours. And it was hot. Texas hot. After a day spent wandering aimlessly in the heat of Dante's Inferno, it was almost our turn. Shortly before our races began we were told what we would be doing. My friend was asked to run the 400 meter dash. I wanted to run the 400 meter dash! I had run that one a bunch of times before, both during off-season workouts and summer camps. I had a strategy for it and thought I'd be able to compete in it. Alas, it was not to be. I was instead asked to run in the next event: The 300 meter hurdles.

For this I had no strategy. The first hurdle of that race was the first hurdle I'd ever tried to clear full speed. And I cleared it by a mile! Which apparently isn't a good thing. Most important to me though, I determined I was NOT going to trip over a hurdle and fall on my face during that race! I ran as fast as I could and as I approached each hurdle, while others with gazelle-like fluidity, glided swiftly over without a hitch in their stride, I slowed, took choppy steps, and leaped with all of my might. I'd land with a thud, regain my balance and try to catch up again only to approach another stinkin' hurdle!

Here are the important facts you need to know: 1. I didn't win the race. 2. I actually didn't come in last! But it was about as close as you can get. 3. Nearing the final straight away I thought I'd finish some-where in the middle. Instead they all separated from me. 4. No matter what my "friends" back in high school tell you, I didn't fall! But I did perhaps stumble a bit and use both my hands to keep from falling forward on that final straight away. 5. I was never invited to a track meet again.

After it was over, I was exhausted. That one race took more out of me than I expected. I was mocked by my friends who watched me. I suppose if I'm honest I didn't really become a track star. You know what got me through the race though? The finish line. I knew I wouldn't look like a fool forever. I knew my legs wouldn't fall off. I knew there was an end in sight. In fact, the whole experience lasted less than a minute. I'm glad there was a finish line.

A Little While

During the farewell discourse, Jesus gives His disciples a riddle. "A little while, and you will no longer see Me; and again a little while, and you will see Me" (John 16:16). This should sound familiar to us. Jesus has said similar things in John 7:33, 14:19, and now again in John 16:16. It should be obvious to the reader and the disciples what the first part means. In a little while Jesus is going away because He is going to be crucified. He is going to die. He will be taken away. And this will happen quickly. The hour has come (John 12:23, 27; 13:1; 16:21; 17:1). What does it mean in "a little while" they will see Him again? The disciples have no clue how to solve the riddle. They don't understand what He means when He says "a little while" or "I go to the Father" (John 16:10, 17–18).

We covered the idea of people misunderstanding Jesus earlier (reflections #8 and #9), but this is part of that same phenomenon. While the disciples do not ask for clarification, Jesus can clearly see they are not getting this. At all. Again. So he gives them an illustration.

Grief Turned into Joy

I've seen my wife give birth to two baby boys. I've never seen such pain before. As, um, beautiful as people say the moment is, it's also quite terrifying. It is absolutely one of the most dangerous things a woman can ever do. There is so much pain, there are so many potential complications, and as excited as I was to meet our sons, I thought a lot about what she would be going through. I prayed a lot about what she would be going through. Both our boys were large. Both were healthy. Both were difficult. The first had a huge head (which resulted in the goofiest newborn conehead I've ever seen in my life). The second turned breech shortly before his due date, and the stubborn little fella refused to turn himself back around. We had high hopes they could get him flipped, but the day came, the doctor tried, after a failed external cephalic version, they had to do a cesarean. That wasn't the plan but as difficult as those moments were on my wife, that's not what she thinks about when she holds our two boys. As I write these words, they are peacefully sleeping in their beds. We went to the park today. We laughed and played games and wrestled and fought crime. They are exhausting and fun and crazy, and we love them with all of our hearts. The anguish and pain of childbirth quickly transformed into a deep and indescribable joy and love.

So it is with the death and resurrection of Jesus. There will be pain. There will be grief. Jesus will suffer. The disciples will be heartbroken. There will be confusion, turmoil, and despair, but the race comes to an end. There is a finish line. Joy follows grief. The resurrection of Jesus vaporized their grief, and they were left with a joy no one will ever take away (John 16:22). The anguish of childbirth results in new life. The grief of crucifixion results in new life—not just the new resurrection life of Jesus, but eternal life for each of His followers. The story of life does not end with death. Rather, in Jesus, the story of death ends with life. The story of grief ends with joy. With reunion. With life.

Reflection Questions

1. Is there benefit to weeping and lamenting and mourning? What is the place of grief and lamentation in the Christian community? In your personal life?

2. Through the resurrection Jesus turned His disciples' grief into joy. In what ways can Jesus still do that for us? Has Jesus ever brought you joy when you least expected it? In what ways can Jesus bring joy to the hurt and grieving through you?

REFLECTION 46

FAREWELL PRAYER

John 16:23–17:26

∼

In My Name

Jesus is finishing one of His longest recorded conversations in all the Bible. He has disclosed what is about to come, He has comforted and promised the Holy Spirit, He has washed His disciples feet as an example of loving service, He has warned about persecution, He has revealed more of His identity, and He has promised divine answers to prayer. He just promised them

> if you ask the Father for anything in My name, He will give it to you
> ... you will ask in My name, and I do not say to you that I will request
> of the Father on your behalf; for the Father Himself loves you,
> because you have loved Me and have believed that I came forth from
> the Father (John 16:23–28; cf. 14:13; 15:7, 16).

Jesus gives comfort and encouragement to go to God in His name.

That is really a remarkable addition to what prayer has always been. Prayer has always been offered to God. Reading through the Hebrew Scriptures there are amazing, insightful, and deep prayers offered by people of faith. However, Jesus has changed the whole world, He's changed everything, including prayer. This is more than just some closing formula to add to your prayers: In Jesus name, amen. This is a radical shift in what it means to address God. This is a remarkable amount of trust Jesus is placing in His disciples. He is allowing them to address God "in His name." If I allow someone to speak for me, or speak in My name, I want to know exactly what they are going to be saying. Jesus, however, is so confident in them He doesn't need to address God for them, they can do it themselves in His name, because He knows His Father loves them, and He knows they believe in Him.

A Closing Prayer

That is not to say Jesus will not speak to God on their behalf (John 17:9). He concludes this conversation by speaking to God for each of them. John 17 is a fitting and beautiful prayer which ultimately concludes His ministry with His disciples. From this prayer they get up and depart to a garden where Jesus is betrayed, arrested, and abandoned by these men. Thank God the final thing He does with them is pray.

This prayer is pretty easily divided into three major sections: Jesus prays for the Father and His glorification (John 17:1–5), for His disciples faith and protection (John 17:6–19), and for the unification of all who will believe through the preaching of His disciples (John 17:20–26). If you are looking for a keyword running through every section of this prayer, it is the word "glory."

The word "glory" or "glorify" is used eight times in this one prayer (John 17:1, 4, 5, 10, 22, 24). The glory of Jesus is a major theme in the Gospel of John, but it is nowhere more vividly depicted than, surprisingly, through being lifted up, exalted high, "glorified" on the cross. While the cross looks like shame to most of the world, Jesus is praying in this fateful hour that God will glorify Him with the glory He had before the world began (John 17:5). In this way, the words are fulfilled which God spoke from heaven. Earlier, after entering Jerusalem for the final Passover, Jesus knows the hour of His impending death has come, and He prays, "'Father, glorify Your name.' Then a voice came out of heaven: 'I have both glorified it and will glorify it again'" (John 12:28). The crowd gathered around Jesus and did not know if it was thunder or an angel which they heard from the sky, but the voice was for them to hear. They needed to know that through the death of Jesus Satan would be cast out of power (John 12:27–33) and God and Jesus would be glorified. He prays this God–given glory would also be lavished upon those who believe in Him, all future disciples and believers, for the sake of a powerful unity which will convict the world (John 17:23).

This prayer defines eternal life (John 17:3), expresses confidence in His disciples (John 17:6–8), and petitions for their continued unity, protection, joy, long life, and sanctification (John 17:11–19). Tragically, Jesus recognizes one of those disciples will miss out on this life and protection. Though unnamed, Jesus calls him "the son of perdition" (John 17:12). Judas has been called a devil (John 6:70–71), a thief (John 12:6), unclean (John 13:10–11), a betrayer (John 13:21), and now a "son of perdition" (John 17:12). That word perdition is used for the destruction of the ancient world through the flood (Luke 17:27), the destruction of Sodom and Gomorrah (Luke 17:29), and plots to destroy Jesus (Mark 3:6). This destruction, or perdition, which is translated as "perish" in the following verses, is something believers are able to avoid. John 3:16: "For God so loved the world, that He gave His only begotten Son, that whoever believes in Him shall not perish, but have eternal life." John 10:28: "I give eternal life to them, and they will never perish; and no one will snatch them out of My hand." Judas could not overcome his lust for earthly wealth. Judas traded his own life for money.

Unity Among Believers

Another theme mentioned is the unity of believers. Jesus wants this unity to be the defining characteristic setting His people apart from everyone else. Jesus is one with the Father and Their unity is the foundation of what all our relationships in Christ are to be. He prays His disciples are "one" as He is with the Father (John 17:11). He prays all future believers will "be one; even as You, Father, are in Me and I in You, that they also may be in Us, so that the world may believe that You sent Me" (John 17:21). He wants us to be "perfected in unity so that the world may know that You sent Me, and love them, even as You have loved Me" (John 17:22).

There are many hurdles to this radical call of unity. Jesus has already hinted at several of them. "I have other sheep, which are not of this fold; I must bring them also, and they will hear My voice; and they will become one flock with one Shepherd" (John 10:16). Jesus wants to open the door to all men, Jew and Gentile alike (see John 7:35). Jesus says, "I, if I am lifted up from the earth, will draw all men to Myself." Even Samaritans, who Jews have no dealings with (John 4:9) and who Jews directly compare to the demon possessed (John 8:48). Jesus comes to unify all.

A beautiful foretaste of this unity is seen in His triumphal entry into Jerusalem. Among those going to the Passover feast were some Greeks who said, "We wish to see Jesus" (John 12:21). Jesus answers with a parable describing how a seed must first die to grow into a plant which produces fruit. Similarly, Jesus will die and will bear fruit. His fruit are any who give up this world in service to Him: "If anyone serves Me, he must follow Me; and where I am, there My servant will be also; if anyone serves Me, the Father will honor him" (John 12:23–26). Jesus opens the door to anyone who serves Him. Jesus is willing to accept these people into His fold and into His service. Are we?

Honoring Jesus' Prayer

Read the prayer of John 17 in its entirety and ask yourself these questions: Am I honoring Jesus' prayer with the life I am living? Am I so enamored with money, wealth, and excess that I am traveling down the road of perdition? (John 17:11). Have I given it my all to keep my ways from the evil one? (John 17:15). Am I seeking to live a life set apart by the truth of the Word of God? (John 17:17). Am I "one" with my brothers and sisters in Christ? Have I prioritized unity over my ambition, desires, and prejudices? Have personal insults caused me to ignore Jesus' prayer? Have politics caused me to ignore Jesus' prayer? Will I only share unity if others agree with me on every point? Can I be united with someone who doesn't have my level of understanding (Or just maybe I don't have theirs)?

I think if we work at putting the unity of the body above ourselves, it will not only be a spiritual encouragement to us, but it will make evangelism indescribably more effective. Perhaps Jesus is right and we can show the world, through our unity, that He truly is from the Father.

Reflection Questions

1. What is the relationship between agreement and unity? How much agreement is necessary for unity to exist? Can you disagree with someone while they remain your brother? Are there issues you cannot disagree about?

2. In what ways can unity change the world? How can our unity impact evangelism? Church growth? The name and reputation of Jesus?

REFLECTION 47
BETRAYED, ARRESTED, AND DENIED

John 18:1–27; 21:15–19

I Am

The prayer has concluded. He has eaten, washed the feet of the disciples, and said everything He needs to say. The hour has come. They all get up from the table and take the short walk to the ravine of the Kidron where there is a garden. The other Gospels let us know this is the Garden of Gethsemane. He's been here before. In fact, He often takes His disciples to this garden. They all know where it is. Including Judas, who left earlier in the dark, after his feet were washed (John 13:30). He didn't hear what Jesus had promised His disciples, nor did he need to. His mind was made up, the "ruler of the world" had filled His heart already. He would betray Jesus in this garden.

Oh, the irony of Satan filling Judas' heart to betray Jesus. Satan's ruin comes through the death of Jesus which he conspired to arrange. And it begins right now. Judas leads both Roman and Jewish soldiers and police to this spot. The world is in darkness at this hour, so they need lanterns, torches, and weapons. A world in darkness always needs weapons.

Jesus is not shocked at their arrival. He knew exactly what was coming that night. He is actually the One who initiates the conversation with the soldiers. "Whom do you seek?" He asks. Remember God in the garden asking Adam a question He already knew the answer to (Gen 3:9)? Here He does it again. "Jesus of Nazareth" they respond. And Jesus simply says, "I AM." Don't let your English Bible fool you. His exact words are "I AM." They hear Him. Judas hears Him.

This has been an important phrase in John's Gospel. It introduces those seven profound identity markers (Reflection #41), but there are also times when Jesus simply says, "I AM" with no description attached to the end: while walking on the sea (John 6:20), arguing at the temple (John 8:24, 58–59; after which they try to stone Him), and during His farewell address (John 13:19). These are non–predicated "I Am" statements and here, in this climactic moment, when His death is most imminent, He says it again. And those powerful, well–trained, brave Roman soldiers, fall to the ground in terror at the statement (John 18:6). It's repeated three times in verses 5–8. Make no mistake, this is the "I Am" statement all the others have been pointing to. The God is Israel (Exod 3:14) is standing in a garden before the Roman armies. The showdown has come. The unthinkable is about to happen.

Jesus Is Arrested

Judas just led the soldiers to Jesus. He heard the "I Am" and watched as they fell to the ground. He may have fallen also. And that moment is the last we read about him in John. There is no mention of his regret, return of the money, or suicide. Just his cowardice in the garden. And the betrayer's story fades away into oblivion.

Jesus asks the trembling soldiers to let His disciples go. If they are only after Him, there is no need for the disciples to be arrested or killed. The way Rome usually put an end to rebellion was not just to kill the leader, but to crucify all involved, leaving their bodies on crosses as a message to every passerby who sees. But Jesus is concerned to make sure none of His disciples are lost (John 18:9; 17:12). Peter will have none of this though. He's not fleeing. He's no coward! He already promised to die for Jesus (John 13:37), now is his chance. With the most powerful army in the world gathered by the hundreds before him, he whips out his sword and begins to strike! He cuts off the ear of the high priest's slave, a man named Malchus.

Jesus emphatically commands him to "put the sword into the sheath" (John 18:11). And I think He means, keep it there. Jesus did not come to take life, to kill, or to destroy. He came to save. When a disciple whips out a sword in defense of Jesus, He has forgotten who Jesus truly is. He has forgotten the mission of Jesus. He has forgotten the love of Jesus. Jesus did not carry a sword and He doesn't need you to either.

Jesus allows Himself to be arrested and is taken to Annas (John 18:12–13) and Caiaphas (John 18:24). Caiaphas appeared earlier in John and accidentally prophesied. I love this story. John 11:47–53 sets in motion the events leading to the crucifixion. It all went back to Jesus raising Lazarus. The sign was too big, and He was too close to Jerusalem and too close to Passover. The Jewish leaders were terrified Rome would come and destroy them because of Jesus, because He got large crowds of Jews to start talking about other kings and Messiahs. Caiaphas, the voice of reason, explains, "It is expedient for you that one man die for the people, and that the whole nation not perish" (John 11:50). Again, the irony. Caiaphas means, by killing Jesus you can save everyone from the Romans. So everyone is saved if Jesus dies. Which is in part true: the death of Jesus does bring the salvation of many, not just Israel, but all who are scattered. Yet it won't save you from the Romans. And the nation is still going to perish.

Peter Denies and Jesus Affirms

All of this is causing Peter's head to spin like crazy. "How can the Messiah be arrested? How can Jesus let this happen? Why didn't He fight? Can He not beat the Romans? Why didn't He defend me? Will I get arrested for being with Him? Will I be crucified for pulling out a sword?" This moment of doubt, fear, and mental fatigue is no time for Peter to make bold proclamations of faith in Jesus. And tragically, that's exactly what he is asked to do. What horrible timing. Why couldn't they have asked him if he was a disciple three weeks earlier? Or right after He fed the 5,000? Why not after the resurrection? Why now? At Peter's weakest moment?

This is important. We don't get to choose the time we're called upon to confess Jesus. The world doesn't wait for us to get prepared. Satan doesn't wait until we're ready. When you are most vulnerable is when you most need to confess. Peter fails. Three times Peter fails. I am not a disciple (John 18:17). I am not a disciple (John 18:25). I was not in the garden (John 18:27). And the rooster crowed.

After the resurrection Jesus doesn't see Judas again. Judas isn't around any longer, but Peter is. Jesus appears to Peter several times. Jesus doesn't appear hurt. (Although how could He not have been?) He doesn't appear angry. (Although He had every right to be.) He appears to forgive, uplift, strengthen, and encourage. The final chapter of the Gospel of John records a famous conversation between Jesus and Peter. Jesus does not give up on him. In fact, He gives Peter three chances to proclaim the love he thrice denied. Read John 21:15–17. Three times Peter says he loves Jesus, but something interesting is happening in this conversation. It's hard to see it in English. The first two times, Jesus asks, do you love (agape) Me? And Peter responds, You know that I love (phileo) You. The third time, Jesus asks, do you love (phileo) Me? And Peter, grieved, says, "I love (phileo) You."

After each of these declarations, Jesus does not rebuke Peter. He does not give up on Peter. Instead, He gives Peter a job: "Tend my lambs ... Shepherd My sheep ... Tend My sheep." The Good Shepherd is calling Peter to be a co–shepherd. A good shepherd. Remember, a good shepherd "lays down his life for the sheep (John 10:11).

Peter loves Jesus, but for some reason He is hesitant to say agape. There are linguistic arguments about how much of a distinction there is in the definition of agape and phileo. This much is clear: the cross is about agape. In moments of fear and confusion, Peter denied Jesus to save His own neck. He needs to learn agape. He'll learn it as a shepherd. And the time will come as he grows older he'll become the shepherd God calls him to be: "You will stretch out your hands and someone else will gird you, and bring you where you do not wish to go" (John 21:18–29). Peter will die. He'll learn agape. He'll shepherd God's people. And he'll glorify God in his death (John 21:19). His failure is not his future. Hope always remains.

Reflection Questions

1. What did the soldiers feel when Jesus said, "I Am"? Why did they fall back? What did Judas feel? What did Peter feel? Why did Jesus tell Peter to put his sword away?

2. Why did Peter deny Jesus? How did he change His mind so quickly? Do you ever implicitly or explicitly deny Jesus in your life, words, or actions? How important is it Jesus gave Peter a chance to confess Him three times after the resurrection?

REFLECTION 48
THE KING AND HIS KINGDOM

John 18:19–19:15

Behold Your King

How did it come to this? There He stands. Exhausted. Beaten. Humiliated. Mocked. He's a bloody mess. His body has been ripped to shreds by a Roman scourge. His face is swollen and bruised from the punches and slaps He has received. Blood is dripping from His head into His eyes. He tries to wipe it but it simply smears, mixing with the sweat and blood on His forearms. He's so exhausted He can barely stand. He hasn't slept. He spent the night with His disciples, serving, teaching, and praying. He went to the garden and was betrayed and arrested. He endured a sham of a trial in the dead of night before Annas where He was accused without evidence and struck when He spoke. He was bound and brought before Caiaphas. Both found Him guilty. Now they've sent Him off to Pilate. Convincing Him is what really matters. He's the Roman in charge of these parts. He's the only one who can get Jesus crucified (John 18:31–32).

But there's a major problem. Jesus hasn't done anything worthy of crucifixion. Healing the sick, feeding the hungry, and raising the dead don't cut it. Pilate talks to Jesus. He considers the matter and finds nothing deserving of crucifixion. "I find no guilt in Him," Pilate says three times (John 18:38; 19:4, 6). Pilate has a difficult job. He can't have a riot on His hands. If he cannot keep the peace, that's on him. He has to answer for it, but he also needs to maintain justice and law. So what happens when maintaining peace means doing something unjust? What do you choose? Pilate isn't ready to decide.

He tries to find an alternative to get himself out of this mess. First, he appeals to their justice. There is a custom where he releases a prisoner to the Jews at Passover. Since Jesus is innocent and the other prisoners are actually guilty, surely their sense of justice will prevail! Surely they'll choose to free Jesus. They don't. Instead they free a known robber, or insurrectionist, Barabbas, whose name ironically means Son (Bar) of the Father (Abbas). Second, he tries to appease their hatred and bloodlust through beating and torturing Jesus. Maybe seeing Him beaten and punished by the Romans will satisfy them, even if He isn't crucified. Maybe wearing that disgraceful crown of thorns beaten into His forehead. Maybe wearing blood soaked royal purple. They slap Him and say, "Hail, King of the Jews!" (John 19:3). Pilate then attempts to rely on their sympathy. He brings Him out, and there He stands. Pilate looks at Him, turns to the crowds, and cries, "Behold the Man!"

They see Him and they shout "Crucify!" All of Pilate's attempts have failed. There must be something more. What horrible thing has He done? What can Pilate possibly crucify Him for? Well, there is one thing. And it's a big deal. It's mentioned all the way back in John 1:49: "Rabbi, You are the Son of God; You are the King of Israel." That is a major problem. The king stuff won't fly with the Romans. Jesus hasn't done anything worthy of crucifixion, but claiming to be a king is serious business. Caesar doesn't like to share. That can get almost anyone crucified. So that's the first thing Pilate asks Jesus, "Are You the King of the Jews?" (John 18:33).

A Kingdom for This World

Jesus is a King. He has a kingdom. It's the most powerful kingdom the world has ever seen, and it's unlike any other kingdom this world has ever seen. Speaking with Pilate, Jesus is about as straightforward and blunt as You ever see Him. He tells Pilate He is a King (John 18:37). He also tells Pilate about His kingdom:

> My kingdom is not of this world. If My kingdom were of this world, then My servants would be fighting so that I would not be handed over to the Jews; but as it is, My kingdom is not of this realm (John 18:36).

Notice a few things about this kingdom. Jesus didn't say His kingdom is not on this world. He didn't say His kingdom is not for this world. His kingdom is certainly a literal kingdom. It's certainly on this earth. And it's certainly for this world. It is just not of or from this world. You know how you can tell? In a few minutes Jesus will stand bloodied and beaten before a crowd of those who hate Him. They'll scream for His crucifixion, and they'll get it. Nailed to a wooden cross, Jesus will suffer miserably and die mercilessly. That's an earthly kingdom. Violence, warfare, and death is the ultimate power behind every earthly kingdom. Perhaps wealth and sex could be thrown in there as well.

That's why it's smart to side with Caesar. No other kingdom on earth uses death as effectively as Rome. There is no enemy more powerful than Caesar. That's why Pilate must crucify Jesus. He tries to get out of it. He tells the Jews to solve this problem themselves (John 18:31; 19:6). He tries to plead with them over and over (John 19:12), but Jesus must be crucified. He gave Himself the title "Son of God" (John 19:7). That belongs to Caesar. Jesus called Himself a King. That belongs to Caesar. If Jesus is Caesar's rival, He cannot be released: "If you release this Man, you are no friend of Caesar; everyone who makes himself out to be a king opposes Caesar" (John 19:12). Pilate simply cannot oppose Caesar. There is too much risk. Caesar has a kingdom which can be seen everywhere you look. It's violent, bloody, and ruthless. It's Babylon the Great reborn. It is the epitome of might, strength, power, and the kingdoms of the earth.

An Upside Down Kingdom

But Jesus' kingdom is not one of those. If it was, "My servants would be fighting" (John 18:36). Nonviolence is a sign of the kingdom of God. When violence seems like the only option, God's kingdom shows you another way. Love conquers hate in the kingdom of God, even if love costs you your life. This is the message Peter struggled with so much. He knew how kingdoms worked! He pulled out His sword in the garden because the one who kills most efficiently wins! That's how revolution happens. That's how independence is won. That's how power is gained. It's vicious and cruel, but it's the way of the world. That's why Jesus' kingdom is so badly needed for this world, but it loses all power when it becomes of this world.

Remember Nicodemus? He was told "unless one is born again he cannot see the kingdom of God" (John 3:3). You don't need to be born again to see the Roman kingdom. You don't need to be born again to realize the wisdom of saying, "We have no king but Caesar!" (John 19:15). They stood and shouted, "Crucify Him!" They saw Him. They were told, "Behold the Man!" and even "Behold your King!" But they couldn't see a King. They saw weakness. They saw failure. They were filled with hatred. They pledged loyalty and allegiance to Caesar and his power and his violence. And the true King of the universe was right in front of them the entire time. The true kingdom from Heaven was right before their eyes. God stood before them and they begged the kingdoms of the world to destroy Him. They saw Rome's power and looked right past God's.

Power in Jesus' kingdom is seen in the Master washing His servant's feet. It's not seen in the luxurious royal purple robe and golden diadem sparkling atop a proud noble head. It's not seen in the sending of a massive well–fortified army to eviscerate enemies. It's not seen in the splendor of the Roman forum or the grandeur of Caesar's throne. It's seen in weakness. It's seen in humiliation. It's seen in the wearied, beaten, and bloodied Man wearing a crown made of thorns. It's seen in Peter sheathing his sword. It's seen in dying rather than killing. It's seen in a King being nailed to a cross.

Reflection Questions

1. In what ways is the kingdom for this world but not of this world? How is Jesus' kingdom different from the kingdoms of earth? How is it "upside down"? How should this impact our view of politics, governments, and kingdoms of this world?

2. Why does Pilate condemn an innocent man? What role does fear play in his judgment? How is this fear similar to Pharaoh in Exodus 1 or Herod in Matthew 2? Does fear ever cause us to deny justice?

REFLECTION 49
CRUCIFIED

John 19:16–42

Crucifixion

The Romans aren't squeamish. You do not slaughter your enemies by the thousands if you can't handle the sight of blood. You don't use the spectacle of unimaginably creative violence in the amphitheatre to pacify the masses if cruelty and violence is not a deeply ingrained part of your social DNA. Yet even for the Romans, the cross was shameful. They wouldn't even entertain the idea such a barbaric practice could have been created by them. It was beneath them. Roman writers speak of the word for "crucifixion" being hard for their ears to take. No matter the crime, Roman citizens were never to be crucified. In fact, the notorious Roman magistrate Gaius Verres was tried and exiled for his crimes and cruelty as a leader in Sicily. Cicero, recorded in *Against Verres*, details his abuses of power including, though not limited to, the crucifixion of Publius Gavius. That was a major problem. He was a Roman citizen. To be a citizen of Rome, like Paul for example, afforded you the respect and dignity of a beheading for capital crimes rather than the disgrace of crucifixion.

Jesus didn't have the honor of Roman citizenship. After His arrest, beatings, and corrupt trials, Pilate "handed Him over to them to be crucified" (John 19:17). John is the only gospel to mention Jesus "bearing His own cross" (John 19:17). The other gospels mention a man, apparently well known to the recipients of Mark's gospel, named "Simon of Cyrene (the father of Alexander and Rufus)" who was ordered "to bear the cross" (Mark 15:21). Tradition developed that Jesus was so battered and physically exhausted as He tried to carry the cross that He repeatedly fell under its load. Thus, the cross was handed to someone standing nearby to carry for Jesus. That Jesus could still stand at all is astonishing.

When Jesus arrives at the Place of the Skull, He is nailed through His wrists to the cross bar, and suspended in the air on the cross. This gruesome moment has been alluded to a number of times by Jesus already. As Moses' healing bronze serpent was exalted high, so the saving Son of Man has been lifted up above the people (John 3:14). In this moment all men are being drawn to the saving power of Jesus and the "ruler of this world," the devil himself, is being defeated (John 12:31–33). God's glory is seen in the exaltation of Christ. Even, or perhaps especially, the exaltation of the cross.

Scripture Is Fulfilled

In John's description of Jesus on the cross, he repeatedly appeals to the fulfillment of Scripture. This continues a trend beginning with Jesus' farewell meal with His disciples (John 12:37–40; 13:18; 15:24–25; 17:12; 19:23–24; 19:28–29; 19:36–37) and culminates with His death on the cross. Even after His death, when He is pierced through with a spear, He is still fulfilling scripture. The crucifixion was not unexpected or some demoralizing failure. It did not catch God off guard. It did not halt the coming of the kingdom. Rather it is fulfilling the long–awaited climax of God's plan. In fulfillment of Scripture, the cross is the means by which God brings His upside–down kingdom into the world.

The first passage fulfilled on the cross is when the soldiers divide up His clothes and cast lots to see who gets to keep His tunic. The passage cited is from Psalm 22:18, a Psalm of David crying to God for help in his time of hopeless despair. You may remember this Psalm is also quoted by Jesus in Matthew and Mark: "My God, My God, Why have You forsaken Me?" (Mark 15:34; Matthew 27:46; Psalm 22:1). The second passage fulfilled is not explicitly stated. It's when Jesus says "I am thirsty," and they give Him sour wine to drink (John 19:28–29). This is almost certainly an allusion back to Psalm 69:21, "And for my thirst they gave me vinegar to drink." This Psalm is also a Davidic cry of distress. It's the Psalm quoted by Jesus when cleansing the temple (John 2:17; Psa 69:9) and fulfilled when Jesus says, "They hate Me without cause" (John 15:25; Psalm 69:4). Like Psalm 22, this is a king's cry of distress which becomes closely connected to the death of Jesus. It is interesting to note over half of all of John's citations come from the Psalms.

The third and fourth passages are closely linked to the spear piercing Jesus' side. The first, "Not a bone of His shall be broken" is clearly a reference to the Passover lamb (Exod 12:46; Num 9:12) on the day of preparation (John 19:31, 35–36, although the wording is also quite close to Psalm 34:20). Finally, John 19:37 directly quotes Zechariah 12:10, "They shall look on Him whom they pierced." If you turn your Bible back to Zechariah 12:10, you'll notice this image is one of Divine protection for the house of David against his enemies, and it is God who says, "They will look on Me whom they have pierced." In fact, "In that day ... the House of David will be like God" (Zech 12:8–10).

These citations inform us this is all part of God's plan. At the cross, more than anywhere else, we need to remember God is still in control. It is not the Roman soldiers, Pilate, the Jews, or Caesar. In these citations, Jesus takes on the role of the Davidic king, the house of David, and the role of the Passover Lamb. On the cross, it is all fulfilled. On the cross, "It is finished" (John 19:36). That famous final phrase of Jesus should give us all pause. That brief three word sentence in our Bibles is actually just one Greek word τετέλεσται (tetelestai). The same word is used just two verses earlier to describe what had been "accomplished (τετέλεσται) to fulfill the Scripture." Those two verses should be read together. On the cross, Jesus fulfilled, accomplished, finished it all. The perfect tense of τετέλεσται indicates it has been and will forever be accomplished, finished, fulfilled. The feasts, the Exodus, the house of David, Messianic expectation, creation and new creation, it has all been anticipating this moment. Jesus, God's chosen King, accomplished it all.

The Death of a King

Jesus is the King who brings fulfillment. He accomplishes what no one else could—not just for one group or one nation, but for the whole world. That's why the sign on the cross itself, written in 3 languages for all men, Jew, Roman, or Greek, the powerful proclamation: "The King of the Jews" (John 19:19–20). He's wearing a crown for a reason. When the Jews ask Pilate to revise the plaque above the head of Jesus, he refuses, "What I have written I have written" (John 19:22). At the trial, Jesus is dressed as a King (John 19:2–3). On the cross, Jesus is proclaimed as a King (John 19:19–22). And after His death, Jesus is buried as a King (John 19:38–42).

Here, Nicodemus makes his final appearance. He's with a man named Joseph, a secret disciple. Nicodemus is a disciple at night and Joseph is a disciple in secret, but at the death of Jesus, they both come forward. They have seen it. They have seen God's King. This is Nicodemus' third appearance in John (John 3:1; 7:50; 19:39). Each time we see him he seems to be getting closer to "seeing the kingdom" (John 3:3). I think this burial gives us reason to be optimistic. Slaves are not buried in beautiful, new garden tombs. Criminals are not decorated with 100 Roman pounds of myrrh and aloes. Joseph and Nicodemus are on a journey. I hope we can meet them one day to ask them about it.

Reflection Questions

1. What do you think about when you see an image of a cross? How is that different than the way Rome used the cross? How has Jesus changed the meaning of the cross?

2. What important things does Jesus do and say on the cross? Who does He choose to watch over His mother? Why a disciple rather than one of His brothers (John 7:1–5)? What does it mean, "It is finished"? What is finished?

REFLECTION 50
THE FIRST DAY OF THE WEEK

John 20:1–18

Black Sabbath

It is no accident Sabbath is the day Jesus spends resting in the cool dark tomb. The darkest Sabbath in human history. The Light of the world has been rejected by the darkness. The Way, the Truth, and the Life has been crucified. The King is dead. The Good News, however, has only just begun. This is the day they were preparing for. This is the day that meant everything.

Remember when they led Jesus to Pilate's residence? They did not want to go inside because He was a Gentile and they didn't want to be defiled (John 18:28). They wanted to be clean for this day. Remember when they asked Pilate to take the bodies off of the crosses? It was "so that the bodies would not remain on the cross on the Sabbath (for the Sabbath was a high day)" (John 19:31). They did not want to be defiled as they condemned an innocent man to death. They did not want to dishonor this "high day" while they dishonored and killed the King of kings. Ceremonial cleansing mattered. Honoring the Sabbath mattered. Eating the Passover mattered. Justice, mercy, and love were all ignored but, hey, at least the Sabbath was honored.

Now Sabbath has come. There is nothing written about this day but you can just imagine. What are the disciples thinking? What is Peter thinking? Are the chief priests celebrating? Is Satan? Does he know he's destroyed himself? Does death know his power is being stolen? Is it known on the cross Jesus took the full brunt of the world's wickedness into Himself so He might destroy it through His death and raise victoriously on the other side? Is it known that on that fateful Sabbath Day, death is enjoying its last day of victory? For the first time death will find out what it means to lose. Sure, Lazarus made death nervous, but Lazarus would fall prey again. For the first time death and hades will see their demise is certain. Satan will be cast out as "ruler of this world." And the King who was beaten and battered just a day before, will burst forth in the glory of His Father, raised to new life which can never be taken again. This is the last day of the old world. A new world is coming with the discovery of an empty tomb.

Apostle to the Apostles

Astonishingly, a woman named Mary from the town of Magdala is the first to discover the tomb. She arrives "while it is still dark" (John 20:1). At these vital moments, John always lets us know when it is "night" and when it is "dark." The Light of the world has not been seen yet. What has been seen is His tomb. The stone rolled away, empty on the inside. That's not what Mary expected to see. Her first thought? Go tell the disciples! Someone moved the body! She quickly finds Peter and the beloved disciple and frantically explains, "They have taken away the Lord out of the tomb, and we do not know where they have laid Him" (John 20:2).

In horror, they sprint to the tomb and the beloved disciple arrives first. Peter is always behind him. The beloved disciple peeks his head inside and sees the burial clothes. Peter barges right in to look around. The linen clothes were lying on the ground but the face cloth was neatly rolled up by itself. Someone had definitely been in there. Why would grave robbers unclothe the body? Why take the time to roll up the face cloth? When the beloved disciple enters the tomb, it dawns on him. He realizes what's happened. He believes (John 20:8). The beloved disciple is the only one said to "believe" before seeing the resurrected Jesus, although it will still take them time to see it in the Scriptures (John 20:9; John 2:17, 22; 12:16).

After the disciples return home, Mary stays by the tomb. She's weeping. Finally gaining the courage to peek inside the tomb to see what the disciples saw, she looks. She sees something amazing. Two angels are seated where Jesus' feet and head had been and they ask her why she is weeping. They know there is nothing to weep about. She still believes the Lord is dead and His body has been stolen. She doesn't know where it is.

Then she turns. She sees someone. She's in a garden, and through her fear and tears she assumes it's the gardener. He asks an interesting question, "Whom are you seeking?" (John 20:15). This is the same question Jesus asked back in the other garden (John 18:4, 7). Mary begs the gardener, if he's moved the body to just tell her where! She'll go and take it. She'll care for it.

Jesus looks at her, clears his voice and says, "Mary!" I can't imagine what that sounded like. She's crying; she's distressed; she knows Jesus is dead. She's trying to solve the problem of the missing body. And she hears that voice calling her name. That voice she's heard so many times before. Like a ton of bricks, it hits her. She sees! She runs! And she grabs Him! "Rabboni!" she screams. It's really Him —a real body you can really grab and hold. He tells her she must let go. He has a job for her. She will be the first person to proclaim the resurrection (John 19:16–18).

In church tradition, Mary has been given the honorific title of the "Apostle to the Apostles." I love that. A woman from Magdala is the first to bring the message of the gospel to the apostles. She's the first to see the empty tomb. She's the first to see Jesus. She's one of the only ones to ever hug the resurrected Lord. What an honor! Women weren't even trusted by courts of law as faithful witnesses. However, the first witness, the witness to the apostles, is a woman. Mary's witness, combined with Joseph of Arimathea's known empty tomb, presents a strong line of evidence Jesus really did rise from the dead, even for those who never get to see it for themselves (John 20:29).

The Gardener

Isn't it interesting this whole scene takes place in a garden? Early in the morning as the sun is rising? It is dark at the beginning of the story (John 20:1) but the sun is shining by its end. I cannot read this passage without those images of New Creation popping back up again. When God created the world, it was in darkness (Genesis 1:2). When this story begins, it is in darkness (John 20:1). When God said, "Let there be light," it was the "first day" of the week (Genesis 1:3–5).

When the Light of the world rises from the darkness of death, it is the "first day of the week" (John 20:1, 19). When God first creates man, He is placed in a garden (Gen 2:8). When the first resurrected man, the first New Man, comes to life, He is in a garden. Adam was called to be a gardener, to tend and protect the garden (Gen 2:15). The first person who sees Jesus suspects He is a gardener as well (John 20:15).

There is a reason Jesus is the "new Adam" (Rom 5:12ff; 1 Cor 15:20–26, 45). Adam was the first man of the old creation. He brought rebellion, sin, and death into it. Jesus is the first man of the New Creation. Of new resurrection life. Of the new world. And He brings forgiveness, salvation, and eternal life. This scene represents the world's new beginning, a new world where God's kingdom is inaugurated through Christ. Like the wheat and the tares, for the time being, the new world seems to grow together with the old, but the "ruler of the world" is changing. And we get to be a part of that. Our world did not begin in Eden. Our world, the one we as Christians now inhabit, began in the garden tomb. That's where our life begins.

Reflection Questions

1. Why is Mary called the "Apostle to the Apostles"? Why is it so important a woman first saw the empty tomb and was the first witness of the risen Jesus? From the beginning women have played a vital role in the life and work of the church. Is this true in your life and church?

2. What is the significance of "the first day of the week"? Why is that day mentioned twice and in all four gospels? Why does the early church meet on this same day (Acts 20:7; 1 Cor 16:2)? How did the world change that day?

REFLECTION 51
DOUBTS AND FEARS

John 20:19–31

~

He Comes with Peace

That first day nothing was certain. Was Mary Magdalene just crazy and hysterical? Why was the tomb empty? Where was the body? Could He really be risen? Where is He? We can't be seen in public right now. They'll blame us! They know we were with Him. Will they kill us? The fear, anxiety, and endless questions drove them to seclusion. They found a safe room to gather together. They locked the door. They had no idea what to do next. And then suddenly, He was there. Right there. He appeared in the room bringing the very thing they needed most. "Peace be with you" (John 20:19).

It's really Him. He showed them His side and hands. They could see the wounds for themselves, and a joy took over them one could hardly imagine. All of the fear, angst, and confusion dissipates in the presence of the Lord. It's time to celebrate (John 16:20, 22). A second time He says to them, "Peace be with you" (John 20:21).

Accompanying this peace is a sign of the Spirit.[1] In His farewell address, Jesus promised the Spirit several times. He also said "If I do not go away, the Helper will not come to you" (John 16:7). The Spirit will be the abiding presence of Jesus after his ascension to the Father. At this appearance in the locked room, Jesus is still with them because He hasn't ascended yet. While among them He breaths on them and commands, "Receive the Holy Spirit" (John 20:22). This is a comforting reminder they will receive the Holy Spirit when Jesus departs. In that way, He will always be with them. When forgiving sin, practicing church discipline, preaching the gospel, they can have assurance Jesus is with them.

Thomas Wasn't There

This amazing confirmation of the resurrection and Christ's victory over the spiritual forces of wickedness in the world was a source of peace to the disciples. They hadn't wasted their time. They were not wrong. Jesus was not a failure. What this means for the future is still uncertain, but Jesus is going to be a part of it no matter what. Except, not all of the disciples were actually there. Mary has seen and believes. The disciples have seen and now believe, yet one disciple wasn't in that room. So he gets his own story.

"Thomas, one of the twelve, called Didymus, was not with them when Jesus came" (John 20:24). Jesus likes nicknames. Peter is a nickname for Simon. Peter and Cephas are the Greek and Aramaic words for "rock." Jesus gives him this nickname in John 1:42. Thomas is a nickname, too. Thomas is the Semitic word for "twin" and Didymus is the Greek word for "twin." So what is his actual name? And who is his twin? Some later non–biblical texts like, The Gospel of Thomas and The Acts of Thomas, suggest his name was "Judas Didymus Thomas" and he was actually the twin brother of (drumroll please) ... Jesus! That, however, is another study for a different day. Just file it away so you can answer a trivia question one day.

In our text, we find Thomas meeting up with the disciples after Jesus departed. They tell him all about it: "We have seen the Lord!"

(John 20:25). They report to Thomas what Mary reported to them (John 20:18). Still, those other disciples were fearful and confused until they saw Jesus for themselves. Thomas is the same way. He cannot accept it. He has ten disciples he's known for years proclaiming the resurrection to him, but he cannot accept it. These trustworthy eye witnesses promise him Jesus is alive, but he cannot believe it. This same Thomas who was willing to die with Jesus just a short time earlier (John 11:16). He cannot believe unless he sees and touches the wounds in Jesus' hands and side. The other disciples were able to see it for themselves. Thomas needs to also.

Thomas, in this moment, is in the situation of those he will later evangelize. He knows the tomb is empty, and he's heard eyewitnesses tell him the Lord has risen. Will he believe it? Thomas has seen Jesus turn water into wine, feed 5,000, walk on water, heal the blind, and even raise the dead. What more will it take? Remember the noble-man's son back in John 4:46–54? That was the second sign Jesus performed in Cana of Galilee. Jesus laments, "Unless you people see signs and wonders, you simply will not believe" (John 4:48). He then heals the nobleman's son without ever seeing him. And the nobleman believes Jesus before ever seeing his son healed. He believed based on the testimony of Jesus. Can Thomas? Can Thomas believe the testimony of those around him?

No. He can't. It's actually not until "after eight days His disciples were again inside, and Thomas with them. Jesus again enters, though the doors are shut, and for the third time says, 'Peace be with you' (John 20:26). Thomas sees. I imagine his eyes have never been wider and his jaw never lower. Jesus looks at him and tells him, "Reach here with your finger, and see My hands; and reach here with your hand and put it into My side; and do not be unbelieving, but believing" (John 20:27). We're not told whether Thomas ever did touch Him. There probably was no need at that point. We are told what he says though: "My Lord and my God!" Now he sees. Now he believes. Now he testifies in the boldest of ways who Jesus is.

The Greatest Sign of All

Jesus wants us to believe as well. He wants us to trust. When He saw Thomas, He didn't rebuke him. He didn't refuse him evidence. He appeared bringing peace and the evidence Thomas needed. Yet Thomas should have believed and trusted the testimony. He should have trusted the signs. He should have trusted what Jesus promised. On this, Jesus challenges him, "Because you have seen Me, have you believed? Blessed are they who did not see, and yet believed" (John 20:29). While that challenge is to Thomas, it is also to me and you and everyone who has heard the story of Jesus without seeing it. Jesus blesses us if we do what Thomas could not. Can we believe the signs based on testimony? This entire Gospel is called "a testimony" of the beloved disciple (John 21:24). Can we believe the one Jesus loved? Can we believe even if we weren't there to see?

John concludes this section with the purpose statement for the whole Gospel: "Therefore many other signs Jesus also performed in the presence of the disciples, which are not written in this book; but these have been written so that you may believe that Jesus is the Christ, the Son of God; and that believing you may have life in His name" (John 20:30–31). Earlier, I wrote a section on the "signs" of Jesus. It was incomplete. The resurrection itself is the greatest sign ever performed. The raising of Lazarus, which proved Jesus is "the Resurrection and the Life" (John 11:25) is merely a shadow of what was to be accomplished by Jesus. Bringing Lazarus momentarily back to life painfully struck death on the heel but the ultimate resurrection to eternal life of Jesus dealt death its crushing blow to the head. Death will never recover. That is the ultimate sign.

There are many other signs which could have been written, but these are sufficient. They portray a picture of Jesus not merely as a good man, a powerful prophet, and even the Messiah, but as Lord and God. I'd love to know the other signs, but the beloved disciple leaves us wondering. He does that a lot actually. And that's fine. He's done enough. Will you believe? Will you take hold of the eternal life found in the name of Jesus?

Reflection Questions

1. Why is Jesus' coming with peace so important? Why do the disciples need "peace" so badly? How can Numbers 6:22–27 connect to these verses?

2. Did any of the disciples believe before they saw Jesus? When did most of them come to believe in the resurrection? Why is Thomas singled out? Which believers are especially blessed?

---

1. See Ben Witherington III, *John's Wisdom: A Commentary on the Fourth Gospel* (Louisville: Westminster John Knox, 1995), 339–41.

REFLECTION 52
FISHING WITH JESUS

John 21:1–25

∾

I Am Going Fishing

Jesus has been raised. What now? The disciples are in awe. They believe in Jesus. They realize who He truly is. They know He promised them the Spirit so what do they do now? Peter looks around at the other disciples and says simply, "I am going fishing" (John 21:3). The other disciples agree to come along, and they get in a boat together. Peter decides to get back to living. He's a fisherman. That's who he's always been. Before Jesus, he was a fisherman; now after Jesus, he'll be a fisherman too. Except he catches nothing. His net is empty. He cannot go back to his old life. There is nothing there anymore. Everything has changed.

During this fruitless fishing excursion someone walks up to the shore and watches them. They don't know who it is. Even when He shouts to them, they don't recognize. Like Mary talking to the gardener, they are talking to the stranger on the shore. They are fruitlessly trying to get back to life as usual when this stranger offers them some advice. "Cast the net on the right side of the boat" (John 21:6). They couldn't even haul the net in. Once this stranger appeared their lives were no longer fruitless. The beloved disciple is the first to realize what's happening. He turns to Peter, "It is the Lord" (John 21:7). This is Jesus' third and final appearance to the disciples in the Gospel of John (John 21:14). Twice inside locked rooms and once on the beach. When Peter hears it's Jesus, he rips off his clothes and dives into the sea, swimming to the Lord as fast as he can. He leaves the fish behind and goes to Jesus.

Breakfast with the Lord

The other disciples go to shore in the boat dragging the massive load of fish. Jesus is cooking on the beach. The fire is already going, He's already cooking fish and has bread. This was the meal, back in John 6:9, Jesus used to feed the 5,000. He could use this to feed His disciples right now. He got breakfast started, and He could turn this into as much bread and fish as He wants. Yet He tells them to bring in their load also. By themselves, they caught nothing, but with Jesus, the disciples are bringing the majority of the fish. 153 to be exact. They have brought in enough fish to feed the masses.

Jesus' ministry has not ended. He got breakfast started but His disciples are to bring the rest of the feast. They can only do it by His instructions. They can only do it when they cast the net where He guides them, but they can do it. Jesus is the Good Shepherd, but in a few verses He will tell Peter to become one who tends, feeds, and cares for the sheep. Jesus is the Bread of Life, but now His disciples are bringing the words which save men's souls. Jesus is the Light of the world, but now His disciples are challenged to open men's eyes to turn from darkness to Light. Jesus got breakfast going, but now we're called to bring the fish.

Jesus invites them to eat with Him (John 21:12). This is fascinating. The resurrection body can be grabbed by Mary, but it can also enter locked doors. It can stand and walk and eat fish and bread. Does it need fish and bread? Can it grow weak and starve? Can it overeat and get fat? We don't know. And neither do His disciples, although I think they have a ton of questions. John describes their confused state by saying, "None of the disciples ventured to question Him, 'Who are you?' knowing that it was the Lord" (John 21:12). What an odd detail. I've never had a meal with somebody I knew and spent the whole time wanting to ask who they were. Why are the disciples having these thoughts? They want to ask, but they can't ask because they know. It's just hard to really grasp them sitting on the seashore eating with Jesus. He was just crucified! He was just laid in a tomb. They mourned for Him, but their mourning was turned to joy (John 16:20–22; John 20:20). Now they eat, as confusing as it may be, knowing it's the Lord. And Jesus breaks bread with them one last time (John 21:13).

A Farewell Challenge

We've discussed this final passage several times already (reflections #4, #5, #6, #47, etc.). John likes 3's. Jesus turned water to wine on the third day. Jesus was raised on the third day. Peter denied three times. Jesus appeared to His disciples three times. Jesus makes Peter affirm his love three times. With each of these, Peter does claim to love the Lord, but he also switches the word "love" from agape to phileo. Jesus is asking for agape. Peter is giving Him phileo. On the third time, Jesus asks about phileo. Peter is grieved about this third question, but again offers Him phileo. What does this mean? It does not mean Peter is unfit to tend God's sheep or become a shepherd of God's people. It perhaps implies Peter is not yet able to give Christ the sacrificial love Jesus challenges us all to have.

Jesus did not give up on His disciples. He did not give up on Thomas. And He does not give up on Peter. He knows Peter will grow. Phileo offers him a little more control, but agape takes him "where you do not wish to go" (John 21:18). Peter will go there though. Peter will have his arms outstretched on a cross in loving, sacrificial discipleship to Jesus. And he will glorify God as Jesus did (John 21:19). Peter must follow.

Do not go back to fishing, Peter. God has called you to something else. Do not turn to the beloved disciple, Peter (John 21:20–22). God has called you to follow. No one else can do it for you. You aren't competing with anyone else. You are not following anybody else. When it comes to washing feet, you follow Jesus. When it comes to leading others to the Light, you follow Jesus. When it comes to the cross, you follow Jesus. "You follow Me!" (John 21:22).

His Testimony is True

The beloved disciple is the one we should thank for gifting us the Gospel of John.

> [He] is the disciple who is testifying to these things and wrote these things, and we know his testimony is true. And there are also many other things which Jesus did, which if they were written in detail, I suppose that even the world itself would not contain the books that would be written (John 21:24–25).

This breath–taking Gospel ends by saying we've barely scratched the surface with Jesus but what we have is enough. The Gospel of John is the testimony of one who was there. His feet were washed by Jesus (John 13:5, 23). He heard Jesus pray (John 17). He saw Jesus beaten and mocked (John 19:1–3). He saw Jesus crucified (John 19:17–18). He spoke with Jesus on the cross and took Mary to be his own mother (John 19:26–27). He saw Jesus die, he saw the spear, he saw the blood and water (John 19:35). He saw the empty tomb (John 21:6–8). He saw the Resurrected Lord. He met with Him in the closed room. He ate with Him on the beach. He walked with Him along the shore. And he told us His story. The story is true. What will you do with it? Will you believe? Will you follow?

> "For God so loved the world, that He gave His only Son, that whoever believes in Him should not perish but have eternal life" (John 3:16).

Reflection Questions

1. How many sets of 3's can you think of in the Passion story? Why might 3 be such an important number?

2. Why is it so important the disciples ate a meal with Jesus? What does a meal mean about His body? Why is a meal with Jesus so important in early Christianity? Do you come to recognize Jesus more fully in the Lord's Supper?

APPENDIX 1
THE WOMAN IN ADULTERY

John 7:53–8:11

∾

Complicated Textual History

You may have noticed I did not discuss one of the most famous stories about Jesus. John 7:53–8:11 records a beloved account of Jesus showing compassion on a woman in sin and criticizing those who hypocritically condemned her. This story has sin, empathy, mystery, forgiveness, and a provocative conclusion. It's no wonder people love it so much. Still, there's a reason it's been moved to an appendix: I'm just not sure what to do with it.

It seems as though this story, while maintaining a powerful impact on Christian thought over the centuries, was not originally part of the Gospel of John. It is in our modern Bibles (usually with brackets or a footnote), but if you were a Christian living in the 2nd century, you would not have seen this account in the Gospel of John. In fact, many of the church fathers who wrote about John: Origen, John Chrysostom, Cyril of Jerusalem, Tertullian, etc. did not write about this account. In Tatian's famous Diatessaron, a 2nd century harmonization of the four gospels into one book, he does not include this story. Why would all of them ignore this incredible story about Jesus? Because it was added to John at a later date. It wasn't in their John.

Also, there was a lot of confusion as to where to add it. It is missing in our earliest manuscripts, both early papyri and the great parchment codices, and once it begins to make an appearance hundreds of years later, it arrives in different places and in different forms. Some manuscripts only contain a shortened form of the story including only John 8:3–11. Some scribes placed it after John 7:36 and some at the end of John. Some scribes, noting how different the writing style and vocabulary is from the rest of John, thought it should be part of Luke, so some manuscripts have it after Luke 21:38 or tacked on to the end. This text is called a "floating text." If floats in many different locations in the manuscript history.

A further clue this account was a later insertion into the text is found in John 8:9–11. All the crowds leave and Jesus is left alone with the woman. He tells her to "Go. From now on sin no more" (John 8:11). Then the next verse, without missing a beat, says, "Then Jesus again spoke to them, saying ..." (John 8:12). Who is the "them"? I thought He was alone? Apparently, there is still a crowd, and He is still at the temple for the Feast of Booths (John 7:14, 37) discussing His divine identity (John 7:40–43, 52; 8:12–13), until they try to kill Him for it (John 8:58–59).

So while it seems like a historically plausible story, it's just hard to know what to do with it or where to put it. One reason Luke has been connected with this story is that reading it in Greek shows language and style more similar to the Synoptic Gospels (Matthew, Mark, and Luke). Many first year Greek students begin by reading John before anything else in the New Testament, because John is noticeably simple and easy to read. Luke, on the other hand, is considerably more difficult. In Greek this passage reads more like Luke than John. It also uses language appearing regularly in the Synoptics but not in John. For example, John 8:3 refers to the "scribes and Pharisees." That description is used all throughout Matthew, Mark, and Luke, but it is never used in John. In fact, this is the only time the word "scribes" would be used in John at all. It's just not John's way of referring to Jesus' opponents. John's preferred phrase, unlike the synoptics, is "the Jews." Since the story is part of ancient historical oral tradition, there were attempts made to find the best place for it. We don't know exactly how it ended up here in John, but it did, and we read it to this day. For further study on this issue, there are many books and commentaries that discuss it in greater detail.[1]

Adultery or Hypocrisy?

While we know it is unlikely John actually wrote this account, we can still learn a lot from it. I think it presents a powerful illustration of the compassion, love, and justice of Jesus. Jesus does not accept or rejoice in iniquity. Adultery is wrong, and Jesus knows this. The crowds know this. That humiliated woman knows this. However, hatred, arrogance, pride, and hypocrisy are wrong, too. It is always so easy to justify ourselves by finding those who are worse than us. "I may lust, lack compassion, be proud and arrogant, overlook those in need, but at least I've never cheated on my wife." This story illustrates self-righteousness to the core.

Think of what the scribes and Pharisees have done here. They found a woman committing adultery. How they found her isn't stated. Was it a sting operation? Entrapment? A Stakeout? We don't know. The details aren't given but they grab her and set her in front of everyone in the center of the court at the temple. They humiliate her as she stands alone. All eyes on her. The religious leaders do not try to help her. They don't try to help her marriage, encourage her to do what is right, listen to how she ended up in this situation. They don't even care if she is stoned to death right in front of them. She doesn't matter to them at all. She's a person with a story. She got in this situation somehow, but no one is interested. She's a pawn. They don't care about her, the adultery, or helping her overcome this sin, they care about trapping Jesus.

They also don't seem to care about the man who was with her. Why isn't he brought before Jesus? They say "the Law of Moses commanded us to stone such a woman" (John 8:5). Does it really? Leviticus 20:10 reads: "If a man commits adultery with the wife of his neighbor, both the adulterer and the adulteress shall surely be put to death." Notice something missing in this story in John 8? Where's the dude? They bring the woman and humiliate her in order to "trap" Jesus, but they care nothing about upholding the Law of Moses or justice, mercy, and faithfulness.

Jesus' Powerful Response

So what does Jesus do? Three things. The first is a mystery. He writes in the sand. What does He write? John doesn't tell us. Many ideas have been suggested. Some say he is writing out the names of those in the crowd. Some say He's writing their sins. Perhaps He's writing the ten commandments with His own finger, in imitation of God's writing of the ten commandments (Exod 31:18; Deut 9:10). In this way Jesus places Himself in the seat of the true Lawgiver and Judge. Maybe that's it. Maybe not. Sometimes we just have to live with ambiguity.

The second thing Jesus does is take the spotlight off of this woman and shine it on the scribes and Pharisees. Jesus wants to focus on the people doing the stoning rather than the one being stoned. He doesn't actually say "Don't stone her!" Instead, He asks who is worthy to stone her. "He who is without sin among you, let him be the first to throw a stone at her" (John 8:7). The problem is not she was innocent or didn't deserve to be stoned. The problem is everyone there that day was guilty and they all deserved to be stoned. Sin has not stained only this woman, but every single person present that day. Don't throw rocks at others which could just as easily be aimed at you. Humbly recognizing our own sins ought to compel us to have sympathy for others. Stones don't show love or mercy, and they will never bring about repentance.

Finally, Jesus switches places with this woman. One thing I love about the placement of this story at the beginning of John 8 is how well it bookends with the end of John 8. The final verse in John 8 says, "They picked up stones to throw at Him ..." (John 8:59). The chapter begins with stones aimed at her but it ends with them aimed at Jesus. If that is not a perfect picture of what Jesus has done for each of us in our sins, then I don't know what is. He defends her, saves her, challenges her, and takes her place. He takes her role as an object of hatred and violence. Not because he committed adultery. He never committed any sin. It was because he conveyed a truth His listeners were unwilling to accept. He painted a picture of Himself they were too blind to see. He is the great I Am (John 8:58). He is the God who suffers and takes the place of the sinner. Though it may not be original, I'm thankful we get to read this ancient story as we make our way through the Gospel of John.

---

1. For further discussion see Bruce M. Metzger, *A Textual Commentary on the Greek New Testament* (Stuttgart: Deutsche Bibelgesellschaft, 1994), 187–89.

APPENDIX 2
DECIDE

Evangelizing with John

In Reflection #2 I mention evangelizing with John. If John was written "that you may believe ... and that by believing you may have life" (John 20:31), then it seems like it'd work quite nicely as an evangelism tract. A God given, divinely inspired guide to evangelism is something you'd think churches would jump all over! It's become my favorite method of studying with those who are intrigued by Jesus. This final appendix is basically how I conclude a study through John's Gospel.

We've seen and heard many signs and testimonies about Jesus. We've gone on a wild ride. We've seen darkness take over the earth but the light of new creation burst forth on the other side. We've seen unparalleled elation and intense sorrow and agony. We've seen King Jesus in all His (surprisingly paradoxical) glory. And no one who met Him got to walk away the same.

They all walked away facing enormous challenges. They all walked away knowing they had some hard decisions to make and, depending on how they chose, some hard things to do. At this point, I'll ask the person or people I am studying with for some examples.

Have we met anyone needing to make really hard decisions? Who was challenged by Jesus?

Who Was Challenged by Jesus?

At this point, there are a hundred different ways the conversation can go. People are often struck by different events or characters. Some might talk about the disciples back in chapter 1. They had to believe the King of Israel was some insignificant man from insignificant Nazareth. Perhaps it's those who watched Him cleanse the temple in John 2. The radical, crazy man who ruined everyone's worship at the temple, who deliriously said He would rebuild the temple in 3 days— were they supposed to just give over their authority to Him? Maybe you think of Nicodemus whose life was the envy of all who met him. Jesus told him to be born again. Maybe you think of the Samaritan woman, or the 5,000 who ate the loaves, or the blind man, or Peter, or Judas, or Pilate. There are so many to choose.

Each of these people and groups had really hard decisions to make. Some of them made the right decisions. Nicodemus, after much trepidation, honored the body of Jesus by giving Him a king's burial after the crucifixion. The Samaritan woman went and told everyone she knew about Jesus. The beloved disciple followed Jesus to the cross. Some of these people made the wrong decisions. The Pharisees tried to silence any who spoke of the great things Jesus did and plotted to kill Him when He couldn't be controlled. Pilate knew Jesus was innocent, but sentenced Him to death anyway. Judas ate with Jesus, saw His signs, even had his feet washed by Jesus, but betrayed Him for a little bit of cash. Some people were a bit of a mixed bag. At times, Peter's loyalty was unquestionable. At other times he denied even knowing Jesus. When the pressure was on, he folded. Based on our knowledge of the rest of the New Testament, while he was never perfect, Peter did ultimately respond positively to Jesus' final challenge of "You follow Me."

What Hard Decisions Will You Make?

Following a discussion of those who were challenged with difficult choices, I think it's imperative to remember the One who had the biggest challenge of all. Jesus. Jesus faithfully responded to God's call even when it cost Him His entire life. He was tortured, mocked, beaten, and ridiculed. Jesus suffered, bled, and died because of His love for each of us. He could have refused at any moment. He could have walked away. He could have given up. Yet when faced with the greatest challenge of His life, the greatest challenge anyone has ever faced, He was brave, determined, and faithful to the end.

At this point, I challenge myself and all who have been part of the study to do something for Jesus. No matter how hard it is, to rise up to the challenge. In my life, I look at what I have been struggling with or failing in, and I challenge myself to follow the example of faithfulness seen in Jesus. I also offer a challenge to other Christians in ways they can grow in their faithfulness to the call of Christ. And to anyone who is not a Christian, I challenge them to put their faith in Jesus, determine to live for Him, and to be baptized that night.

It's easy to see the characters in John and judge their weaknesses, fears, and failures from afar. It's harder when the challenge of Jesus is laid before us. How will we respond to it? Will we be a Pilate? Will we be a Peter? Will we be a Samaritan woman? Now is the time to decide. If you are reading this, I want to challenge you also. Decide what you are going to do with Jesus. Are you a follower? What does that look like in your life? Has it changed your attitude towards service? Generosity? Love? Purity? Faithfulness? Are you living on autopilot, just cruising along each day apathetically wearing the name of Christ? When is the last time you've really been challenged by the Gospel? The last time you were uncomfortable? The last time you gave up something meaningful to you because you knew it was the best thing to do? Look into your life and look into your heart. Do you see a cross? Do you see King Jesus?

If you are not a follower. I challenge you to become one today. Follow Jesus. Call up a Christian you know and tell them you want to talk. Hey, send me (Travis Bookout: bald guy, preacher) a message on Facebook. I'd love to talk to you. Don't walk away from Jesus today. Change your life. Change your Lord. Believe. Be born again of water and Spirit. Receive abundant, eternal life. See the Kingdom. Worship your King. I love you. God loves you more. Decide.

BIBLIOGRAPHY

Beasley-Murray, George R. *John*. Word Biblical Commentary 36. Waco: Word Books, 1987.

Evans, Rachel Held. *Inspired: Slaying Giants, Walking on Water, and Loving the Bible Again*. Nashville: Nelson Books, 2018.

Ferguson, Everett. *Baptism in the Early Church: History, Theology, and Liturgy in the First Five Centuries*. Grand Rapids: Eerdmans, 2009.

Hays, Richard B. *Echoes of Scripture in the Gospels*. Waco: Baylor University, 2017.

———. *Reading Backwards: Figural Christology and the Fourfold Gospel Witness*. Waco: Baylor University, 2014.

Metzger, Bruce M. *A Textual Commentary on the Greek New Testament*. Stuttgart: Deutsche Bibelgesellschaft, 1994.

Powell, Mark Allan. *Introducing the New Testament: A Historical, Literary, and Theological Survey*. Grand Rapids: Baker Academic, 2009.

Witherington III, Ben. *John's Wisdom: A Commentary on the Fourth Gospel*. Louisville: Westminster John Knox, 1995.

———. *What Have They Done with Jesus? Beyond Strange Theories and Bad History—Why We Can Trust the Bible*. San Francisco: Harper-Collins, 2006.

Wright, Tom. *John for Everyone: Part 1 Reflections 1–10*. Louisville: Westminster John Knox, 2004.

———. *John for Everyone: Part 2 Reflections 11–21*. Louisville: Westminster John Knox, 2004.

SCRIPTURE INDEX

Genesis

I	8, 64, 98, 130
1:2	240
1:2–3	9
1:2–5	9
1:3	8
1:3–4	64
1:3–5	240
1:5	8, 98
1:6	8
1:8	8
1:9	8
1:11	8
1:14	8
1:20	8
1:22	8
1:24	8
1:26	8
1:28	8
1:29	8
2:8	240
2:15	240
3:9	223
9:12	52
9:13	52
16:13	140
17:11	52
18	173
18:4–5	173
24	140
28:12	65
28:17	66

29:1–12	140

Exodus

2	140
3:14	89, 152, 223
6:2–3	152
10:1–2	39
12:46	166, 234
13:21	9
14	36, 149
14:11	149
15:24	149
16:2	149
16:4	149
16:7	149
16:8	149
16:12	149
20:8–11	143
20:17	133
25:8	65
25:9	65
31:18	255
33:18	9
33:22	9
40:35	9

Leviticus

15:19–33	135
20:10	255
23:34–44	148

Numbers

6:22–27	246
9:12	166, 234
14:1–4	149
21	128, 129
21:5	149
25:6–13	204

Deuteronomy

5:14–15	144
7:13	56
9:10	255
11:14	56
14:23–26	56
14:26	57
16:13–15	148
18:15–18	79, 87
28:39	57
28:51	57
33:28	56
34:10–12	79

2 Kings

18:4	131

Esther

9:20–32	39

Job

42:7–8	93

Psalms

22	234

22:1	234	34:2	160	14:50	21
22:18	234	34:4	160	15:21	233
33:6	8	34:10	160	15:34	234
34:20	166, 234	34:11–16	160	15:36	61
42	188	34:23–25	160		
43	188	34:25	161	**Luke**	
69	60	34:31	161	6:27–36	177
69:4	234			17:27	219
69:9	61, 173, 234	**Hosea**		17:29	219
69:21	234	9:2	57	20:2	60
78	80	13:4–6	81	21:38	253
78:21–24	80			23:12	199
78:24	80, 82	**Joel**		23:36	61
104:14–15	56	1:4	56	24:27	173
107:23–32	89	1:5	56	24:44–45	173
116	116	1:7	56	24:50–51	124
116:4–9	116	2:19	56		
116:15	116, 117	2:22	56	**John**	
		2:24	56	1	18, 130, 258
Proverbs		2:25	56	1:1	5, 64,
8	7, 8			169, 200	
8:12	7	**Amos**		1:1–5	9
8:22	7	5:11	57	1:3	8, 64
8:23–31	7	9:12	57	1:4	III, II2, 145,
		9:13–14	57	159	
Isaiah				1:4–5	130
5	196	**Zephaniah**		1:4–9	94
5:2	196	1:13	57	1:5	9, 43, 64
5:4	196			1:6	104
5:7	196	**Haggai**		1:6–7	17, 146
20:3	52	2:9	65	1:7	17
28:15	111			1:8	146
28:18	111	**Zechariah**		1:9	98, 130,
35:1–8	191	12:8–10	234	192	
40:3–5	191	12:10	234	1:9–11	43
43:16–21	191			1:10	46, 58
51:10–14	191	**Matthew**		1:10–11	64
52:1–12	191	5:11–12	118	1:12	42, 90
55:12–13	191	21:23	60	1:12–13	43
		27:34	61	1:13	42, 48, 126
Ezekiel		27:46	61, 234	1:14	9, 64, 65,
4	101			170	
4:1–8	52	**Mark**		1:15	17
10:4	65	2:22	57	1:18	9, 172
10:18	65	3:6	219	1:19	17, 47
11:23	65	4:10–12	44	1:21	79
18:32	116	4:21–25	44	1:27	17
20:20	52	4:33–34	44	1:29	17, 64, 108,
34	38, 160,	10:6–8	99	165	
161		11:28	60	1:30	17

1:32	17	3:3	xiii, 42, 43,	4:46	68
1:32–33	209		48, 49, 53, 130, 230	4:46–54	67, 72, 75,
1:34	17		130, 230, 235		164, 244
1:35	17, 64	3:3–4	42	4:48	12, 69, 70,
1:36	17, 30,	3:3–5	104		244
	108, 165	3:4	51	4:50	69, 111
1:37	17, 31	3:4–10	xiii	4:51–54	103
1:38–39	28	3:5	49, 103, 126,	4:53	68
1:39	xv, 27		183	4:53–54	12, 72
1:41	17	3:5–8	209	4:54	50, 68
1:42	231, 243	3:8	127, 209	5	18, 102
1:43	28, 31, 64	3:9–12	49	5:1	35, 72
1:45	17, 28	3:12–13	126	5:3	68, 72
1:46	26, 28, 149	3:13	5, 49	5:3b–4	74
1:47	xiii	3:14	233	5:5	68, 72
1:47–49	103	3:14–15	83, 128	5:6	74
1:49	17, 28, 29,	3:16	14, 129, 219,	5:7	73
	228		250	5:8	74, 102
1:50	28, 54, 70	3:17	104	5:9–10	159
1:51	xiii, 65	3:17–18	129	5:13	45, 75
2	13, 59, 63, 163,	3:19	99	5:14	75
	164, 187, 194, 258	3:22	163	5:15	75
2:1	58, 72	3:22–23	126, 183	5:16	143
2:1–11	xii, 54	3:23	126	5:16–17	xiii, 145
2:6	56	3:31	5, 42, 125	5:17	75, 144
2:9	56, 57, 58	3:34	209	5:18	144
2:10	55, 56, 57	4	13, 139, 140,	5:18–30	18
2:11	12, 50, 56,		159, 164	5:19–30	145
	58, 68, 70, 72	4:1–3	163	5:20	145
2:12–13	68	4:4	132	5:21	145
2:13	35, 59, 66,	4:7	67, 69	5:22	145
	163	4:9	133, 135, 220	5:23	145
2:13ff	159	4:10	84	5:24	145
2:13–22	36	4:10–11	209	5:25–30	145
2:17	61, 234, 239	4:10–14	103, 126	5:28–29	113, 146
2:18	51, 52, 60	4:10–15	42, 51	5:31	146
2:19	58, 60	4:12	138, 139, 151	5:31–47	18
2:19–20	51, 63	4:14	84, 183	5:33–35	146
2:19–21	41	4:19	108	5:36	104, 146, 162
2:20	60	4:20	135	5:37–38	146
2:21	60, 63, 66	4:24	126	5:39	147
2:22	61, 173, 182,	4:28–29	139	5:39–47	83, 146
	239	4:29	18, 28, 140	5:43	90
2:23	51, 68, 72	4:39	18, 28	5:46	107, 147
2:24–25	67, 68	4:39–42	72	5:47	147
2:49–50	69	4:40	28	6	13, 36, 58, 91
3	128, 150, 159	4:41–42	29	6:1	164
3:1	67, 68, 235	4:42	18, 29, 108	6:1–15	87
3:1–2	xiii	4:43–45	72	6:2	32, 78
3:2	12, 18, 51	4:45	68, 70		

6:4   35, 36, 59,
   78, 88, 164
6:5–6   78
6:7–9   78
6:14   12, 18, 50,
   79, 87, 108, 149
6:15   79, 88
6:16–21   36, 149
6:20   89, 193, 223
6:21   90
6:26   32, 58, 80
6:26–66   42
6:26–71   87
6:27   51, 84
6:29   104
6:30   13
6:30–31   80
6:31   80
6:32   47, 80, 84,
   192
6:32–35   78, 149
6:32–40   5
6:35   18, 36, 58,
   80, 85, 193
6:40   84
6:40–44   159
6:41   36
6:41–42   82
6:42   6
6:44   84
6:44–45   83
6:47–51   84
6:48   18, 36, 193
6:51   5, 84
6:53–58   104
6:54–56   58, 85
6:58   85
6:63   209
6:66   32
6:68   18, 145
6:69   149
6:70–71   219
7   123, 164
7:1   149, 164
7:1–2   164
7:1–5   236
7:2   35
7:5   149
7:12   149
7:14   253

7:20   149
7:27   149
7:28   47
7:29   104
7:31   12, 52, 150
7:33   215
7:35   220
7:36   253
7:37   253
7:37–39   42, 103,
   126, 149, 183, 209
7:40   79
7:40–41   18, 52, 150
7:40–43   253
7:41   149
7:41–42   5
7:43   105, 106
7:50   235
7:50–51   150
7:52   5, 149, 253
7:53–8:11   252
8   255, 256
8:3   253
8:3–11   253
8:5   255
8:7   255
8:9–11   253
8:11   253
8:12   18, 31, 130,
   193, 253
8:12–13   253
8:12–19   18
8:13   150
8:18   18
8:24   193, 211, 223
8:30   150
8:31   150
8:31–32   150, 192
8:32   166
8:32–33   47
8:32–34   42
8:33   150
8:34   166
8:34–36   151
8:37–59   151
8:48   150, 220
8:51–59   139
8:53   139, 151
8:58   5, 89, 152,
   164, 256

8:58–59   223, 253
8:59   6, 112, 149,
   161, 256
9   14, 45, 53, 94,
   97, 111
9–10:21   164
9:2   93, 108
9:3   94, 104
9:3–4   94
9:3–5   98
9:4   94, 99
9:4–5   98
9:5   9, 18, 45, 95,
   130, 193
9:7   104, 126, 183
9:8–9   106
9:12   103
9:13–15   159
9:14   102, 106
9:15–16   159
9:16   106, 153
9:17   107, 108
9:22   107
9:23   125
9:25   107, 108
9:28   107
9:30–34   154
9:32   107
9:32–33   100
9:35–39   108
9:35–41   45
9:37   103
9:38   95
9:39   99, 152
9:39–41   95
10:1   154, 157
10:4   159
10:4–5   32
10:5   154, 157, 159
10:6   48
10:6–7   42
10:7   18, 155, 193
10:9   18, 155, 193
10:10   155
10:11   19, 193, 226
10:13   156
10:13–15   156
10:14   19, 193
10:16   156, 220
10:17–18   156

10:19 105, 106
10:19–20 47
10:19–21 159
10:20 200
10:22 35, 37, 38, 164
10:22–24 159
10:24 38
10:25 159, 162
10:26 159
10:27 32, 159
10:27–28 145
10:28 219
10:28–29 161
10:30 6, 161, 173
10:31 6, 112, 152, 161, 164
10:40–42 164
11 14, 22
11:3 22, 111
11:4 112, 117
11:6 111
11:8 112
11:11–13 42, 51, 111
11:16 112, 244
11:21 111
11:23 113
11:25 19, 111, 145, 155, 159, 193, 245
11:32 111
11:33 185
11:34 27
11:35 118
11:36 21, 22, 111
11:40 112, 117, 118
11:45–48 13
11:47–53 224
11:50 224
11:53 112, 164
11:54 112
11:55 59, 112, 164
12:1 35, 164
12:1–2 21
12:3–6 179
12:6 219
12:9 21
12:12 35
12:12–26 164

12:16 239
12:20 35
12:21 220
12:23 117, 164, 215
12:23–26 220
12:26 32
12:27 164, 186, 215
12:27–33 219
12:28 166, 219
12:31 166, 211
12:31–33 166, 233
12:32–33 83
12:37 12
12:37–40 233
12:38–41 12–13
12:42 124
12:43 124
12:48 145
13 22, 163, 177, 179, 181
13–17 208
13:1 35, 163, 164, 174, 215
13:2–5 178
13:5 250
13:6–11 181
13:8 103, 126, 174, 178
13:8–10 178
13:10–11 197, 219
13:12–15 171
13:13 193
13:14–15 174
13:16 201
13:18 233
13:19 223
13:20 90
13:21 186, 219
13:21–30 178
13:23 20, 250
13:23–25 23
13:27–29 42
13:30 222
13:34 171, 176, 201
13:34–35 156, 169, 196, 201
13:36 190

13:36–37 32
13:37 224
13:36–38 184
13:38 174
14 185
14:1 185, 186
14:2–3 186, 187
14:3 190
14:3–6 42
14:5 190
14:6 19, 47, 145, 155, 159, 192, 193
14:8–11 173
14:9 185
14:13 217
14:16 208
14:17 208, 209
14:19 215
14:23 187
14:26 187, 208, 209
14:27 186
14:30 166, 211
15:1 47, 192, 194
15:1–11 19, 193
15:2 194, 197
15:3 197
15:4–5 194
15:4–7 195
15:5 195
15:5–6 195
15:6 197
15:7 195, 217
15:8 194
15:9–10 194
15:10 195
15:12 195, 201
15:13 201
15:14 195, 198
15:15 200, 201
15:16 195, 217
15:17 195, 201
15:19 203
15:20 201
15:24–25 233
15:25 61, 234
15:26 209
16:1–4 203–204
16:6 186

16:7	243
16:7–11	210
16:10	215
16:11	166, 211
16:13	207, 209
16:16	215
16:16–18	42
16:17–18	215
16:20	242
16:20–22	249
16:21	215
16:22	186, 216, 242
16:23–28	217
16:25	48
16:27–29	5
16:28–30	48
17	218, 221, 250
17:1	215, 218
17:1–5	218
17:3	219
17:4	218
17:5	218, 219
17:6–8	219
17:6–19	218
17:8	104
17:9	218
17:10	218
17:11	220, 221
17:11–19	219
17:12	219, 233
17:15	221
17:17	221
17:18	104
17:20	194
17:20–26	218
17:21	220, 224
17:22	218, 220
17:22–23	156
17:23	219
17:24	218
18:3–11	184
18:4	239
18:5–8	89, 223
18:6	223
18:7	239
18:9	224
18:10–11	32
18:11	224
18:12–13	224

18:15	33
18:15–16	20, 23
18:16	33
18:17	32, 225
18:24	224
18:25	225
18:25–27	32
18:27	225
18:28	237
18:31	229
18:31–32	228
18:33	229
18:36	49, 130, 204, 229, 230
18:36–37	42
18:37	229
18:37–38	48, 192
18:38	28
18:39–40	166
19:1–3	250
19:2–3	235
19:3	228
19:4	228
19:6	228, 229
19:7	229
19:12	199, 229, 230
19:15	230
19:16–18	239
19:17	233
19:17–18	250
19:19–20	235
19:19–22	235
19:22	235
19:23–24	233
19:25–27	21, 23
19:26	33
19:26–27	250
19:28–29	61, 233, 234
19:31	35, 165, 234, 237
19:31–37	36
19:33	165
19:34	103, 126, 183
19:35	16, 33, 250
19:35–36	234
19:36	165, 234
19:36–37	233
19:37	234
19:38–42	131, 235

19:39	124, 235
20:1	238, 240
20:2	22, 238
20:2–4	20
20:4	23
20:5–7	113
20:8	23, 239
20:9	239
20:14	45
20:15	239, 240
20:18	244
20:19	240, 242
20:20	249
20:20–29	13
20:21	104, 242
20:21–22	209
20:22	243
20:24	243
20:25	244
20:26	244
20:27	244
20:27–28	70
20:28	6, 19, 108
20:29	19, 27, 28, 29, 70, 240, 245
20:30	16
20:30–31	11, 14, 50, 68, 245
20:31	114, 257
21:2	21
21:3	247
21:4	45
21:4–7	23
21:6	248
21:6–8	250
21:7	248
21:12	248, 249
21:13	249
21:14	248
21:15–17	33, 225
21:18	33, 209, 249
21:18–19	226
21:19	33, 117, 209, 226, 249
21:20	24
21:20–22	250
21:21	24
21:22	24, 27, 250
21:22–23	22, 42
21:24	16, 20, 245

21:24–25	250	**1 Thessalonians**	
21:25	51	4:13	115
Acts		**1 Timothy**	
1:20	61	5:10	181
4:32–37	179		
5:41	118	**Hebrews**	
8:4–8	142	2:9	117
8:36	190	2:10	117
9:1	205	3:19	149
9:2	190		
9:17	190	**1 Peter**	
15:16–18	57	4:12–16	118
18:26	190		
19:23	190	**1 John**	
20:7	241	3:16	201
22:3–4	205		
		Revelation	
Romans		7:15	65
5:12ff	240	20:14	117
5:18	99	21:3	9, 65
11:9–10	61	21:22	66
12:14–21	206		
15:3	61	**Ancient Literature**	
1 Corinthians			
2:6–16	49	**Ecclesiasticus**	
3:16	61	32:1–2	55
15:20–26	240		
15:26	116	**1 Maccabees**	
15:45	99, 240	1:52	37
15:54–55	116	2:17–18	205
16:2	241	2:24–27	205
		8:11–12	199
2 Corinthians		8:17	199
3:14–16	173	8:20	199
Galatians		**Mishnah Niddah**	
1:13–14	205	4.1	134
		7.4	135
Ephesians			
2:19–22	61	**Wisdom**	
		9:1–2	8
Philippians			
1:21–23	115		
1:29	118		
2:5–8	170		
3:6	204, 205		
3:10	118		

CPSIA information can be obtained
at www.ICGtesting.com
Printed in the USA
LVHW110903250421
685283LV00026B/148